DUNS SCOTUS, METAPHYSICIAN

**Purdue University Press Series
in the History of Philosophy**

General Editors
Arion Kelkel
Joseph J. Kockelmans
Adriaan Peperzak
Calvin O. Schrag
Thomas Seebohm

DUNS SCOTUS, METAPHYSICIAN

William A. Frank and
Allan B. Wolter

Purdue University Press
West Lafayette, Indiana

Copyright ©1995 by Purdue University Research Foundation.
All rights reserved.

99 98 97 96 95   5 4 3 2 1

∞ The paper used in this book meets the minimum requirements of American National Standard for Information Sciences—Permanence of Paper Printed Library Materials, ANSI Z39.48-1992.

Printed in the United States of America

Interior design by Anita Noble

Library of Congress Cataloging-in-Publication Data
Frank, William A.
    Duns Scotus, metaphysician / William A. Frank and Allan B. Wolter.
        p. cm. — (Purdue University Press series in the history of philosophy)
    Includes bibliographical references and index.
    ISBN 1-55753-071-8 (alk. paper). — ISBN 1-55753-072-6 (pbk. : alk. paper)
        1. Duns Scotus, John, ca. 1266–1308. 2. Metaphysics.
    3. God—History of doctrines—Middles Ages, 600–1500.
     4. Knowledge, Theory of. I. Wolter, Allan Bernard, 1913– .
    II. Title. III. Series.
    B765.D74F73 1995
    189'.4—dc20   95-6138
                                                            CIP

CONTENTS

vii PREFACE

1 CHAPTER ONE
Life and Works

18 CHAPTER TWO
The Nature of Metaphysics
18 Text: *Questions on the Metaphysics,* prologue;
Reportatio I A, prologue, q. 3, a. 1
28 Commentary

40 CHAPTER THREE
Parisian Proof for the Existence of God
40 Text: *Reportatio* I A, d. 2, qq. 1–4
74 Commentary

108 CHAPTER FOUR
Three Questions about Knowledge
108 Text: *Ordinatio* I, d. 3, qq. 1–2;
Lectura I, d. 3, q. 3
134 Commentary

184 CHAPTER FIVE
Two Metaphysical Questions
184 Texts: *Ordinatio* II, d. 3, qq. 5–6;
Questions on the Metaphysics book 9, q. 15
196 Commentary
196 Individuation, Universals, and
Common Nature
197 On the Will

209 SELECT BIBLIOGRAPHY

219 INDEX

PREFACE

In this book we present John Duns Scotus's metaphysical treatment of God. As a philosopher, Scotus was above all a metaphysician, and his metaphysics was ordered finally toward the rational knowledge of the first being. Since the purpose of this series in the history of philosophy is to present the fundamental ideas of the great thinkers—and Scotus is certainly one of the greatest thinkers of the medieval West—we think there can be no more direct access to his basic thought than through a critical study of his philosophical treatment of God. Many readers will be familiar with Thomas Aquinas's Five Ways or with Anselm's famous *Proslogion* argument. Scotus's proof, however, is altogether of another order of complexity. Indeed, it amounts to a *summula metaphysicae*, or little "summa," of first philosophy. The texts and commentaries we present draw out the critical, systematic sweep of his philosophical vision.

Chapters 3 and 4 constitute the core of our book. In chapter 3, we take up the actual proof for the existence of God. Our text is drawn from the *Reportata parisiensia,* which is a report—rather like a scribe's transcript—examined and approved by Scotus himself, of his lectures at Paris. This mature treatment of the God question is distinguished within Scotus's works for its self-conscious holistic approach to what was conventionally a series of separate topics. In chapter 4 we discover the underlying principles of Scotus's philosophical theory of knowledge. When taken together in their systematic totality, the issues dealt with there enable us to see the historical uniqueness and speculative daring of Scotus's metaphysics. Among the medieval philosophers who accepted Aristotelian scientific theory, he is perhaps the first to realize fully its negative consequences for the philosophical doctrines of illumination and the analogical concept of being.

This central unit on the knowledge of God is preceded by chapter 2, with its brief introduction to Scotus's theory of metaphysics—or first philosophy, as it is sometimes called. As with all of the great philosophers, Scotus had an ordered view of the whole of reality, one in which God is but one—albeit the most important—topic. Our intent is to introduce the discipline or science by which Scotus will subsequently carry out his primary investigation. Our final chapter examines the issue of individuation and universals and that of the nature of free will. The first of these questions establishes the principles of Scotistic realism, and the second introduces the ontological foundation for contingency and for the particular splendor that moral goodness gives to the world.

History has been stingy with facts concerning the details of Scotus's life. During his own lifetime, his intellectual daring seems to have made him a target for certain vengeful fellow scholars. Several centuries after his death, at least in England, "Duns" became a term of opprobrium, dunce. Only in this century have we distinguished his authentic works from a number of titles spuriously attributed to him. Chapter 1 takes stock of what we know of Scotus's life and works in the light of current historical and textual studies.

Our commentaries serve the primary purpose of bringing out the philosophical meaning of Scotus's text. To this end, we provide the historical context, discuss the requirements of the genre, elaborate the various arguments, explain technical terms, reestablish dialectical contexts, and correlate particular passages with complementary Scotistic texts. Because he was dealing with perennial philosophical issues, we also try to shed light on them by alluding to contemporary strategies for dealing with similar problems. It is our conviction that Scotus's metaphysical thoughts can stand above the historical contingencies in which he shaped them. We hope our book will be as much a spur to philosophical thought as a guide to a splendid moment in its history.

We gratefully acknowledge support from the Earhart Foundation and the University of Dallas. We also wish to thank both the Catholic University of America Press for its permission to reprint the text and translation of the material on the will in chapter 5 and *Franciscan Studies* for its permission to reprint the text and translation of chapter 3. We gratefully recognize the permission of Hermann Schalüch, O.F.M, Grand Chancellor of the Pontifio Ateneo Antonianum, to use the many texts from the Vatican edition of Scotus's *Opera omnia,* which is the corporate work of the Scotus Commission.

Our readers should know that we—and they—are much indebted to the diligence and sober judgment of our editor, Margaret Hunt, who in innumerable details has improved our work.

We two philosophers could hardly ask for a more supportive community than that offered by the Franciscans at Old Mission, Santa Barbara, during our work in the fall of 1993. Finally, we acknowledge the faithful encouragement given us throughout our labors by Therese Chicherio and the Frank children, Clare, Joseph, Jude, Abraham, and William.

CHAPTER ONE | Life and Works

| Biographical Notes

In the Conventual Franciscan Church in Cologne, the ornate catafalque containing the mortal remains of John Duns Scotus bears the inscription "Scotia me genuit, Anglia me suscepit, Gallia me docuit, Colonia me tenet." Taken from the opening lines of a poem honoring this philosopher and theologian, this epitaph reads in English translation: "Scotland begot me, England reared me, France taught me, Cologne holds my remains." This capsule biography may serve to organize the relatively few details we know of the life of this intellectual giant, who was known to his contemporaries as the "Subtle Doctor" and regarded as father of the philosophical school of Scotism.

| Scotland Begot Me

First called the "Scot" or Scotus when he studied at the University of Paris, John Duns was born in the village bearing his family's name, nestled between the Lammermuir and Cheviot Hills, close to the North Sea and the Scottish-English border, in the district of Berwick. The Tweed River runs nearby. To the northwest of the present town stands Duns Castle. Near the pavilion gate marking the entrance to the castle grounds is a historical marker that reads: "John Duns Scotus, the Subtle Doctor, and Member of the Franciscan Order, was born on this site in 1266. Wherever his distinguished name is uttered, he sheds luster on Duns and Scotland, the town and land which bore him. Erected by the Franciscan Order on the Seventh Centenary of his Birth, Sept. 1966."[1] In the town's public park, a striking bronze statue of the thinker, depicted as drawing inspiration from above, bears a similar inscription, with the added line "Hic magni spirat imago viri [Here breathes the spirit of a great man]."

England Reared Me

Writing in the sixteenth century, the Franciscan theologian John Major confirms the village of Duns as Scotus's birthplace, "eight miles distant from England and separated from my own home by seven or eight leagues only." Major adds that when Scotus "was no more than a boy, but had already been grounded in grammar, he was taken by two Scottish Minorite [Franciscan] friars to Oxford, for at that time there existed no university in Scotland." Major goes on to say: "By the favour of those friars he lived in the convent of the Minorites at Oxford, and he made his profession in the religion of Blessed Francis."[2] Like the Dominicans, the new mendicant order of Franciscans were not known as monks or clerics but as friars (a term derived from the way the English pronounce *frères*). Their convents, known as "friaries," had spread throughout England and Scotland. Major's remark that young Scotus was taken to England by Scottish friars—probably by an uncle or other close relative in the family who recognized his exceptional intellectual abilities—suggests that Scotus was interested early in life in joining the Franciscans.

Boys as young as twelve could begin their studies at Oxford,[3] and Scotus's observation about a thirteen-year-old's knowledge of sacred matters may be indicative of his own experience as a young man.[4] Like the Dominicans, or Order of Preachers, the Franciscans were interested in studying theology to enhance their ministry of preaching. They welcomed candidates, especially from the faculty of theology, into their brotherhood, and it was in this way that these two newly founded mendicant orders first obtained chairs of theology at the universities at Paris and Oxford. It was customary to first obtain a master of arts (the program of arts, philosophy, and the natural sciences) before entering the program of studies leading to a master of theology. The mendicant friars, however, generally did not incept (that is, begin their careers as masters in a formal ceremony), determine, or reign as masters of arts but preferred to study philosophy and the natural sciences in their own study houses rather than as artists enrolled with a regent master in the faculty of arts. Franciscans especially were loath to be called "masters," since their rule of life was based on a literal following of the Gospels, and they took seriously the evangelical admonition "Ne vocemini magistri, quia Magister vester unus est Christus [Avoid being called masters, for one is your master Christ]" (Mt 23.10). A university graduate and master himself, Bonaventure, as minister general, or head, of the Franciscan order, had earlier written a beautiful sermon on Christ as the one master of all that was taught at the university of Paris in his day. It is not surprising, then, that we have no record of Scotus becoming a master of arts, but we would be mistaken to believe that his philosophical commentaries on Aristotle's works necessarily represent the fruit of an introductory stage in his academic career. The Spanish Scotist Antonius Andreas, for example, who studied at the University of Paris, declares his own logical works to be what he learned there from Scotus: "Haec de dictis magistri fratris Ioannis Duns, natione Scoti, sedentis super cathedram magistralem, ut potui, colligens, in unum compilavi [From the words of Master Brother John Duns, of the Scottish nation, occupying the magisterial chair, as far as I have been able to collect these and compile them into one work].[5]

Our first certain date in Scotus's Oxford academic career, however, is that of his ordination to the priesthood on 17 March 1291 at nearby Northampton.[6] At the time he would have been well into studies leading to a mastership in theology. Theological subjects were studied and taught in a methodical way according to the sequence of topics in Peter Lombard's four books of the *Sentences.* "*Sententia*" is the Latin term for "opinion," and Peter's work is a twelfth-century theological synthesis of the opinions of the fathers of the church. Since these ranged over the whole field of theology, Peter's *Sentences* had been adopted by the middle of the thirteenth century as a kind of official textbook by the faculty of theology at both Oxford and Paris. As a bachelor preparing for inception as master, the student of theology had to present a series of original questions[7] as the basis of his lectures. Since these followed the sequence of topics in the *Sentences,* the student's original and comprehensive work on theology was somewhat inappropriately called a "commentary on the *Sentences.*" The several "commentaries" made by Scotus are found in the form of an original lecture (*lectura*), as the transcript by a student or a scribe who recorded the actual lectures conducted by Scotus (*reportatio*),[8] or in a final revision dictated for distribution by the booksellers (*ordinatio*).

In Scotus's case, this *ordinatio,* or "ordered" revision, was dictated to secretaries. We know from the date Scotus gives in the second question of its prologue that he had begun this revision of his earlier Oxford lectures by the summer of 1300. As the editors of the Vatican edition of Scotus's *Opera omnia* note, the date seems to be an allusion to both Albumazar's prophecy about the duration of the Islamic religion and the news of the defeat of the Egyptians at the battle of Medjamâa-el-Mordûj.[9] At the time,

Scotus would have been living at the Oxford friary when Hugh of Hertilpole, the English provincial, on 26 July 1300 recommended him with twenty-one other members of that Franciscan study house to Bishop Dalderby to hear confessions of the pilgrims that thronged to the friars' church. Though he was not among the eight chosen, the very presence of Scotus's name on the list seems a solid argument that he would be in Oxford during the coming academic year at least, if not longer.

Scotus did not remain long at Oxford, however: a note in Codex 66 of Merton College, Oxford, indicates that Scotus "flourished at Cambridge, Oxford, and Paris."[10] It is still not clear when Scotus was at Cambridge,[11] though we are somewhat better informed about his academic career in Paris. Source material from all of the earlier bachelor lectures, however, found its way into the Paris *ordinatio,* Scotus's major contribution to theology.

| France Taught Me

Scotus did not take his formal first step as a master of theology at Oxford; on the recommendation of the English provincial, he was selected to read the *Sentences* at the more prestigious University of Paris, which had three times the enrollment of Oxford. According to a manuscript of one of the earliest of Scotus's Parisian lectures on the *Sentences,* he began in the fall of 1302, probably some time around the end of September or the first week in October. Gonsalvus of Spain was the regent master of the Franciscans, and Scotus probably participated as a bachelor in the famous disputation between Gonsalvus and the Dominican Master Eckhart.[12] Before Scotus's first year in Paris ended, however, the long-smoldering feud between Pope Boniface VIII and King Philip IV (the Fair) over the taxation of church property to finance the king's armies eventually invaded the university and caused it to be shut down.[13] The trouble began in March when Philip, with the advice of his chief minister, Nogaret, called a council that set in motion the crown's official policy to have Boniface deposed as an illegitimate pope. In the months that followed, he won over the French clergy and universities to his cause. A great antipapal demonstration took place on 24 June 1303. The following day royal commissioners examined each friar at the Franciscan convent to determine who sided with the king. Some seventy friars, mostly French, signed in favor of Philip, while the rest (some eighty-odd) remained loyal to the pope. We find Scotus's and Gonsalvus's names on two lists of the latter. The penalty for such opposition to the king was exile from France within three days. Boniface countered on 15 August 1303 with a bull whereby he suspended the university's right to give degrees in theology and canon and civil law. On 8 September Nogaret with an army invaded the papal palace at Anangi in an effort to force the pope's resignation but was eventually driven off by an angry populace. Boniface, a sick and broken octogenarian, never recovered from the attack and died on 11 October.

It was not until the following April that Pope Benedict XI, in the interests of peace, lifted the ban on the university, and Philip expedited the return of the exiled students.[14] Scholars differ as to where Scotus might have gone after leaving Paris. Some suggest Cambridge, but Oxford seems more likely, since we have manuscript evidence of additional lectures apparently given there that refer to what he taught previously in Paris.[15]

Scotus was back in Paris before the end of 1304. Probably he returned by May, and in accordance with university regulations, he would have begun commenting on book 4 of the *Sentences,* completing these lectures by the end of June. This chronology would explain the references to the papal documents of Benedict XI, one of which Scotus claimed to have seen with his own eyes.[16]

Scotus would have participated as bachelor respondent when Gilles de Ligny was promoted as the new Franciscan regent master when the university reopened.[17] Gonsalvus had meanwhile been elected minister general of the Franciscan order. And in a letter dated 18 November 1304, Gonsalvus indicates that he was appointing Scotus, his former student, to follow Gilles as regent master:

> Since, according to the statutes of the Order and the statutes of your convent, the bachelor to be presented at this time should belong to some province other than the province of France, I assign to you Friar John Scotus, of whose laudable life, excellent knowledge, and most subtle ability, as well as his other remarkable qualities, I am fully informed, partly from long experience and partly from report which has been spread everywhere.[18]

Scotus probably incepted as master early in 1305. That Scotus had not been at Paris the customary four years before being licensed as master was undoubtedly due to one of the many papal privileges granted to the mendicant friars.

The major task of a regent master of theology was to lecture on the Scriptures, but on certain days these and other lectures were suspended so that the students could attend, and participate as opponents or respondents in, a public disputation under one of the masters. These were known as "ordinary disputations," since the various masters took regular turns and usually confined the questions disputed on such occasions to a particular subject. These ordinary disputations were distinguished from the more solemn "quodlibetal disputations," which a master could hold during Advent or Lent, which anyone (*quislibet*) could attend and at which one could raise any question (*quodlibet*) on any theological topic (*de quolibet*); the master conducting the disputation would give his answer and arguments. Later, in the quiet of his study, he would prepare a systematic edition of the various questions raised.

During his regency as the Franciscan master of theology, Scotus conducted both types of disputations. It is not clear whether his Parisian disputation with William Peter Godin, the Dominican master, on the question of whether matter is the principle of individuation was an "ordinary disputation" held when he was regent master or whether he was a bachelor participating in the ceremonies of Gilles's installation as master.[19] Since his regency was short, we only have evidence of his "ordinary disputations" in marginal notes that indicate he incorporated material from them into his final *ordinatio*.[20] Scotus's one solemn "quodlibetal disputation" was probably held during Advent of 1306 or Lent of 1307.[21] Subsequently the twenty-one quodlibetal questions raised on this occasion were arranged under the general heading of "God and Creatures." Scotus's regency at Paris was cut short, so we have only one *quodlibet*.

Scotus was sent to be lector of theology to the Franciscan study house in Cologne. The last record of his life is a document that he signed there, dated February 1308. This would imply that he must have left Paris in time to begin teaching there by the autumn of 1307.

Scotus's tenure in Paris was abbreviated, in part because of two of his controversial teachings: the rationale for the incarnation of the second person of the Trinity as Jesus Christ; and the question of whether Mary contracted original sin as a descendant of Adam. Scotus regarded the human nature of Christ, united to the divine nature through the second person of the Trinity, as the culmination, the supreme work of creation. Though Christ played a redemptive role, this was incidental to his coming into the world created in God's image and likeness as the Son of God. It was only to show his love as the firstborn of creation that Jesus submitted to the crucifixion as a prelude to his resurrection and glorification.

More controversial than this belief in the primacy of Christ was Scotus's defense of the immaculate conception of Mary, the mother of the God-man. Theologians universally believed that God, in view of the future merits of Jesus Christ, sanctified Mary and John the Baptist in the womb, so that both were born with God's sanctifying grace. The popular feast of Mary's conception, celebrated on 8 December, honored this belief but also raised questions among theologians as to how "conception" was to be interpreted, since as a descendant of Adam she would have contracted original sin. Though the soul of Christ was exempt from such sin by reason of the virgin birth, Mary was conceived naturally, like John the Baptist. According to the commonly held view, anyone seminally conceived would inherit the essential guilt of Adam's sin at the moment of his or her conception. But if Mary were immaculately conceived, she would need no redemption, and Christ would then not be the universal redeemer. How could one explain the apostle Paul's claims that since Christ "died for all, all died" (2 Cor 5.15) and "just as through one man's disobedience all became sinners, so through one man's obedience all shall become just" (Rom 5.19)?

Scotus argued that original sin, which falls on every descendant of Adam, consists in a lack of justification or the loss of the soul's upright order to its Creator. Moreover, the disorder can only be rectified when one is baptized into Christ's death and given grace in virtue of his redemptive merits. Therefore, God could have given such grace, and hence, in anticipation of those merits, conferred justification or right order on Mary's soul at the moment of its creation. Scotus proposed such an immaculate conception as a theological possibility on the grounds that it represented the most perfect form of mediation, and Christ was a perfect mediator. Far from compromising Christ's dignity as universal redeemer, such a preredemption of his mother would have been most fitting.

In view of the general consensus of theologians that Mary had contracted original sin, however, Scotus prudently worded his personal theological opinion as to how Mary was conceived:

> I say that God could have brought it about that [1] she was never in original sin, or [2] she was in sin for only an instant, or [3] she was in sin for some period of time and at the last instant of that time was purged of it. . . . Which of these three possibilities is factually the case, God knows—but if the authority of the Church or the authority of Scripture does not contradict such, it seems probable that what is more excellent should be attributed to Mary.[22]

Even this carefully crafted statement initially provoked a storm of opposition at Paris. The Dominicans, who had earlier adopted Aquinas as their "common doctor" by taking his teaching as the norm for their theological studies, were quick to oppose it, especially Master Hervé de Nédélec. Secular masters, too, declared it heretical, such as Jean de Pouilly, who proposed that "one should proceed not by arguments but otherwise" against such an audacious and presumptuous theologian.[23]

This suggestion that the secular arm be invoked has led some to believe that Scotus's defense of Mary's immaculate conception or his opposition to Philip the Fair's iniquitous measures to suppress the Knights Templar[24] may have been the reason why Scotus was sent to Cologne. As Andrew Little argues, Scotus had "formidable enemies" in Paris, and "his old friend, the minister general Gonsalvo, may have sent him elsewhere either to put him out of danger or to allay the controversies caused by his presence in Paris."[25]

Cologne Holds My Remains

Why Cologne was chosen, however, is another question. Earlier biographers of Scotus suggest there was some special need in this German metropolis that would explain why such a talented theologian at the height his career was dispatched to this particular study center, made famous earlier by Albert the Great and Aquinas, to be sure, but inferior by far in prestige to Paris.[26] Later historians, lacking specifics, have presented a number of widely different reasons for his presence in Cologne. Luke Wadding cites four early-fourteenth-century theories that, individually, seem insufficient to warrant him going there, but taken as a whole, might well justify the selection of Cologne as the most useful place for Scotus to be sent, especially if he had to be removed from Paris.[27]

Whatever the reason, William Vorilong, who was learned in Scotistic lore and lectured in Paris in 1430, indicates that Scotus's departure was both hasty and urgent. When the letter from the minister general came to him when he was relaxing with his students in Pré-aux-Clercs, outside the walls of the city, he set off immediately for Cologne without even returning to the convent to collect his books or belongings.[28] This may be one of the reasons why all of his major works seem to have been left incomplete with his departure from Paris. Friary records list him as the thirty-sixth lector of Cologne, who died on 8 November 1308.[29] Reverenced as a saint, he was buried in the friary church.

As devotion to Mary as immaculately conceived spread, so too did respect increase for the "subtle and Marian doctor" who had solved the principal theological objections to her prerogative. His relics were moved successively to places of greater prominence in the church, first beneath the floor before the main altar and later encased in an elaborate catafalque just behind. During World War II, when the city was reduced to rubble and the church gutted, Scotus's relics were preserved in the underground vaults of the nearby cathedral. With the restoration of the Minoritenkirche, they now rest in the left aisle of the main body of the church.

His cult from time immemorial and his reputation for heroic virtue were officially recognized by the Roman Catholic Church on 6 July 1991, when Pope John Paul II confirmed his status as blessed by conferring liturgical honors in a solemn vespers service in the Basilica of St. Peter on 20 March 1993.

Principal Works

It is unfortunate that Scotus's early death left almost every one of his major works in an incomplete state and in various stages of development. So great was his fame and following, however, that his dictated works or reports of his lectures, in whatever form they existed, were treasured, copied, and recopied by disciples. Thus a rich manuscript tradition of various writings still exists, but understandably it reflects his thought at various stages of his career. And even his monumental *Ordinatio,* meant to be his final commentary on the *Sentences,* seems to have gone through more than one revision; the Vatican edition's version omits significant areas of his thought and may need to be supplemented with earlier, partially revised materials that he intended to incorporate eventually.

Scotus's *Ordinatio* and his *Quodlibet,* which—with the exception of the last question—was in its final form,[30] are largely responsible for his reputation as a theologian and philosopher as well. They contain his latest and most fully developed philosophical opinions, and his shorter commentaries on Aristotle's writings need to be read in the light of these two major works. The *Ordinatio,* which is divided into four books, will run to fifteen volumes in the Vatican edition, which was begun in 1950; it will be many decades before it is published in its entirety.

An English translation of the entire *Quodlibet* is available under the title *God and Creatures.* The Latin text of the work is at present accessible in the Vivès reprint of Wadding's *Opera omnia* edition of Scotus's works and in Felix Alluntis's 1963 Biblioteca de Autores Cristianos edition.

The Wadding-Vivès edition is still a major source of most of Scotus's hitherto edited works. Though it contains several selections now regarded as unauthentic,[31] it still needs to be used by scholars—albeit with caution—until it is completely replaced by the ongoing Vatican edition of his theological works and by the edition of his philosophical works in progress at the Franciscan Institute of St. Bonaventure University.[32] Besides the first seven volumes, which contain Scotus's philosophical commentaries on Aristotle's logical,[33] psychological,[34] and other philosophical works, and the last two volumes, which are dedicated to the *Quodlibet,* the remaining portion of Wadding-Vivès edition is devoted to the *Ordinatio*—also known as the *Opus oxoniense*—and the *Reportata parisiensia.* A word needs to be said about each of these two works as found in this widely used edition.

Scotus left the *Ordinatio,* as we indicated, in an unfinished state. But his secretarial staff, eager to make this legacy available to the public, completed those questions he had failed to dictate before his mission to Cologne by incorporating original reports, or transcripts, that students or scribes had made of his lectures. Since it began, at least, as a revision of his bachelor lectures at Oxford, it is known as Scotus's *Oxford Commentary,* or *Opus oxoniense,* to distinguish it from the presumably later *Paris Commentary,* or *Reportata parisiensia.* The Vatican edition has sought critically to extract the original *ordinatio* as personally revised at the time of Scotus's death from the *Opus oxoniense* as edited by his secretaries.

Scotus commented on the *Sentences* at Paris, both before and after his exile from the city. A highly significant work, though still largely unedited, is the personally examined and corrected report of his questions on book 1, which is known technically as *Reportatio* I A. Though the Vatican edition makes continual references to this work in footnotes, it will be some years before the entire work is published. We have taken Scotus's proof for the existence of God from portions of this work that we have previously edited and translated.

In his edition of the four books of the *Reportata parisiensia,* Wadding chose for the first book not the *Reportatio* I A but rather the carefully edited version of Scotus's Paris lectures made by William of Alnwick, Scotus's secretary, known today as the *Additiones magnae* on book 1. Alnwick also recorded a version, as yet unpublished, of book 2 of Scotus's Paris lectures. Comparison of these *additiones,* especially of book 2, with certain manuscripts of the *ordinatio* supports the theory that Scotus took with him to

Paris as much of the *ordinatio* as he had completed. As occasion warranted, he used some of these revised questions in his Paris lectures on the *Sentences*. Hence, Alnwick could refer to these *additiones* as extracted from both Scotus's Oxford and Paris lectures.[35] The scribe of Codex A, however, indicates that some of these questions that the scribe of Codex V expressly declares are an integral part of book 2 of the *ordinatio* are missing in the *Liber Scoti*, which is Scotus's personal working manuscript, from which his secretaries, or scribes, would compose the finished work. This implies that Scotus may have wanted to do further revisions on these questions after coming to Paris, and that more than one version of the *ordinatio* exists. There is also evidence from Alnwick that the revision of the five integrated questions from distinction 39 of the *lectura* that the Vatican edition has relegated to an appendix[36] and cited as the work of a disciple was done by Scotus himself, probably before going to Paris. Codex A indicates that the *Liber Scoti* has a blank for this section, which again suggests that Scotus may have wanted to do further work on this portion, leaving space for his final revision to be inserted. This particular section is important, since it has been used to determine Scotus's theory about God's foreknowledge of contingent events.

The Vatican edition has also published the hitherto unedited Oxford bachelor lectures on the first two books of the *Sentences*. These *lecturae* are found in volumes 15–19.[37] There is reason to suppose that Scotus also commented on books 3 and 4 before going to Paris,[38] but manuscripts of these *lecturae* may have been obliterated by Thomas Cromwell's express effort to eradicate Scotus's works and influence from Oxford during the first half of the sixteenth century.[39]

The *Tractatus de primo principio* is a short but important compendium of Scotus's natural theology. It seems to be one of his latest works, and he may have prepared it with the help of an associate; it draws heavily on the proof for the existence and unicity of God found in the *Ordinatio*.[40]

The *Collationes parisiensis et oxonienses* represent a collection of much shorter disputed questions—the sort of private disputations it was customary to conduct within the Franciscan study houses every week or fortnight as a method of reviewing the material covered in daily studies. Wadding believed that they represented some of Scotus's Paris disputations and published thirty-nine of them.[41] Charles Balić showed that forty-six such disputations exist, nineteen from Paris[42] and the rest from Scotus's Oxford period. He proved that of the seven missing from the

Wadding collection, one had been published inadvertently by Wadding elsewhere under another name,[43] and Balić edited three additional *collationes* he considered important,[44] one clarifying Scotus's notion of the univocity of being as applied to God and creatures.

NOTES

1. *Acta Ordinis Fratrum Minorum* 85 (1966): 504.
2. Though Marianus Brockie's account of Scotus's parentage and early life is recognized as unreliable, he undoubtedly did not make up his *Monasticon Scoticanum* entirely out of whole cloth. Thus his claim that Scotus had some close relative in the order and received his schooling in grammar at Haddington may have some historical foundation. As Major affirms, who else but a relative would have recognized so early his exceptional talent and taken him to Oxford? See *A History of Greater Britain as Well England as Scotland Compiled from Ancient Authorities by John Major, by Name Indeed a Scot, but by Profession a Theologian,* trans. Archibald Constable, 206–7.
3. Andrew G. Little, *The Grey Friars in Oxford,* 191.
4. "In the primitive church, boys were not immediately instructed in those things that pertain to the clergy or the divine office. Indeed one could well say that adults were insufficiently educated in such matters. But now boys are at once given instruction and engage in such matters, and therefore some already at thirteen years of age are even more adequately instructed in such actions than perhaps an uneducated person of twenty-five would have been then" (*Ordinatio* IV, d. 25, q. 2 [Codex A, fol. 248ra/b]).
5. P. Sagüés-Azcona, "Apuntes para la historia del escotismo en España en el siglo XIV," 4.
6. See Efrem Longpré, O.F.M., "L'ordination sacerdotale du bx. Jean Duns Scotus: Document du 17 mars 1291." Of the forty-eight priests ordained that day in the Priory of St. Andrew in Northampton, five were Franciscans or Minorites, including "Fr. Johannes Dons." Andrew G. Little indicates that though Bishop Sutton ordained in numerous other places throughout his diocese between May 1290 and December 1292, he did not at Oxford itself ("Chronological Notes on the Life of Duns Scotus," 571n). This would explain why friars studying at Oxford, as Scotus was at the time, would have had to travel to some place nearby where the bishop was holding ordination ceremonies. Scotus's ordination has been used to estimate the probable date of his birth: since Bishop Sutton ordained nearer to Oxford than Northampton on 23 December 1290, André Callebaut, O.F.M., argued that Scotus must have come of canonical age for ordination somewhere after that date and before 17 March 1291. This would place his birth late in 1265 or, more probably, early in 1266. See Callebaut, "A propos du Bx. Jean Duns Scot de Littledean: Notes et recherches historiques de 1265 à 1292," 319.
7. The usual literary form used by the medieval Scholastics was that of the tripartite disputed question, which began with a brief summary of the pros and cons, known as *argumenta principalia,* followed by the central body, called the *corpus,* and concluded with an *ad argu-*

menta, or answer to the introductory arguments to the contrary. "Question," therefore, is more like a chapter in a book when applied to a Scholastic treatise.

8. We have one report of Scotus's Paris lectures that he personally examined and corrected (*reportatio examinata*).

9. *Doctoris Subtilis et Mariani Ioannis Duns Scoti, Opera omnia,* 1:77 n. 2. The battle took place on 23 December 1299, but the news did not reach Oxford until the following summer.

10. Little, "Chronological Notes," 571.

11. The *Lectura Cantabrigiensis,* the title of Scotus's lectures delivered at Cambridge, is found in the manuscripts Codex Tuderti 12 and Civ. Vat. Borgh. lat. 50, 89.

12. R. Klibansky, *Commentarium de Eckhardi magisterio,* xxx–xxxiii.

13. Little, "Chronological Notes," 575–77.

14. See Little, "Chronological Notes," 577, for more details.

15. The editors of the Vatican edition cite a manuscript of *Lectura* III, d. 5, q. 5: "Dixi Parisius primo quod . . ." See "Prolegomena" to volume 19, 33*.

16. See, e.g., Little, "Chronological Notes," 577. In the *Ordinatio* IV, d. 25, q. 1, Scotus refers to a document that probably was issued on 31 January 1304; in *Reportata parisiensia* IV, d. 17, he cites Benedict's "new constitution *Inter cunctas,*" issued 17 February 1304.

17. F. Pelster argues that Scotus is the respondent. In addition to Gilles, the Franciscan Alanus and Godfrey of Fontaines also participated in the event. He also suggests that the dispute that Scotus held with the Dominican Master William Peter Godin fits in well with the description given by the statutes of the disputation in which two masters dispute with each other ("Handschriftliches zu Skotus mit neuen Angaben über sein Leben," 11–15). Cf. A. G. Little and F. Pelster, S.J., *Oxford Theology and Theologians circa A.D. 1282–1302,* 47 n. 1. Also see Clemens Stroick, "Eine Pariser Disputation vom Jahre 1306: Die Verteidigung des thomistischen Individuationsprinzips gegen Johannes Duns Scotus durch Guillelmus Petri de Godino OP."

18. Little, "Chronological Notes," 577–78.

19. Pelster, "Handschriftliches zu Skotus," 15–16.

20. Codex A indicates that he was still working on his *ordinatio* during his tenure in Paris and left it incomplete when he departed for Cologne.

21. P. Glorieux, *La littérature quodlibétique,* 153.

22. Scotus, *Ordinatio* III, d. 3, q. 1, in *John Duns Scotus: Four Questions on Mary,* trans. A. B. Wolter, 43, 45.

23. In his Bibliotheca Mariana Medii Aevi, Charles Balić has edited the Mariology of Duns Scotus (*Ioannis Duns Scoti Theologiae Marianae Elementa*) as well as those of two of his contemporaries who criticized his views: *Ioannis de Polliaco et Iohannis de Neapoli, Quaestiones disputatae de immaculata conceptione Beatae Mariae Virginis.* These questions are interesting because they indicate the theological opposition to the doctrine of the immaculate conception at this period of church history. Jean goes so far as to brand Scotus's carefully worded defense of Mary's prerogative as heretical: "Primo volo declarare quod non potest dici probabiliter nec teneri pro opinione probabili quod beata Virgo de facto non contraxit originale peccatum. Immo salve cuiuscumque reverentia, videtur quod debeat hereticum reputari" [First I want to say that a person cannot say in the mode of probability, nor can he hold as a probable opinion, that the blessed Virgin did not actually contract original sin. Indeed, for the sake of all that is holy, this ought to be branded as heretical] (2). See also A. Callebaut, "La maîtrise du bx. Jean Duns Scot in 1305: Son départ de Paris en 1307 durant la préparation du procès contre les Templiers."

24. In an attempt to take over the treasury of the Knights Templar to raise funds for his military campaigns, the unscrupulous lawyers advising Philip suggested trying the grand master and other knights on charges of heresy. Heresy was a crime that only a board made up of regent masters from the faculty of theology were competent to judge. Scotus would have had to sit on such a board, but he was already persona non grata in the eyes of the king's lawyers and advisors because of the position he had taken against the crown in the Boniface affair.

25. Little, "Chronological Notes," 582.

26. Matthew Ferchius (Ferkic), writing in the seventeenth century, suggests this was the case. See the following note.

27. First, Cologne was undoubtedly the most important study center in Germany. Though the Dominican order had lost Albert through death in 1280, Cologne still housed numerous disciples of this great teacher, and the city had aspirations to become a university center like Paris. In 1388, at the request of Archbishop Frederick III of Cologne and the German Senate, Pope Urban VI sent Dominican legates to establish the university by pontifical decree. The inaugural lecture, given by the Parisian theologian Gerard Calcariensis, indicated that this university was built on earlier foundations set by such learned men as Albert, Aquinas, and Scotus. Second, in 1305 the Franciscans had lost William, their official lector of theology, and a competent replacement was required in view of the crisis developing there. Third, the heretical sect of Beghards, which had practically died out elsewhere in Europe, was very aggressive in Germany. They had become arrogant and insolent, interrupting the preaching of the Dominicans and Franciscans, who were entrusted by Archbishop Henry II of Cologne to prevent heresy from infecting the souls in his charge. Fourth, Albert's disciples had reopened the fight and controversy about the conception of Mary, and Scotus, who had never been vanquished in debate, was sent to defend this prerogative with the dexterity and subtlety he had manifested at the University of Paris (Wadding, *Annales Minorum*, 6:121–24).

28. "Narratur de Doctore Subtili qui in Prato clericorum, visa Generalis Ministri obedientia, dum actu Regens esset in scholis Parisiensibus, aut pauca aut nulla de rebus habita dispositione, Parisiis exivit ut Coloniam iret, secundum Ministri sententiam" [It is said of the Subtle Doctor that he was in the Prato of the clerics when he saw the orders of the minister general, even though he was currently the regent master. He left Paris and went to Cologne according to the minister's directive, encumbered by few, if any, possessions] (William Vorilong, *Opus super IV libros Sententiarum* II, d. 44, q. 1, fol. 161va).

29. "Deinde in eadem tabula post trigesimum quintum sequitur Reverendus Pater frater Joannes Scotus sacrae Theologiae professor, Doctor Subtilis nominatus, quondam Lector Coloniae, qui obiit anno

MCCCVIII, VI Idus Novembris" [Then in the same register, after the thirty-fifth there follows Reverend father brother John Scotus, professor of sacred theology, called the Subtle Doctor, a certain lector at Cologne, who died in 1308 on the eighth of November] (Wadding, *Annales,* 122).

30. Question 21 is only partially revised. The manuscript Clm 8717 from the Bayerische Staatsbibliothek in Munich ends abruptly with the words: "Tertium membrum" [the third part], referring to the third of the three parts of Scotus's answer, and the marginal note: "Finis. Quodlibet repertum in sui quaternis. Quod sequitur est de Reportatione" [The end of the *Quodlibet* found in his quaternary manuscript sheet. What follows is from the *Reportatio*] (fol. 85vb).

31. The following philosophical works found in the Wadding-Vivès edition are definitely spurious: *Grammatica speculative* (Thomas of Erfurt), *Quaestiones in librum I et II priorum Analyticorum Aristotelis, Quaestiones in librum I et II posteriorum Analyticorum, Expositio et quaestiones in VIII libros Physicorum Aristotelis, Meteorologicorum libri quatuor, Expositio in XII libros Metaphysicorum Aristotelis seu Metaphysica textualis* (Antonius Andreas), *Conclusiones utilissimae ex libris Metaphysicorum Aristotelis collectae, Quaestiones disputatae de rerum principio* (Vital du Four), *Quaestiones miscellaneae de formalitatibus* (except the first question which contains the "Logica Scoti"), *De cognitione Dei tractatus imperfectus. Tractatus de perfectione statuum* seems to be an open question.

32. The third and fourth volumes of this edition contain the *Quaestiones super Metaphysicam Aristotelis* and the *Theoremata*.

33. The following are generally accepted as genuine logical works of Scotus: *Quaestiones super Universalia Porphyrii, Quaestiones in librum Praedicamentorum, Quaestiones in I et II librum Perihermenias, Opus secundum sive octo quaestiones in duos libros Perihermenias,* and *Quaestiones in libros Elenchorum.*

34. *Quaestiones in libros Aristotelis De anima.*

35. Codex V (Vatican 876), which contains the first two books of the *ordinatio,* also contains the two books of the *Additiones magnae* of Scotus's Paris lectures, all penned by the same scribe. The explicit to the second book says: "Expliciunt Additiones secundi libri magistri Ioannis de Duns, subtilis doctoris extractae per magistrum Willelmum de Alnewyk, de Ordine Fratrum Minorum, de Lecturae Parisiensi et Oxoniensi praedicti magistri Ioannnis, cui propitietur Deus" [Here is set forth the Additions of the second book of master John of Duns, the subtle doctor, which have been taken by William of Alnwick, of the Order of Friars Minor, from the Paris and Oxford lectures of master John, since taken by God].

36. See *Doctoris Subtilis et Mariani Ioannis Duns Scoti Opera omnia,* vol. 6 (1964), 401–44.

37. The only other unpublished Oxford lecture is known as the *Lectura completa,* on book 3, which he apparently completed after his first year in Paris, probably during 1303–4. This is found in three manuscripts, two by John Reynbold of Monte Ornato, in 1453 and 1462. See "Prolegomena," *Opera omnia,* vol. 19 (Vatican, 1993), 33*.

38. Frequent references in book 4 to "another *ordinatio*" in Codex A (Assisi 137) suggest he lectured on all four books at Oxford and was revising the last of these before leaving for Paris.

39. In a letter to Cromwell about his 1535 visit to Oxford University, Richard Layton gives this graphic description of the destruction of Scotus's writings: "We have set Duns in Bocardo [the Oxford prison], and have utterly banished him from Oxford for ever, with all his blind glosses; and is now made a common servant to every man, fast nailed upon posts at all common houses of easement: *id quod oculis meis vidi.* And the second time we came to New College, after we had declared your injunctions, we found all the great quadrant court full of the leaves of Duns, the wind blowing them into every corner" (quoted in R. W. Dixon, *History of the Church of England from the Abolition of the Roman Jurisdiction,* 1:303).

40. The Latin text is available in a modern critical edition by M. Mueller, O.F.M., but as one of the casualties of World War II, existing copies of this edition are rare. The Latin text is reprinted with a Spanish translation by Felix Alluntis, O.F.M., in *Juan Duns Escoto: Tratado acerca del Primer Principio* (Madrid: Biblioteca de Auctores Christianos, 1989); with an Italian translation and commentary by Pietro Scapin, *Il Primo Principio degli esseri* (Padua: Liviana editrice, 1973); and with a German translation and commentary by Wolfgang Kluxen, *Johannes Duns Scotus: Abhandlung über das erste Prinzip* (Darmstadt: Wissenschaftliche Buchgesellschaft, 1974). An edition and English translation was done by Evan Roche, O.F.M., *The De Primo Principio of John Duns Scotus: A Revised Text and Translation* (St. Bonaventure, N.Y.: The Franciscan Institute; Louvain: E. Nauwelaerts, 1949). A. B. Wolter's *John Duns Scotus: A Treatise on God as First Principle* contains a bilingual edition and a paragraph-by-paragraph commentary on the text.

41. Wadding-Vivès 5:131–317.

42. These include questions 1–4, 6–11, 20, 36–39 in the Wadding edition; Charles Balić, "De Collationibus Ioannis Duns Scoti, Doctoris Subtilis ac Mariani."

43. Balić, ibid., 197 states that Wadding published an Oxford *collatio* as question 1 among the "Quaestiones Miscellaneae de Formalitatibus" (Vivès 5:338–53.). Codex Vat. lat. 876 indicates that this question is also known as the *Logica Scoti.*

44. Balić, "De Collationibus," 201–19. These three were discovered and published independently by C. R. S. Harris, *Duns Scotus,* 2:361–78.

CHAPTER TWO | The Nature of Metaphysics

Text
[Scientia Metaphysicae]

Sic, si omnes homines natura scire desiderant, ergo maxime scientiam maxime desiderabunt. Ita arguit Philosophus I huius cap. 2.[1] Et ibidem subdit: "quae sit maxime scientia, illa scilicet quae est circa maxime scibilia." Maxime autem dicuntur scibilia dupliciter: vel quia primo omnium sciuntur sine quibus non possunt alia sciri; vel quia sunt certissima cognoscibilia. Utroque autem modo considerat ista scientia maxime scibilia. Haec igitur est maxime scientia, et per consequens maxime desiderabilis. . . .

[M]axime scibilia primo modo sunt communissima, ut ens in quantum ens, et quaecumque consequuntur ens in quantum ens. Dicit enim Avicenna I *Metaphysicae* cap. 5 a[2] quod "ens et res imprimuntur in anima prima impressione, quae non acquiritur ex aliis notioribus se." Et infra b: "quae priora sunt ad imaginandum per se ipsa sunt ea quae communia sunt omnibus, sicut res et ens et unum. Et ideo non potest manifestari aliquod horum per probationem, quae non sit circularis." Haec autem communissima pertinent ad considerationem metaphysicae secundum Philosophum in IV huius in principio:[3] "Est scientia quaedam quae speculatur ens in quantum ens, et quae huic insunt secundum se," etc.

Text from the prologue, *Questions on the Metaphysics* nos. 16–18, 32–33. Currently this text is accessible in Vivès, vol. 7; a critical edition, upon which our text is based, is forthcoming from the Franciscan Institute.

1. Aristotle, *Metaphysics* 1.2.982a30–b3.
2. Avicenna, *Liber de Philosophia prima sive Scientia divina* 1.5, in *Avicenna Latinus,* ed. S. Van Riet, 31–33.
3. Aristotle, *Metaphysics* 4.1.1003a21–22.

[The Science of Metaphysics]

If all men by nature desire to know, then they desire most of all the greatest knowledge or science. So the Philosopher argues in chap. 2 of the first book of this work [*Metaphysics*]. And he immediately indicates what the greatest science is, namely, that science which is about those things that are most knowable. But there are two senses in which things are said to be maximally knowable: either because they are the first of all things known, and without knowing them nothing else can be known; or because they are what are known most certainly. In either way, however, this science is about the most knowable. Therefore, this is most of all a science and, consequently, most desirable. . . .

What is most knowable in the first way is what is most common, such as being as being and its properties. For Avicenna says in book 1, *Metaphysics,* chap. 5: that (a) "being and thing are impressed in the soul with the first impression, and they are not acquired from anything more knowable than themselves"; and below (b) "those prior things that are imagined through themselves are the things that are most common of all, such as thing and being and one. And hence they cannot be made evident through any proof that is not circular." These most common things are considered by metaphysics, according to the Philosopher in the beginning of book 4 of this work [*Metaphysics*]: "There is a science that deals theoretically with being as being and with what characterizes it as such," etc.

Cuius necessitas ostendi potest sic: ex quo communissima primo intelliguntur—ut probatum est per Avicennam[4]—sequitur quod alia specialiora non possunt cognosci nisi illa communia prius cognoscantur. Et non potest istorum communium cognitio tradi in aliqua scientia particulari—quia qua ratione in una, eadem ratione in alia (cum ens et unum dicantur aequaliter de omnibus, X huius),[5] et ita idem multotiens inutiliter repeteretur—igitur necesse est esse aliquam scientiam universalem, quae per se consideret illa transcendentia. Et hanc scientiam vocamus metaphysicam, quae dicitur a "meta," quod est "trans," et "ycos"[6] "scientia," quasi transcendens scientia, quia est de transcendentibus.

[L]oquimur de materia "circa quam" est scientia, quae dicitur a quibusdam[7] subiectum scientiae, vel magis proprie obiectum, sicut et illud circa quod est virtus dicitur obiectum virtutis proprie, non subiectum. De isto autem [subiecto vel] obiecto huius scientiae ostensum est prius quod haec scientia est circa transcendentia; ostensum est autem quod est circa altissimas causas. Quod autem istorum debeat poni proprium eius obiectum, variae sunt opiniones, ideo de hoc quaeritur primo: Utrum proprium subiectum metaphysicae sit ens in quantum ens (sicut posuit Avicenna)[8] vel Deus et Intelligentiae (sicut posuit Commentator Averroes).[9]

---

4. Avicenna, *Liber de Philosophia prima sive Scientia divina* 1.5.
5. Aristotle, *Metaphysics* 10.2.1053b25–26.
6. Cf. Lambert of Auxerre, *Logica (Summa Lamberti)* c. 1, ed. F. Alessio, 4: "Dicitur autem logica a logos quod est sermo et ycos quod est scientia, quasi scientia de sermone" ["Logic" derives from "logos," which is speech, and "ycos," which is science, which makes the science of speech]; and Lambert of Auxerre, in *Les Auctoritates Aristotelis,* ed. Jacqueline Hamesse, 310: ". . . unde icos est propositio quae scitur esse vera ut in pluribus, ut odire odientes et amare amantes" [whence "icos" is a proposition that is known to be true, as in many things, as, for example, to hate is in those who hate, and to love is in those who love].
7. Henry of Ghent, *Summa quaestionum ordinariarum* art. 19, q. 1, vol. 1, fol. 115H–I.
8. Avicenna, *Metaphysica* 1.2 (*Avicenna Latinus,* 12).
9. Averroes, *Metaphysica* 4, comm. 1, in *Aristotelis Opera cum Averrois Commentariis* (1562; reprint, Frankfurt: Minerva, 1962), vol. 8, fol. 64; *Physica* 1, comm. 83, in ibid., vol. 4, fol. 47.

The Nature of Metaphysics

The need for this science can be shown in this way: from the fact that the most common things are understood first, it follows—as Avicenna proves—that the other, more particular things cannot be known unless these more common things are first known. And the knowledge of these more common things cannot be treated in some more particular science, because the very reason that one particular science could treat them would allow all others to do so as well (since being and one are predicated equally of all, according to chap. 3, book 10 of this work), and thus we would have many useless repetitions. Therefore, it is necessary that some general science exist that considers these transcendentals as such. This we call metaphysics, which is from *"meta,"* which means "transcends," and *"phycos,"* which means "science." It is, as it were, the transcending science, because it is concerned with the transcendentals. . . .

We speak of the matter [of this science] in the sense of its being what the science is about. This is called by some the subject of the science, but more properly it should be called its object, just as we say of a virtue that what it is about is its object, not its subject. As for the object of the science in this sense, we have indicated above that this science is about the transcendentals. And it was shown to be about the highest causes. But there are various opinions about which of these ought to be considered its proper object or subject. Therefore, we inquire about this first. Is the proper subject of metaphysics being as being, as Avicenna claims, or God and the Intelligences, as the Commentator, Averroes, assumes?

[Ens ut Subiectum et Deus ut Finis Metaphysicae]

Hic tria videnda primo si primus et supremus habitus naturaliter perficiens intellectum viatoris cuiusmodi est habitus metaphysicae, habeat Deum pro primo obiecto suo? . . .

De primo est controversia inter Avicennam et Averroem. Posuit enim Avicenna quod Deus non est subiectum in metaphysica, sed aliquid aliud ut ens, quia nulla scientia probat suum subiectum esse; metaphysicus probat Deum esse et substantias separatas esse; ergo etc. Averroes reprehendit Avicennam in commento ultimo I *Physicorum;*[10] supposita maiori Avicennae, quod nulla scientia probat suum subiectum esse, quae est communis utrique, capit quod Deus est subiectum in metaphysica et quod Deum esse non probatur in metaphysica sed in physica, quia nullum genus substantiarum separatarum potest probari esse nisi per motum, quod pertinet ad physicam.

Sed Avicenna bene dicit et Averroes valde male. Et accipio propositionem utriusque communem, scilicet: "Nulla scientia probat suum obiectum esse," quae vera est propter primitatem subiecti ad scientiam, quia si esset posterius, posset ipsum probari esse in illa scientia in qua habet rationem posterioris et non obiecti adaequati. Sed maiorem primitatem habet subiectum respectu scientiae posterioris quam prioris; ergo si scientia prima non potest probare suum subiectum esse, quia

---

Text from *Reportatio* I A, prol. q. 3, a. 1. i (Vienna, Österreichische Nationalbibliothek, cod. lat. 1453, fol. 8va–b).

10. Averroes, *Physica* 1, comm. 81, in *Aristotelis Opera cum Averrois Commentariis,* vol. 4, fol. 47va: ". . . declaratum est in *Posterioribus Analyticis* quod impossibile est aliquam scientiam declarare suum subiectum esse, sed concedit ipsum esse, aut quia manifestum per se, aut quia demonstratum in alia scientia. Unde Avicenna peccavit maxime, cum dicit quod primus Philosophus demonstrat primum principium esse, et processit in hoc in suo libro de scientia Divina per viam quam existimavit esse necessariam, et essentialem in illa scientia, et peccavit peccato manifesto" [it is explained in the *Posterior Analytics* that it is impossible for some science to declare the existence of its own subject. Rather, it concedes its existence, either because it is self-evident or because it has been demonstrated in another science. Accordingly, Avicenna maximally errs when he says that the first philosopher demonstrates the existence of the first principle and then goes on in his book to do this through a way he thinks to be necessary and essential within the science. In this he errs by a clear error].

[Being as the Subject and God as the Goal of Metaphysics]

Here we must first see whether metaphysics, as the first and highest of the naturally acquired habits perfecting man's intellect in this present life, has God as its first object. . . .

On this point there is a controversy between Avicenna and Averroes. Avicenna claims that not God, but something else, such as being, is the subject of metaphysics. For no science proves the existence of its own subject, yet the metaphysician proves that God exists. In his final comment on book 1 of the *Physics,* Averroes attacks Avicenna, using the same major premise, admitted by both, that no science proves the existence of its subject. God is the subject of metaphysics; but his existence is not proved there but in physics, for it is only by means of motion that any sort of pure spirit can be proved to exist, and motion pertains to the science of physics.

Avicenna has spoken well, however, and Averroes very badly, and against him I use the basic proposition that they both hold, namely, "No science proves the existence of its subject." This is true because of the priority that a subject has with respect to the science. For if it were posterior, its subject could be proved in a lower science, where it would be conceived under some inferior aspect inadequate for its role as the object [of the higher science]. But a subject enjoys a greater priority over a lower science than over its own, higher science. If the highest science, therefore, cannot establish the existence of its subject, since this is first or

est subiectum primum, ergo multo magis nec scientia posterior; ergo si metaphysica non potest probare Deum esse, multo magis nec physica.

Probatio minoris, quia duplicem primitatem habet subiectum prioris scientiae ad posteriorem respectu scientiae prioris. Item, si Deum esse est demonstratum in physica et suppositum tamquam subiectum in metaphysica, ergo conclusio in physica est simpliciter principium, quia principium in scientia est ex subiecto eius et per consequens physica erit simpliciter prior metaphysicae; quae omnia sunt absurda.

Item, ex omni proprietate manifesta in effectu potest concludi causam esse, si talis proprietas non ponitur in esse nisi solum a tali causa vel a tali causalitate. Sed non solum huiusmodi proprietates quae considerantur in physica, ut motum esse, manifeste concludunt causam esse moventem, sed etiam proprietates consideratae in metaphysica, ut ens posterius, ens possibile, ens finitum, prout sunt in effectu, concludunt de causa primitatem simpliciter, actualitatem et infinitatem, et huiusmodi, ex quibus potest demonstrari esse de primo ente potius quam ex ratione motus.

Dico ergo ad quaestionem quantum pertinet ad istam articulum quod Deus non est subiectum in metaphysica, quia ut supra probatum in prima quaestione[11] de Deo, potest tantum esse una scientia, quae non est metaphysica. Quod probo sic: De omni subiecto scientiae subalternatae praecognoscitur ex sensibus an est vel si est, ut patet de subiecto perspectivae. Licet enim linea visualis, quae est subiectum in perspectiva, possit demonstrari tamquam conclusio geometriae, tamen si est subiectum alicuius scientiae subalternatae, de eo oportet statim esse notum si est, sine ulteriori inquisitione ex sensu vel experientia, scilicet quod sibi non repugnat esse; sicut enim principia statim sciuntur apprehensis terminis, et cum subiectum sit causa principii et per consequens prius eo in entitate et cognoscibilitate, ita cum subiectum non sit posterius suo principio nec ignotius, oportet ipsum esse statim notum ex sensibus si est; sed nulla ratio propria conceptibilis de Deo potest statim esse nobis nota si est; ergo nulla notita viatoris acquisita naturaliter a nobis potest esse de Deo sub aliqua ratione eius propria. Minor patet, quia prima ratio propria de Deo quam concipimus est quod sit primum ens; sed primum ens non est primo notum ex sensibus, sed oportet prius concipere

---

11. *Rep.* I A prol., q. 1, a. 4.

highest, still less can an inferior science do so. Therefore, if metaphysics cannot prove the existence of God, much less can physics.

The minor premise is proved because of the double primacy that the subject of a higher science has in regard to a lower science's relationship to a prior science. Also, if God's existence is something demonstrated in physics and presupposed in metaphysics as a subject, then—to put it simply—a conclusion in physics is the starting point of metaphysics, for any science starts with its subject. Hence, physics will be prior to metaphysics—all of which is absurd.

Also, if any property can exist only in virtue of such and such a cause, from every such property that appears in an effect we can infer the existence of its cause. Now, it is not just such properties of the effect considered in physics—such as that something is moved—that lead one to conclude the existence of a moving cause, but the same is true of properties considered in metaphysics. If an effect represents something posterior, possible, or finite, such properties imply that their cause enjoys an unqualified primacy, actuality, infinity, and the like. It is from properties of this sort rather than from the nature of motion that the existence of a first being can be demonstrated.

So far as this question is concerned, then, I say that God is not the subject of metaphysics, for as we proved earlier in the first question [*Rep.* I A, prol., q. 1, a. 4], there can be but one science about God as first subject, and this is not metaphysics. And I prove this in the following way. The senses tell us whether or not any subject of a subordinate science exists, as is clear in the case of optics. For although a visible line, which is the subject of optics, could be demonstrated as a conclusion of geometry, nevertheless if it is the subject of some subordinate science, one needs to be able to know immediately, without any further experience or investigation by the senses, whether or not it exists, namely, that there is nothing incompatible about its existence. Just as principles are grasped immediately once the terms are apprehended through the medium of the senses, so too the existence of the subject must be known immediately from the senses. For the subject is not posterior to, or less known than, the principle, since the subject is its cause and hence prior to the principle in entity and knowability. But no knowledge acquired naturally in this life represents any characteristic of God that is proper to him. The minor premise is evident, for the first proper notion we have about God is that he is the first being. "First being," however, is not something initially known from the senses, for we must first

possibilitatem unionis terminorum, et antequam sciamus hanc compositionem esse possibilem, oportet quod aliquod ens demonstretur esse primum.

Concedo ergo cum Avicenna quod Deus non est subiectum in metaphysica; nec obviat dictum Averroris I *Posteriorum*,[12] nec illud I *Metaphysicae*,[13] quod metaphysica est circa causas altissimas, quia loquitur sicut consuevit I *Priorem*,[14] cum dicit: "Primum oportet dicere circa quid et de quo, quoniam circa demonstrationem et de disciplina demonstrativa," i.e., universali scientia demonstrandi. Unde "circa" notat proprie circumstantiam causae finalis, sicut ly "de" circumstantiam causae materialis; unde metaphysica est circa causas altissimas finaliter ad quas terminatur ipsius speculatio.

---

12. Aristotle, *Posterior Analytics* 1.1.71a10–12.
13. Aristotle, *Metaphysics* 1.2, passim.
14. Aristotle, *Prior Analytics* 1.1.24a, 10ff.

ascertain that the combination of these two terms makes sense. Before we can know that this combination represents something possible, we need to demonstrate that some being is first.

Hence I concede with Avicenna that God is not the subject of metaphysics. Nor is this contradicted by the dictum of Averroes [about prior knowledge of the existence of the subject] (from the *Posterior Analytics,* book 1), nor the statement that metaphysics is concerned with the highest causes (from *Metaphysics,* book 1). For the Philosopher speaks there as he did in the *Prior Analytics* I, where he says: "First we need to determine what this is concerned with and is about, for it is concerned with demonstration and is about the demonstrative branch of learning, i.e., it is about the general science of demonstrating." Hence "concerned with" denotes properly the circumstance of the final cause, just as the word "about" designates the circumstance of the material cause. Consequently, metaphysics is concerned with the highest causes as its goal and ends with the theoretical knowledge of them.

Commentary

Introduction

Although the central focus of this book is Scotus's proof for the existence of God, this needs to be situated within a larger line of investigation. The argument is meant to be taken as science, but what science is it that collects and weighs the evidence that leads to a rational judgment about the existence and nature of God? For Scotus, as with the Schoolmen in general, it was metaphysics, which from its beginning has tested the limits of reason by daring to comprehend the intelligibility of the Divine Being. This is not to identify metaphysics with theology or the philosophy of religion but rather to acknowledge the historical fact that by and large metaphysics, as a distinct region of philosophic inquiry, finds itself in one fashion or another confronting the natural intelligibility of a first principle. In fact, the place of God in metaphysics is one of the major questions of the discipline.[1]

For Scotus there was little doubt about the existence or possibility of Aristotle's "first philosophy." The medievals, at least those of the thirteenth and fourteenth centuries, considered metaphysics to be a science of reality, with its own principles, method, and evidences. As such, it was able to portray entities and features of the world insofar as they fell within its scope. God was but one such object, although he of course enjoyed a certain primacy. Nevertheless, within the broad confines of a commitment to the scientific rationality of this most exalted division of philosophy, the question of the nature of the discipline was much disputed.[2]

Our first set of texts introduces the nature of Scotistic metaphysics. In much of what he says, Scotus reflects a received tradition. Within the limits of the heritage, he crafted a unique approach epitomized in his doctrine of the transcendental objects of metaphysics. The subsequent proof for the existence of God is to be understood as a development from within that science. His celebrated univocal notion of being figures prominently in the systematic scheme in an interesting way, which we shall bring out in chapter 4.

Questions on the Metaphysics

In our first passage, Scotus considers the nobility and causes of metaphysics. He takes as his text the first sentence of Aristotle's *Metaphysics:* "All men by nature desire to know." Between the first sentence of the *Metaphysics* and its famous climax in book 12 with self-thinking-thought as the first principle, there lies a complex philosophical story. It is a tale about Aristotle's perplexing book and also about metaphysics itself, and perhaps not simply because so much of Western philosophy developed under the influence of "the Philosopher"—as the medievals called him—but because he expressed in his seminal work something that anyone must come to see who tries to understand the world at the limits of its intelligibility. And it begins with the observation of the universal human desire to understand. Curiosity and a sense of wonder are impulses as inveterate to human nature as the need for nourishment and society. Although Aristotle believed that all knowledge perfects the knower, be it sense cognition, baseball statistics, history, or mathematics, some knowledge is better than others, depending upon the rank of its object in a hierarchy of values. The *Metaphysics* is a quest for the highest of intelligibles.

Behind his idea on the good of knowledge lies an assumption that is not altogether familiar to our way of thinking. The medievals understood knowledge as a discipline, a disposition toward reality, residing in the intellect as a qualitative perfection and possessed of objective necessity, one that is acquired through acts of thought and that can be spelled out as an organized network of concepts, principles, and conclusions. The generic name for such qualities of the soul is *habitus,* which we translate with some reluctance as "habit."[3] What is to be emphasized is that knowledge, ontologically speaking, is an acquired power of the intellect. The desire that Aristotle referred to, therefore, aims at acquiring this qualitative addition to the soul, this power to "see" the world from the point of view of certain pervasive, intelligible features. The simple acquisition of the *habitus* does not suffice, however. In the language of virtues and habits into which Scotus draws us, one ultimately strives to exercise the virtue, to actualize the acquired potentiality. Actually knowing something, employing one's capacity for thinking clearly about things, is the more immediate desideratum. The contemplative life, the philosophy extolled in the *Nicomachean Ethics* (1177b18–25) as the happiest of lives, refers to precisely this sort of activity with respect to the most worthy object.

Assuming that each of us, in virtue of our essential humanity, is teleologically ordered toward acquiring and exercising the capacity to understand the world around us, Scotus then follows Aristotle in arguing that we would naturally "desire most of all the greatest knowledge or science." The question, of course, is, What is the greatest? It is "maximally knowable" with respect to two criteria: that which is foundational, namely, those concepts and principles that are themselves without presupposition and yet presupposed in all other knowledge;[4] and that which is stable or certain, namely, those rational commitments about which we could not be wrong without our losing hold on the complex whole of our practical and theoretical worldview.[5] With respect to the first criterion, Scotus observes Aristotle insisting that the most universally present ideas are those dealing with "being as being and its properties." The science that develops around these as its primary concerns achieves foundational knowledge.

Regarding the second criterion, he insists that the many particular sciences, such as physics, psychology, or politics, commonly presuppose the intelligible reality of such features as unity, sameness, and being. It would be inefficient for each investigator of a particular realm of experience to have to clarify these common presuppositions. Fair enough, one might object, but the mathematician and biologist could advance mathematics or biology just fine with presuppositions; there is no need to divert one's energies toward the philosopher's concerns. In reply, the philosopher would agree that in most cases, perhaps even in all, knowing by presupposition is adequate from within the particular science, but there still remains an unexplored region of intelligibilities. Moreover, understanding the presuppositions of one's special science has not only speculative interest but also practical consequences. So long as the science advances on presuppositions that are not clarified from within the science itself, then one's convictions must be tentative, a condition that is neither desirable nor necessary. In this way, Aristotle and Scotus draw upon our desire for certainty in our knowledge to push us toward an anticipation of metaphysics.

Scotus concludes this introduction by stating: "it is necessary that some general science exist that considers these transcendentals as such." The expression "transcendentals as such" refers to those fundamental realities that transcend Aristotle's basic categories[6] because they either cut across several categories or belong to no category at all. "Same" would illustrate categorial transcendence, for we speak in mathematics of the "same number" (in the category of quantity) and in biology of the "same bacteria" (in the category of substance). The analysis of sameness belongs to a discipline other, and more fundamental, than either mathematics or biology. As predicates, such attributes would pertain to being prior to its division into the categories, to what Aristotle would call "being as being."[7] Part of Scotus's uniqueness as a philosopher is tied up with the way he conceives of the transcendentals.[8] What is no doubt clear is that the science of metaphysics finds its raison d'être in the intelligibility of the most common of objects, namely, being and the properties that belong to it precisely insofar as it is being. It is also distinguished by its engagement with God, the highest of causes. How these two are interconnected is broached in our next selection.

Being as the Subject and God as the Goal of Metaphysics

The question at issue in this text is whether metaphysics has God as its first object. We have excerpted this passage from the prologue to the *Reportata parisiensia,* one of Scotus's several commentaries on Peter's *Sentences.* Its prologue comprises three questions: Can God be the subject of some science? Can per se knowable truths about God be known by us in our present state? and Can a human in this state know by purely natural reason all the truths that can be known about God? In the process of addressing these questions, Scotus considers the possibility of a knowledge of God that is not dependent upon the gift of faith or special revelation. If the *habitus* of metaphysics is fundamental among naturally acquired dispositions, and if it is supremely perfective of one's intellect in this life, then it makes sense to ask whether it has God as its first object, as Scotus does in the first article of the third question. The selection here is the whole of the article. Ultimately, the answer will depend on how God figures into the metaphysical science of the transcendentals.

No one characterizes Scotus's philosophy as easy. His sobriquet, the Subtle Doctor, reflects the difficulty of his thought as well as its sinuous discrimination. This difficulty helps one sympathize with the humanists and reformers whose exasperation at it caused them to introduce the word "dunce" as a term of opprobrium.[9] Charles Sanders Peirce championed Scotus and claimed that the humanists could not digest him because they were "weak thinkers. Some of them no doubt might have been trained to be strong thinkers; but they had no severe training in thought. All their energies went to writing a classical language and an artistic expression. They went to the ancients for their philosophy; and mostly took up the easiest of the ancient sects of philosophy."[10]

We will concern ourselves with five issues in this selection. The first describes the formative tradition of great commentaries on Aristotle's *Metaphysics*. The second deals with certain terms expressing the logical nature of Aristotelian science. The third and fourth analyze the two central proofs of Scotus's thesis. In the fifth, we build on certain of his remarks to amplify his notion of metaphysics as a science of the transcendentals.

❙ Avicenna contra Averroes

Scotus develops his doctrine within a tradition of interpreting the *Metaphysics*. As regards the question of what is the proper subject of metaphysics, Aristotle's text is sufficiently ambiguous to generate a variety of different readings, most of which can be arranged in reference to the two most compelling theories. The first took on its classical form in the first half of the eleventh century with the great Islamic philosopher Avicenna (ibn-Sina, as he was known to his contemporaries), who insisted that being as being is the first subject of metaphysics. A century and a half later, another Muslim, the equally great Averroes (ibn-Rushd) gave the other interpretive pole its most famous expression by arguing that God is its first subject. The Aristotle that so charged thirteenth-century Christian philosophers and theologians was delivered along with the glosses of these two preeminent thinkers.[11] Scotus rehearses this dialectic at great length in his *Questions on the Metaphysics*.[12] In the text at hand, which is probably later than his formal study of the *Metaphysics*, we have a shortened version of the same classical debate.

In his *Posterior Analytics*, Aristotle laid down three requirements for the subject of scientific knowledge, which Scotus then uses to guide his treatment of the issue in *Questions on the Metaphysics*. Aristotle insisted that both the existence and quiddity of its subject be foreknown or presupposed in the investigations (*Post. Analy.* 1.71a10–15, 76a25–35). In this case, either God or being as being would have to be taken for granted at the outset as an existent reality and grasped in its essential intelligibility. In *Questions on the Metaphysics*, Scotus invokes this criterion in saying that no science proves the existence of its subject.[13] Secondly, Aristotle held that the subject of science has attributes that can be demonstrated of it (71a11–13; 76b12–20). Applied to the theories of Averroes and Avicenna, this would mean that either God or being as being would have properties or attributes that can be demonstrated to inhere necessarily in it. Finally, the subject of any science must have principles and parts (87a31–38), and the question then becomes how we can say this of either God or being as being. Even though he judges that Avicenna has the stronger argument, Scotus finds both theories wanting in the final analysis and thus proposes his own metaphysics of the transcendentals. He rejects the principle held by both Islamic commentators that no science proves the existence of its own subject because he thinks that there is a legitimate sense in which God, whose existence is proved in a demonstration of the simple fact,[14] is included under the object "being." He does agree with Avicenna against Averroes in rejecting that God is the foreknown object that anchors all subsequent metaphysical demonstrations.

Aristotelian Science

To appreciate what is at issue, we need to reflect upon what is meant by the terms "subject" (or "object"), "science," and "first." The basic sense of "subject" is grammatical. It means that part of speech in a sentence that is qualified by the predicate, such as, for example, "man" in "The man thinks." The subject is that about which we are speaking. Usually expressed as a noun, it is endowed with a constant identity across a variety of predications, for we can say, to continue our example, the man is tall, was born in Kansas, and so on. Although the list of predicates can be extended unendingly, all are ordered to the single subject, to the one thing about which we speak.[15] Any proposition represents a relationship obtaining between its subject and predicate. The intelligible content of what is conceived in the terms, that is, their meaning, is referred to as the object. The object comes to be expressed as the subject of a proposition. If the paradigmatic meaning of "subject" is syntactical, then perhaps we can say that "object" is semantic. Scotus is here trying to determine what object or subject is the origin of metaphysical knowledge.

He uses the term *scientia* (scientific knowledge) in a technical sense. In the Aristotelian scheme of things, one has knowledge rather than probable opinion when one sees things in their necessities. Such knowledge, represented in the propositional form S is P, claims that the predicate, P, necessarily inheres in the subject, S. Broadly speaking, there are two ways one can come to such propositions. Either the inherence is evident to one who sufficiently grasps the meaning of the subject term, or the necessary connection between the two terms has to be inferred.[16] Ultimately the inference comes to rest on propositions that are immediately known. Scientific knowledge (*scientia*), strictly speaking, names the truths we come to through inference, which is why Aristotle called it the *habitus* of a demonstrative conclusion.[17]

Finally, what do we mean by the "first object (or subject) of a science"? If it is "first," an object must contain in itself with a primary virtuality all those truths of the *habitus* that it engenders.[18] To begin with, the object contains the immediate propositions, since in the subject of those truths are contained their predicates. Moreover, the immediate propositions contain the conclusion that one might deduce from them. In this sense the subject of the immediate propositions contains all the truths of that *habitus*. It would be easy to mistake Scotus's idea of the "first object" as some kind of Leibnizian monad pregnant with all truths that can be cranked out, as it were, with the proper algorithm. Actually, he has two things in mind. First of all, he wants to hold to the primary sense of scientific knowledge as the *habitus* of a syllogistic conclusion. He also wants to acknowledge that when we speak of geometry, physics, and metaphysics as sciences, we understand that each contains many principles and conclusions, which have a unity greater than a sheer aggregation of many habits or "sciences" taken in the strict sense.[19] The idea seems to be that through the *habitus* acquired in the act of scientific knowledge (of, say, proposition p), especially where one has a quidditative grasp of its subject, one is thereby inclined to think about any proposition in which p is virtually contained.[20] The point can be suggested with an analogy. If one were to possess the skill of tennis, it would not mean that one has the exact stroke for every play in the match the way, for instance, an archer has arrows in a quiver; rather it means one has acquired the power, the virtuality, to materialize the appropriate stroke during the actual play. In fact, a move made in the heat of competition may never have occurred before, but still it derives from the same habit. The many distinct conclusions of a science are similarly united in the *habitus* virtually to think about all those propositions whose necessity reposes mediately or immediately in the first subject of the science.

Fortified with these background observations, we can now consider the argument of the text. Recall that the proposition to be proved is that God is not the first object of metaphysics. The article breaks down into two larger arguments.

Argument 1: Using the Logic of Containment

In order to adjudicate between Averroes and Avicenna, Scotus appeals to what we mean by "prior" when we say that a subject is first or one science is prior to another. Let us suppose we have an instance of scientific knowledge, say, "S is P." Can we hold both that S is the first object of that science, and that the existence of S is proved in an inferior science? According to Scotus, this is what Averroes holds when he insists both that God is the first subject of metaphysical knowledge and that his existence is proved in physics. To refute the claim, Scotus appeals to the principle that where sciences are ranked hierarchically—for instance, where "S is P" is prior to "S' is P'"—the subject in an inferior science cannot serve as the first object of the superior science. The principle follows from the rationale of an object's or subject's priority. In essence, an object is prior in the degree to which it contains within itself, essentially or virtually, the immediate, self-evident truths, which then would contain within themselves subsequent mediate or demonstrated truths. Averroes falls foul of the transitive, non-symmetrical logic of containment. His claim runs into a contradiction in the following way. According to him, "God exists" is scientific knowledge demonstrated in physics, a science inferior to metaphysics. But presuming we have the fairly primitive demonstrated metaphysical truth "God is one," according to the priority relationship of the two *scientiae,* metaphysics' "God is one" contains physics' "God exists," and thus its subject, God, contains the truths of physics, including "God exists." Hence it has a first subject prior to the demonstration that God exists. However, if the subject of metaphysics' "God is one" is demonstrated in physics' "God exists," then "God exists" contains "God is one." The contradiction is obvious, since the subject of physics, "God," cannot both contain and be contained by the "God" of metaphysics.

| Argument 2:
| Using the Hiddenness of God

The second argument begins with the conviction that there is a science that has God as its first subject. It is theology, which is rooted in divine revelation and not to be confused with metaphysics, which depends solely on natural reason. Scotus established these claims earlier in the prologue. In the excerpt here, the question is raised whether the same object can figure as first subject in different sciences, particularly in those cases where one science is subalternate to another. Why could God not be the first subject of metaphysics, even if we grant that he is also the first subject of theology? Scotus gives the example of geometry and optics: because optics is subalternate to geometry, optics borrows many of its principles from geometry; and more importantly, they each have the line as their first subject. Could metaphysics be analogous to optics? This suggestion turns the Averroistic argument on its head: perhaps God is the subject of the first of philosophical sciences because metaphysics is subordinated to a science that is superior to philosophy.

The comparison fails, however, because of the special way that God differs from lines. The line can be seen and immediately understood in such a way that thoughtful attention will perceive its necessary attributes. With respect to God, by contrast, "no knowledge acquired naturally in this life represents any characteristic . . . that is proper to him." Theology overcomes this deficiency by privileged evidences specially granted by God outside the ordinary course of things, whereas metaphysics, by its very nature a strictly philosophical science, is restricted to such evidence as is available to natural reason. Scotus, of course, is no skeptic regarding our philosophical knowledge of God. The point is simply that all of our certain and necessary philosophical knowledge of God is *scientia*. Our grasp of the truth "God is the first being," for example, is the result of demonstration. First we prove "Some being is first," then we can justifiably attribute the predicate "first being" to the subject "God." The initial meaning of "God" available to the metaphysician precisely in his capacity as a philosopher does not contain the basis for the unmediated attribution of God's proper characteristics.

I God in Metaphysics

Scotus only establishes the negative proposition that God is not the first subject of metaphysics. He does not necessarily agree with Avicenna that the primary subject is being as being, but he does not deny that God is a subject in first philosophy. Indeed, Scotus believes that divinity is a subject proper to metaphysical knowledge, but it is sought and, in part, achieved as its goal. The path toward this end is indicated in the text. We commonly infer the existence of causes from the existence of effects in fields of experience as various as medicine, forensics, and physics. The principle is a general one and finds its application in metaphysics as well. Properties such as posteriority, possibility, or finitude, which belong to entities that are effects, allow us to conclude that the corresponding attributes of simple firstness, actuality, and infinitude belong to the responsible causal entity. Working out the details of the argument constitutes a proof for the existence of God.

For our current purposes, we note that among the primitive, irreducible terms are a subject (*ens*) and a set of attributes arranged as pairs of disjunctive opposites (posterior/prior, possible/ actual, finite/infinite, and effect/cause). There are two other sorts of terms that belong to the group we have begun to describe, namely, the attributes known as the coextensive transcendentals (one, true, good) and the pure perfections (e.g., wisdom, life, knowledge, will). Taken as a whole, these four sorts of intelligibilities define the field of transcendentals. As a family of concepts, expressed as subject (being) and attributes (coextensive and disjunctive predicates and pure perfections), they capture the intelligibility of reality prior to its division into the categories.[21] It is in this sense that Scotus says, as he does in our first selection, "this science is about the transcendentals."

Metaphysics is brought to its completion in the knowledge of the ultimate causes. In the order of eminence or perfection, therefore, God is the first subject of the science. We emphasize, however, that the scientific knowledge of God is a conclusion to be arrived at. The very possibility of its demonstration shows the rich potentiality implicit in our fundamental transcendental concepts. Properly understood, Scotus's metaphysics, his science of the transcendentals, is a theologic.[22] The *habitus* which begins with the grasp of being and its attributes and seeks out the necessary interrelationships between them is drawn by its own logic to a philosophical knowledge of God. Starting with our most common, transcendental notions, Scotus, the metaphysician, leads the mind into an understanding of the first principle as the Infinite One.

NOTES

1. The chief terms of this discussion are present in interpretations of Aristotle's *Metaphysics,* the founding work for all subsequent metaphysics. In contemporary terms, the question is posed by asking about the relationship between Aristotle's ideas on universal ontology (i.e., the study of being as being, its forms, and the forms of the forms, as well as their respective opposites [1003b22–23]) and his theology (or study of immaterial substances [1026a29–30]). See Walter D. Ludwig's discussion of the major interpreters over the last hundred years, "Aristotle's Conception of the Science of Being."

2. Albert Zimmermann, *Ontologie oder Metaphysik? Die Diskussion über den Gegenstand der Metaphysik im 13. und 14. Jahrhundert: Texte und Untersuchungen.*

3. Yves Simon carefully distinguishes the nest of concepts including habit, *habitus,* opinion, science, and moral virtue in his *Definition of Moral Virtue.*

4. In the latter half of this century, the philosophical academy has called into question the legitimacy of any foundational view of knowledge. The critique is epitomized in Wilfred Sellars's "Empiricism and

the Philosophy of Mind," and Willard Van Orman Quine's "Two Dogmas of Empiricism." Among the strategies of those who have felt the full force of the contemporary critique but still insist upon rationally justified intellectual moorings are those championed by Alvin Plantinga, with his "properly basic beliefs," in "Reason and Belief in God"; and Alasdair MacIntyre, with his recovery of classical dialectical inquiry, in *First Principles, Final Ends and Contemporary Philosophical Issues* and *Three Rival Versions of Moral Enquiry, Encyclopaedia, Genealogy, Tradition.*

5. Chapter 4 will deal with Scotus's defense of our certain knowledge against the claims of fundamental skepticism.

6. Aristotle's various lists of the categories were soon collected into the traditional ten: substance, quantity, quality, relation, position, action, affection, place, time, and habit or state. His main treatment of them is in *Categories.*

7. Aristotle sketches this view of metaphysics in *Metaphysics* 4.1–2.

8. For instance, Scotus expands the field of transcendental concepts, which traditionally includes the "one," "true," and "good"—which are logically coextensive with "being"—by adding three additional sorts of concepts: "being" itself; disjunctive pairs, such as "actual and potential," "finite and infinite," and "contingent and necessary"; and pure perfections, such as "life," "wisdom," and "will" (*Ord.* I, d. 8, nos. 113–15 [Vat. 4, 205–7]; Allan B. Wolter, *The Transcendentals and Their Function in the Metaphysics of Duns Scotus*).

9. See the entry for "dunce" in the *Oxford English Dictionary;* one is struck by the hostility at the origin of the word.

10. *Collected Papers of Charles Sanders Peirce,* ed. Charles Hartshorne and Paul Weiss (1931), 1:4–5.

11. On the transmission of Aristotle to the West, see F. E. Peters, *Aristotle and the Arabs: The Aristotelian Tradition in Islam,* and Fernand Van Steenberghen, *Aristotle in the West: The Origins of Latin Aristotelianism.*

12. Book 1, q. 1.

13. Book 1, q. 1 (Vivès 7:11–39).

14. Aristotle distinguished a demonstration of the reasoned fact (*propter quid*) from a demonstration of the simple fact (*quia*) (*Posterior Analytics* 1.13–14). In the second type, although one proves that the predicate belongs to the subject of the conclusion, it is done without explaining in the process the ontological cause or reason behind the truth.

15. On the extended senses of the term in logical, epistemological, and metaphysical contexts, see Newton Garver, "Subject and Predicate."

16. Each dividing part is subject to further division. For instance, self-evident propositions can be in what the medievals called either the first or the second mode, depending upon whether the predicate represents an essential or nonessential attribute of the subject. For their part, the deductive conclusions divide into *propter quid* or *quia,* depending on whether or not the inference is based on insight into the ontological reason or real cause of the predicate's relationship to the subject.

17. "We suppose ourselves to possess unqualified scientific knowledge of a thing, as opposed to knowing it in the accidental way in which the sophist knows, when we think that we know the cause on which the

fact depends, as the cause of that fact and of no other, and further, that the fact would not be other than it is. Now that scientific knowing [*scientia*] is something of this sort is evident. . . . The proper object of unqualified scientific knowledge is something which cannot be other than it is. . . . By demonstration I mean a syllogism productive of scientific knowledge, that is, the grasp of which is *eo ipso* such knowledge" (*Posterior Analytics* 1.2.71b8–12, 14–15, 17–18; trans. G. R. G. Mure in *The Basic Works of Aristotle*, ed. Richard McKeon, 111–12).

    18. *Ord.* prol. p. 3, q. 3, nos. 142–43 (Vat. 1:96–97); *Rep. par.* prol., q. 1, art. 2, no. 3 (Vivès 22:9).

    19. *Questions on the Metaphysics* book 6, q. 1, no. 2 (Vivès 7:303).

    20. Ibid., no. 8 (308).

    21. *Ord.* I, d. 8, no. 115 (Vat. 4:206–7); Wolter, *Transcendentals*.

    22. Allan B. Wolter, "The 'Theologism' of Duns Scotus," in *The Philosophical Theology of John Duns Scotus*, by Allan B. Wolter, 209–53.

CHAPTER THREE
Parisian Proof for the Existence of God

Text

[Prima Pars: De Exsistentia Dei]

Circa esse Dei propono tres quaestiones. Prima est utrum sit aliquod ens primum simpliciter in universitate entium; secunda utrum primitas simpliciter possit competere entibus alterius rationis; tertia utrum sit aliquod ens simpliciter et actu infinitum. . . .

Quantum ad quaestiones istas, primo ostendo quis sit ordo inter illas, secundo quomodo una dependet ab alia.

Quantum ad primum dico quod, ut dictum est prius, de Deo secundum nullum conceptum nobis possibilem de eo in via est per se notum de eo esse [nec notum] demonstratione propter quid, quia medium ad demonstrandum de eo esse est nobis ignotum, scilicet essentia Dei ut haec vel deitas sub ratione deitatis; et ideo haec propositio "Deus est" non est per se nota nec nobis nota propter quid, nec est desperatum a nobis cognosci. Ergo demonstratione quia tantum potest a nobis cognosci modo, ut medium sumitur ab effectu. Immediatius autem sunt nobis notae proprietates respectivae in causa quam proprietates absolutae, quia secundum proprietates respectivas dicimus eum respicere omnem effectum ut secundum proprietates causalitatis et productibilitatis; et ideo ex huiusmodi proprietatibus primo propositum est ostendendum.

This text is from Scotus's personally examined report of his lecture as a bachelor candidate for a master of theology degree at the University of Paris, known as *Reportatio* I A. The Latin text and translation is an excerpt from the four questions in distinction 2 of this work, the complete text of which is available in Allan B. Wolter and Marilyn McCord Adams, eds., "Duns Scotus' Parisian Proof for the Existence of God."

[Part One: The Existence of God]

Regarding the existence of God, I propose three questions. First, in the world of beings, is there some being that is first in an unqualified sense? Second, could several different sorts of being possess such primacy? Third, is some being actually infinite in an unqualified sense? . . .

As for these questions, I show first how they are ordered and second how one depends upon the other.

As for the first, I say as I did before about God, that according to no concept of him that we have in this life is his existence known per se [or] by a demonstration of the reasoned fact, because the middle term needed to demonstrate this, namely, God's essence as precisely "this" or as deity qua deity, is unknown to us. And for us the proposition "God exists" is therefore neither self-evident nor known as a reasoned fact. But we need not despair of knowing it altogether. Indeed, at present we can know it only by a demonstration of the simple fact, where the middle term of the demonstration is taken from what God effects. Those properties related to his causal activity, however, are known more immediately than are his absolute properties, because we say he relates to every effect in virtue of the relational properties of causality and producibility. And therefore it is on the basis of these properties that we must first establish our proposed thesis.

[1. Responsio ad primam quaestionem]

Respondeo ergo ad primam quaestionem quod est aliquod primum simpliciter omni primitate quae non includit aliquam imperfectionem, cuius est primitas materiae vel formae respectu compositi; pars enim semper est imperfectior toto et tamen prior; pars enim participat entitatem totius et non est ipsum totum. Aliae enim sunt primitates quae non includunt aliquam imperfectionem, ut primitas eminentiae et triplicis causalis independentiae, scilicet efficientis, formalis vel exemplaris, et finalis. Primitas autem eminentiae non est primitas causalitatis; non enim ex hoc quod unum ens praeeminet alteri, est causa illius. Nam primum in quolibet genere praeeminet alteri posteriori illius generis, et tamen non est causa illius. Primitas etiam exemplaris non distinguitur a primitate efficientiae, quia primum exemplans alia in esse intelligibili, non est nisi primum efficiens per intellectum; et sicut naturale efficiens non distinguitur contra efficiens, immo continetur sub eo, sic nec exemplaris distinguitur ab efficiente. Sunt ergo duae causalitates contra se distinctae, scilicet causae efficientis et finalis. Et istae primitates omnes, quae attribuimus Deo, nullam includunt imperfectionem.

[i. Quod Deus sit primum primitate efficientis]

Quod autem Deus sit primum omnium ista primitate probo: et primo de primitate efficientiae sic: Aliquod ens est effectum, quia productum; aut igitur producitur a se, vel a nihilo vel ab alio. Non a nihilo, quia nihil nullius est causa; nec a se, quia nihil est quod seipsum gignat vel producat, I *De Trinitate*, capitulo nono.[1] Ergo, ab alio. Si ab alio, ergo illud producitur a nihilo vel a se vel ab alio, et sic procedetur in infinitum. Ergo oportet stare ad aliquid non productum, nec virtute alterius producens sed virtute propria; et hoc voco primum.

[*Duae instantiae*] Contra istam rationem insto dupliciter:

Primo, quia non est inconveniens procedere in infinitum in productionibus eiusdem rationis, secundum philosophos—ut quod filius iste sit ab isto patre et iste ab alio, et sic in infinitum. Ignis etiam ab igne potest esse in infinitum.

---

1. Augustine, *De trinitate* 1.9.

[1. Reply to the first question]

I reply then to the initial question that there is some being that is simply first in every way that does not include some imperfection, such as that of the primacies of matter and form with respect to their composite, for a part [such as matter and form] is always less perfect than the whole, since the part shares the entity of the whole and yet is not the whole itself. But there are other ways of being first that do not include any imperfection, such as the primacy of excellence and of causal independence in a threefold sense, namely of having no efficient cause, no formal or exemplar cause, and no final cause. Now the primacy of excellence is not a primacy of causality, for it does not follow that if one being is more perfect than another, it is also the cause of that other. For the most eminent [species] in any genus excels each less eminent [species] and yet is not its cause. Note also that the primacy of exemplarity is not distinguished from that of efficiency, because for the first to model another in thought is nothing other than a first efficient cause endowed with an intellect. Now just as a natural efficient cause is not distinguished from efficient cause—indeed it is a subdivision thereof—so neither is the exemplar cause. Hence, there are only two sorts of causality that are distinct from each other, namely, what pertains to an efficient cause and to a final cause, respectively. And each primacy that we attribute to God includes no imperfection.

[i. That God is first as an effective agent]

I prove that God is first of all things by each such primacy, and I begin with the primacy of efficiency thus: Some being is an effect because it is produced. Now either nothing produces it, or it produces itself, or it is produced by another. It is not produced by nothing, for nothing is the cause of nothing. Neither does it produce itself, for according to book 1, chapter nine of Augustine's *De trinitate,* "nothing begets itself." Therefore it is produced by another. If by another, then this other is produced by nothing, by itself, or by another—and so the process would continue indefinitely. Consequently, one must stop with something that is not produced but that produces by its own power and not in virtue of any other; and this I call the first.

[*Two objections*] I raise two objections to this reasoning:

First, it is not incongruous that productions of the same sort should continue indefinitely, according to the philosophers. Thus this son is from that father, and the latter from another father, and so on ad infinitum. Fire, too, can come from fire indefinitely.

Item, omnis demonstratio non demonstrans quia sed propter quid est ex necessariis; haec non est ex necessariis sed ex rationibus producentis et producti, quae sunt termini contingentes; ergo non demonstrans.

[*Solutio primae instantiae*] Excludo primam consequentiam: dico quod non est processus in infinitum in essentialiter ordinatis; nec umquam philosophi in talibus concesserunt infinitatem, licet in accidentaliter ordinatis hoc concesserint, ut patet per Avicennam,[2] VI *Metaphysicae,* capitulo quinto.

Ad hoc autem demonstrandum praemitto unum, scilicet quod non est idem loqui de causis per se et per accidens, et de causis essentialiter et accidentaliter ordinatis. Nam in primo est tantum comparatio unius ad unum, scilicet causae ad effectum, et est causa per se quando aliquid secundum naturam propriam et non secundum aliquid sibi accidens causat, ut subiectum est per se causa suae passionis, et in multis aliis, ut album disgregat et aedificator aedificat; sed causa per accidens est e converso, ut Policletus aedificat.

In secundo autem est comparatio duarum causarum inter se in quantum ab eis est aliquod tertium ut causatum, et tunc different causae per se sive essentialiter ordinatae a causis accidentaliter ordinatis tripliciter, ex qua triplici differentia habebitur triplex demonstratio ad probandum aliquid simpliciter primum efficiens.

Prima differentia est quod in causis per se et essentialiter ordinatis causa secunda, in quantum causat, dependet a prima; in accidentaliter ordinatis non sic dependet in causando licet in esse vel in aliquo alio dependeat. Filius enim licet secundum esse dependeat a patre, non tamen in causando, quia patre mortuo potest agere sicut ipso vivo.

Secunda differentia est quia in per se et essentialiter ordinatis est causalitas alterius rationis et alterius ordinis, quia superior causa est perfectior eo quod eius virtute causat causa secunda; sed non sic est in accidentaliter ordinatis, quia ita potest filius generare sicut pater, nec dependet in causando nisi a causa eiusdem rationis, non a causa perfectiori.

---

2. Avicenna, *Metaphysica* 66 (*Opera latina, Venetiis,* 1508, fol. 94rb–va).

There is also this objection. Every demonstration not demonstrating the simple fact but rather the reason for the fact begins with something necessary. But this argument does not, for it uses the notions of producer and produced, which are contingent terms; hence the argument does not demonstrate.

[*Solution to the first objection*] I refute the first objection thus: in things essentially ordered, I declare, there is no progression to infinity, nor do any philosophers admit such, though they do concede this where accidentally ordered things are concerned, as it clear from Avicenna's *Metaphysics,* book 8, chapter 5.

To demonstrate this, however, I introduce one prefatory remark, namely, to speak of per se and per accidens causes is not the same as speaking of essentially ordered and accidentally ordered causes. For in the first case, there is a one-to-one comparison, namely, of a cause to its effect. And we have a per se cause when something causes by virtue of its proper nature, not by something incidental to it. Thus a subject is the per se cause of its proper attribute; and there are many other instances, such as when something white expands [the diaphanous medium] or a builder builds. But the converse is true of a per accidens cause, such as Polycletus building.

In the second case, however, there is a comparison of two causes with each other insofar as some third thing is caused by them. And then it turns out that per se or essentially ordered causes differ from those accidentally ordered in three ways. And this triple difference provides a threefold demonstration for proving that something is a first efficient cause in an unqualified sense.

The first difference is that with causes that are essentially ordered, the second cause, insofar as it causes, depends upon the first, whereas in accidentally ordered causes the second does not depend upon the first in this way, though it may be dependent on the first for its existence or in some other respect. For though a son depends upon his father for his existence, he does not depend upon him in causing, since when his father is dead he can act as effectively as if his father were alive.

There is a second difference, since the causality of per se and essentially ordered causes is of different sorts and is ordered [to the effect] in different ways. For the superior cause is more perfect inasmuch as the second cause causes by virtue of the former. But this is not so with accidentally ordered causes, for a son can procreate, just as a father can; and he does not depend in this except upon a cause of the same sort—not upon a more perfect cause.

Tertia differentia est quia omnes causae per se et essentialiter ordinatae simul necessario requiruntur ad causandum effectum; quia, si non, aliqua causalitas essentialis et per se deesset effectui; sed talis simultas non requiritur in accidentaliter ordinatis, sed successive una post aliam.

Ex prima differentia arguo sic: in causis essentialiter ordinatis, ubi ponit adversarius infinitatem, secunda in quantum causat dependet a prima. Si ergo essent causae infinitae ita quod quaelibet alia—non solum quaelibet posterior—dependet a sua proxima priori, sed universitas causatorum ab alia causa priori, non ab aliqua causa quae est aliquid illius universitatis, quia tunc esset aliqua causa sui. Tota enim universitas dependentium dependet et non ab aliquo illius universitatis, quia quilibet dependet; ergo ab aliquo quod non est aliquid illius universitatis, et hoc voco primum efficiens. Si igitur sunt infinitae, adhuc dependent ab aliqua, quae non est illius infinitatis.

Ex secunda differentia arguo sic: si causae essentialiter ordinatae sint alterius ordinis, semper causa superior est perfectior; ergo causa in infinitum superior, erit in infinitum perfectior. Si igitur sunt infinitae tales, erunt infinitae causae perfectae. Sed nulla talis simpliciter perfecta causat virtute alterius; ergo non sunt essentialiter ordinatae. Dato enim quod causaret virtute alterius, non esset simpliciter suprema et perfecta.

Ex tertia differentia arguo sic: si causae ordinatae essentialiter in infinitum concurrant ad productionem alicuius effectus, et ex ista differentia omnes causae essentialiter sint simul, sequitur quod infinita actu sunt simul ad causandum hunc effectum, quod non conceditur ab aliquo philosopho.

[*Argumenta persuasiva*] Ad hoc etiam adducuntur duae aliae persuasiones. Prima talis: si sit processus in infinitum in causis essentialiter ordinatis, omnes erunt causatae; ergo ab aliqua causa, et si illa non sit prima, omnes erunt aequaliter mediae causae, nam non ponitur alia prima respectu cuius alia possit dici propinquior vel remotior alia; et sic est verum quod tenet ratio Philosophi, II *Metaphysicae*,[3] et est eadem ratio virtualiter cum illa quae accepta est ex prima differentia.

---

3. Aristotle, *Metaphysics* 2.2.994a17–19.

There is a third difference, because all the per se and essentially ordered causes are needed simultaneously to cause the effect; were this not so, some per se and essential causality would be lacking the effect. But such simultaneity is not required where accidentally ordered causes are concerned, for they exercise their causality successively, one after the other.

From the first difference I argue thus: In essentially ordered causes, where our adversary postulates an infinity, each second cause, insofar as it is causing, depends upon a first. If there were an infinity of causes, therefore, it would be such that each one of them—not just each posterior cause—depended upon its immediately prior cause. Rather, the whole collection of what is caused depends upon some other prior cause that is not a part of that collection, for then something would be a cause of itself. Since the whole collection of dependents depends, it does so not upon something that is part of that collection, because everything there is dependent. Consequently it depends upon something that is not part of that totality. And this I call the first efficient. Hence, even if there is an infinity of causes, they still depend upon something that is not a part of that infinity.

From the second difference I argue thus: If all essentially ordered causes are of a different order, because they are of different orders, the higher will always be more perfect. Therefore a cause that is infinitely superior will be infinitely more perfect. Hence if there is an infinity of such, there will be infinite causes that are simply perfect. But no cause that is simply perfect causes by virtue of another; therefore if there is an infinity of causes, then they are not essentially ordered. For if you grant that they cause by virtue of another, none would be simply supreme or perfect.

From the third argument I argue thus: If an infinity of essentially ordered causes would concur in the production of some effect, and—by virtue of this third difference—all such must act at once, it would follow that an actual infinity is simultaneously causing this effect—something that no philosopher admits.

[*Two persuasive reasons*] Two other persuasive arguments are adduced to prove this [primacy of efficiency], the first of which is this. If in essentially ordered causes, the process went on to infinity, each would be caused, and hence by some cause. If this were not a first cause, then all would be equally intermediate causes, for there would be no first with reference to which one could be said to be more proximate or remote than another. And hence the argument given by the Philosopher in book 2 of the *Metaphysics* would hold good. This is virtually the same as the argument derived from the first difference.

Secunda ratio est ista: omne effectivum nullam imperfectionem includit; sed quod nihil imperfectionis includit, potest poni inter entia sine imperfectione. Sed si nulla causa est sine dependentia ad aliquid prius, in nullo est sine imperfectione; ergo effectibilitas potest inesse alicui naturae, et illa natura est simpliciter prima. Ergo effectibilitas simpliciter prima est possibilis et, si potest esse et non ab aliquo alio, ergo a se.

Sed dices quod istae rationes non concludunt supponendo ordinem essentialem causarum. Sed negabitur tibi ordo essentialis, et dicetur quod omne quod producitur, producitur sufficienter a causa particulari eiusdem rationis sicut a causa totali, ut filius a patre, et sic in infinitum.

Contra: hoc productum aut producitur a causa alterius ordinis, et sequitur ordo essentialis, aut a causa eiusdem rationis, et tunc fuit possibile produci a causa a qua producitur, et ista ab alia et illa ab alia a qua producitur, fuit possibilis produci, et sic in infinitum. Semper enim natura habebit eundem modum essendi in quolibet eiusdem rationis, ita quod, si unum fuit productibile, et quodlibet in infinitum successive. Sed nulla successio potest in infinitum continuari nisi in virtute alicuius permanentis in infinitum cum tota successione illa, eo quod nulla difformitas perpetuatur nisi in virtute alicuius uniformis quod non est aliquid illius successionis, quia nulla pars successionis potest permanere cum tota successione, eo quod tunc non esset pars eius. Ergo est aliquid essentialiter prius tota successione, cum tota successio dependeat ad ipsum. Omne ergo quod dependet a causa accidentaliter ordinata, dependet essentialius a causa per se et essentialiter ordinata. Immo negato ordine essentiali negabitur ordo accidentalis, quia accidentia non habent ordinem nisi mediante fixo et permanente, et per consequens nec multitudinem in infinitum. Et sic exclusa est prima instantia, scilicet quod non est procedere in infinitum in accidentaliter ordinatis nisi fuerit status in essentialiter ordinatis.

[*Solutio secundae instantiae*] Ad secundam instantiam quae dicit quod non demonstro, quia procedo ex contingentibus, cum dico: aliqua natura est producta vel effecta, ergo aliquid est

The second reason is this. To be an efficient cause does not imply imperfection. But what includes no imperfection can be assumed to exist without imperfection in some being. But if no cause exists that is not itself dependent upon something prior, then no cause exists without imperfection. [Since this negates our initial assumption], it follows from that assumption that effectibility could exist in some nature that is simply first. Therefore, effectibility that is first in an unqualified sense is possible, and if it can exist and yet cannot be from another, then it exists of itself.

You may object that these reasons are valid only if one assumes an essential order among the causes, something you deny and avow instead that everything produced is adequately accounted for by some particular total cause of the same sort, like a son produced by a father, and so on ad infinitum.

I say against this: Either this product is produced by a cause of some other order, and then it follows that an essential order does exist, or else the product is caused by something of the same sort. As such it would be a possible to be produced by the cause that produces it, and that cause, too, would be only a possible to be produced by some other cause, which in turn was only a possible to be produced by something else, and so on ad infinitum. For where all are of the same sort, their natures would have the same sort of existence, so that if one were only something able to be produced, then all would be such successively. But no succession can continue indefinitely except by virtue of something permanent that is coextensive with the succession as a whole. For no change in form [i.e., from possibility to actuality] is perpetuated save by virtue of something uniform that is not a part of the succession itself, since no part can persist throughout the entire succession and still be only just a part of it. Therefore, there is something that is essentially prior to the whole succession, since the latter depends upon it. Hence everything that depends upon an accidentally ordered cause also depends upon a per se and essentially ordered cause as well. Indeed, if this essential order is denied, the accidental order will also be denied, because the accidentals have no order except in relation to something fixed and permanent. Neither would a multitude, then, have any order proceeding to infinity. And in this way the first objection is refuted, namely, that there will be no infinite process of accidentally ordered causes unless there be a stage where the essential order ends.

[*Solution to the second objection*] The second objection claims that I have no demonstration when I argue: "Some nature is produced or effected, hence something is producing or effecting it,

producens vel efficiens, etc., respondeo quod in demonstratione quia possum accipere praemissam de inesse vel de possibili. Si accipitur de inesse, est demonstratio contingens et non ex necessariis; ut cum dico: "Aliquid est productum, ergo aliquid est producens"; ostensum enim est ad sensum. Si autem accipiatur praemissa pro possibile esse sic: "Aliqua natura est possibilis fieri, sive effectibilis vel productibilis, ergo aliqua natura est effectiva vel productiva," est demonstratio ex necessariis. Nam antecedens est necessarium et consequens similiter, quia aliquod subiectum est mutabile et aliquod entium est possibile—distinguendo possibile contra necessarium. Et concludit probatio istis rebus de esse quiditativo vel de esse possibili sic: "Aliquid potest fieri, ergo aliquid est productivum et causativum eius; et si aliquid simpliciter primum effectivum, erit actu existens."

Probo sic: cuius rationi repugnat esse ab alio, illud si potest esse, potest esse a se; sed rationi primi simpliciter effectivi repugnat esse ab alio, quia non est effectum vel productivum ab alio, nec virtute alicuius alterius est productivum vel effectivum vel producens; et potest esse; ergo est. Si enim potest esse, aut ergo a se, vel ab alio; non ab alio, quia ponitur primum; si a se, habetur propositum, quia si potest esse, est. Ergo concludo quod in causis efficientibus est dare essentialem ordinem et per consequens aliquod efficiens primum simpliciter.

[ii. Quod Deus sit primum primitate eminentiae]

Ex isto secundo infero quod est aliquod ens simpliciter in eminentia, quia in ordine essentiali causarum essentialium semper est causa aequivoca respectu sui effectus, quia est alterius ordinis ab effectu. Causa autem aequivoca semper est nobilior suo effectu, cum non potest esse aeque perfectum nec minus perfectum; sic enim dicerem quod omnia alia perfecta corpora possent produci a musca, quia per te non requiritur in causa aequivoca maior perfectio quam in eius effectu.

etc., since I start out with contingent terms. To this I reply: In a demonstration of the simple fact [such as from effect to cause], I can take as a premise a statement of what exists or of what is only possible. If I take only the assertoric statement of what exists, my demonstration will be contingent and not based on necessary terms. Such would be the case if I say: "Something is being produced, therefore something is producing it," for this is something that sense perception reveals. But if the premise is taken from what is possible, then the demonstration begins with what is necessary, in this way: "It is possible that some nature comes to be, i.e., it is effectible or producible; hence some nature is able to effect or produce it." For here the antecedent, and the consequent as well, are necessary, because some being is mutable, and among beings something is possible—where "possible" is contrasted with "necessary." And the proof infers these things from what is essential to existence, i.e., its possibility, in this fashion: "Something can come to be, therefore something can produce or cause it." But if something can cause effectively in a simple or unqualified sense, then it will be actually existing.

This I prove as follows: If it is repugnant to the very notion of something that it be from another, then if it can exist, it can exist of itself. But that it stem from another is repugnant to the very notion of an efficient agent that is first in an unqualified sense, since it is not an effect, nor does it have its productive capacity from another; neither is it producing or able to be effective or productive only by virtue of something else. Furthermore, it can exist. Therefore it actually does exist. For if it can exist, then it either is of itself or is from another. It is not from another, because it is assumed to be first. If it is of itself, we have what we set out to prove, since if it can exist, it does exist. Therefore, I conclude that in efficient causes an essential order represents what is given, and from this it follows that some efficient cause is simply first.

| [ii. That God is first in excellence]

From this I infer secondly that some being is simply unexcelled. For in an essential order of essential or per se causes, a cause is always equivocal with respect to its effect, since it is of a different order than the latter. An equivocal cause, however, is always nobler than its effect, since, as equivocal, it can be neither less perfect nor only equal in perfection with its effect. For this would be equivalent to saying that every other more perfect organism could be produced by a fly, since—according to you—no greater perfection is required of an equivocal cause than exists in its effect.

[iii. Quod Deus sit primum primitate finalitatis]

Ex hoc etiam sequitur tertio—si est aliquod primum efficiens—quod est aliquis primus finis non ordinabilis ad alium finem nec virtute alterius finitivum, quia omne per se agens et efficiens agit propter finem—habetur hoc ex II *Physicorum*[4]—et prius efficiens propter priorem finem, ergo primum efficiens propter ultimum finem; sed propter nihil aliud a se principaliter agit et ultimate, ergo propter se sicut propter finem. Et sic sequitur quod primum efficiens erit ultimus finis, sive primus. Si enim ageret per se propter finem alium a se, tunc aliquid esset nobilius primo efficiente, quia finis, qui est aliquid remotum ab agente intendente finem, est nobilius eo.

[iv. Quod Deus sit primum exemplans]

Quarto et ultimo dico quod primum efficiens est primum exemplans respectu effectibilium, quia, ut prius dictum est, primum efficiens agit propter finem per se, nam omne per se agens agit propter finem, etiam agens per naturam, de quo minus videtur, II *Physicorum*.[5] Vel ergo propter finem quem cognoscit, vel in quem a cognoscente dirigitur. Non secundo modo, quia primum efficiens non potest ab alio dirigi vel ordinari. Ergo propter finem quem cognoscit. Sed agens per cognitionem ordinat effectum in finem cognitum, sed hoc non est aliud quam effectum exemplari. Sed non ordinat rem in aliquem finem secundarium cognitum alium a se, quia tunc non esset primus finis, ut dictum est; ergo ordinat in se exemplando tamquam in finem ultimatum immediate. Et sic sequitur quod est primum exemplans....

[2. Responsio ad secundam quaestionem]

Ad secundam quaestionem qua quaeritur utrum primitas simpliciter posset competere entibus alterius rationis, respondeo: ista quaestio videtur habere duplicem intellectum:

---

4. Aristotle, *Physics* 2.5.196b17–22.
5. Ibid., 8.198b10–199b33.

[iii. That among final causes God is also first]

From this a third point also follows. If something is first as an efficient agent, then something also exists that is first as an end, i.e., something that cannot exist or function as final cause only by virtue of some other end. Every per se agent or efficient cause acts for the sake of some end. This we glean from book 2 of the *Physics*. Now a prior efficient agent acts for the sake of some prior end; therefore, the first efficient agent acts for the sake of the final end. But such an agent never acts principally or ultimately for anything other than itself. Hence, it acts for the sake of itself as end. Thus it follows that the first efficient agent will also be the ultimate or first end. For were an agent to act for the sake of some end other than itself, then something would be nobler than the first efficient agent, because anything that is removed or distinct from an agent intending the end is nobler than that agent.

[iv. That God is the first exemplar cause]

Fourth, and finally, I say that the first efficient agent also functions as the first exemplar cause of all that can be effected, because, as was stated earlier, the first efficient acts for an end per se, for every per se agent acts for an end. Even one that acts by nature acts for some end where the teleology is less obvious, according to book 2 of the *Physics*. Now either the first agent acts for an end that it is aware of, or else it is directed to its end by one who is aware of it. But it is not in the second manner, for a first efficient cause cannot be directed or ordered by another. Hence it acts for the sake of some end that it has in mind. An agent that acts knowingly orders its effect to the end that it has mind; but this is nothing else than to function as the exemplar cause of that effect. Such an agent, however, does not order a thing to some known secondary end distinct from itself, for then it would not be the first end that we claimed it to be. Therefore, in modeling the thing in its mind, it immediately orders it to itself as ultimate end. And thus it follows that the first efficient agent plays a primary role as exemplar....

[2. Reply to the second question]

The second question asked whether this primacy in an unqualified sense could pertain to beings of different sorts. To this I reply: The question, it seems, could be understood in two ways. One

unum comparando primitatem ad primitatem, ut primitatem eminentiae ad efficientiae vel finis, quae sunt alterius rationis; sed iste intellectus non est ad propositum, quia probatum est prius quod cui competit primitas rationis unius, et alia alterius rationis, quia nulla istarum concludit aliquam imperfectionem. Est igitur idem primum efficiens, primum exemplans, primum eminens et primum finiens, sive primus finis.

Alius intellectus quaestionis est an omnes illae quattuor possunt competere essentiis alterius rationis, et respondeo quod non, quod probo: loquamur modo exempli gratia de primitate efficientiae. Si duae essentiae alterius rationis possent esse primae efficientes simpliciter, aut ergo respectu eorumdem effectuum vel effectibilium posteriorum, vel respectu aliorum. Non possunt esse causae primae efficientes respectu eiusdem effectus, quia eiusdem causati non possunt esse plures causae totales eiusdem generis vel ordinis; ergo multo minus possunt esse duae causae efficientes totaliter, quia istae non essent eiusdem generis et ordinis, et neutra dependeret ab altera in causando aliquem effectum. —Probatio assumpti, scilicet quod respectu eiusdem causati non possunt esse duae causae totales. Sint a et b duae causae totales efficientes respectu eiusdem effectus. Ex quo ergo a est totalis causa alicuius effectus, posito a sufficienter ponitur effectus, quia effectus non dependet nisi a causa eius totali; et ita, circumscripto b, potest iste effectus sufficienter poni ab a. Sed secundum te b est totalis causa illius effectus; ergo aliquid erit totalis causa alicuius, quo non posito non minus esset effectus et a quo effectus non dependeret. Consequens est impossibile. Ergo oportet dare quod sint duae causae totales respectu diversorum effectuum. Sed hoc similiter est impossibile, quia aut sunt diversorum effectuum eiusdem speciei, aut alterius speciei; non eiusdem speciei, quia ista possunt esse a causa eiusdem speciei; nec requirunt causas distinctas speciei; nec secundo modo, quia si illi effectus sunt diversae speciei, ergo habent ordinem essentialem, quia species universi sunt sicut numeri. Ergo et omnia quae habent ordinem essentialem reducuntur ad unum principium a quo dependent, quod est quadruplici primitate primum, sicut ostensum est in praecedente quaestione.

would be to compare one primacy with another, for example that of eminence with that of efficiency or that of final cause, which are primacies of different sorts. But this sense of the question is not relevant to what we have in mind. For it was proved earlier that the subject to which one sort of primacy pertains also has the other sorts, since none of these ways of being first implies any imperfection. The first efficient cause is the same being as the first exemplar cause and is also the most excellent and is the first end or final cause as well.

Another sense of the question is whether all four of these ways of being first could pertain to different sorts of essences, and to this I reply that they could not. I give a proof for this. Take, for example, the primacy of efficiency. If two essences of different sorts could both be first efficient causes in an unqualified sense, it would be either with respect to the same actual or possible effects or with respect to different effects. Both could not be first efficient causes of the same effect. For if the same effect cannot have several total causes of the same kind or order, much less could essentially different agents be total efficient causes of the same effect, since they are not of the same kind or order, nor does one depend upon the other in causing the same effect. Proof of the antecedent that the same effect cannot have two total causes [of the same kind] follows. Let a and b be two total efficient causes of the same effect. Then from the fact that a is the total cause of some effect, it follows that if a is given, this suffices to place the effect in existence, because the effect depends only on its total cause. Thus, even if b were written off completely, the same effect could exist because a would suffice to accomplish it. But according to you, b is the total cause of this effect; therefore, something will be the total cause of a thing that—even if it were not given—would not prevent the effect from existing, since the effect does not depend upon it for its existence. But the consequent is impossible. Therefore, the two total causes must be causes of diverse effects. But this, too, is impossible, because either these are effects of the same species or of different species. They are not of the same species, because these can stem from a cause of the same species and do not require specifically distinct causes. But neither are the diverse effects of different species, for if they were, an essential order would exist among them, since all the species in the world are like numbers. And then it would follow that all these things that have an essential order would be traced back to one principle, from which they depend. And this—as we showed in the previous question—would be the principle that is first by a quadruple primacy.

Item, hoc probatur per rationem Philosophi XII *Metaphysicae*.[6] Si sunt prima entia alterius rationis habentia sub se diversas coordinationes, ita quod coordinata ad unum primum non haberent ordinem ad coordinata in alia coordinatione ad aliud primum, tolleretur natura boni ab universo, quae natura boni consistit in ordine partium universi ad invicem et ad primum. Unde ponentes plura principia prima alterius coordinationis, "inconnexam faciunt universi substantiam," sicut dicit ibidem Philosophus.[7]

Item, tertio hoc probatur specialiter de primitate eminentiae, nam sicut in omni genere est stare ad aliquam unam naturam quae est mensura omnium posteriorum in illo genere, ita in genere totius entis necesse est stare ad aliquam naturam simpliciter primam quae est ratio et mensura omnium entium, ut patet ex X *Metaphysicae*.[8]

Ex dictis sequuntur duo corollaria: unum quod est primum efficiens non tantum est primum secundum quid respectu omnium effectibilium unius coordinationis, sed etiam est primum respectu omnium effectibilium et etiam primum eminens et primum finis. Unde sequitur quod aliquod ens simpliciter primum est unius rationis, ex quo patet necessitas istius quaestionis, nam ex rationibus praecedentis quaestionis non est probatum nisi aliquod primum unius coordinationis. Posset enim aliquis dicere aliam coordinationem esse habentem suum primum efficiens et sua effectibilia. Unde cum arguitur in praecedente quaestione quod hoc productum producitur ab aliquo et non in infinitum, ergo est stare ad aliquod primum, diceret aliquis quod hoc est verum ad primum illius coordinationis, ut ad solem; sed praeter ista sunt alia productibilia alterius rationis, quae non habent suum primum utpote lunam. Ideo necesse fuit postea quaerere, an possint esse duo prima alterius rationis, et probare quod est tantum unum ens simpliciter primum unius rationis, quod pertinet ad istam quaestionem. An autem tale sit, aut unum numero vel plura, pertinet ad quaestionem sequentem de unitate Dei.

Secundum corollarium est quod cum ista primitas tantum convenit uni essentiae, nihil faciens unum per accidens cum ista essentia requiritur ad primitatem istius essentiae, quia si requiretur, tunc ista primitas non convenit tantum uni essen-

---

6. Aristotle, *Metaphysics* 12.8.1074a31–37.
7. Ibid., 12.10.1076a1.
8. Ibid., 10.1.1052b17–18.

The reasoning of the Philosopher in book 12 of the *Metaphysics* provides another proof of this. If each of two different sorts of first beings has under it its own group of ordered effects that is distinct from, but coordinate with, that of the other, the goodness of the universe would be destroyed. For what makes the universe good is the orderly way that all its constituent parts hang together and depend upon one being that is first. Hence, those who postulate several first principles, each with a distinct but coordinate group of effects, "dismember the substance of the universe," as the Philosopher says in that same book.

Also, there is a third proof that refers in particular to the primacy of excellence, for just as in every category we end with some one nature that is the measure of all the others in that category, so in the category of the whole of being, it is necessary to end with some nature that is first in an unqualified sense and is the measure of all beings, as is evident from book 10 of the *Metaphysics*.

Two corollaries follow from what has been said. One is that the first efficient agent is not only first in a qualified sense, i.e., with respect to all that can be effected in one coordination; it is also first with respect to everything whatsoever that can be effected and is also the first in excellence and is the first end. Hence it follows that there is but one kind of being that is simply first. From this we see why this question was necessary, since the arguments of the previous question only establish the fact that there is something first with respect to one coordination, for one could say that the other coordination has its own first efficient cause and what it can effect. Hence, when we argued in the preceding question that this product is produced by something, and that, since the productive process cannot be infinite, one must end with something first, someone could object that this is true only of what is first in this coordination, for instance the sun, but besides this there are other things of a different sort that could be produced that would not have this as their first cause, for example, the moon. Therefore it was necessary to ask further whether there could be two such firsts of different sorts. Proving that there is but one kind of being that is first in an unqualified sense was the task of this question. Whether the number of such is one or several pertains to a later question about the unicity of God.

The second corollary is that inasmuch as this primacy belongs to but one sort of essence, nothing that constitutes something that is only accidentally one with it is required for this essence to be first. For if it were, then this primacy would not pertain to only one essence but rather to a certain aggregate of two

tiae, sed cuidam aggregato ex duabus essentiis, et tunc nihil unum esset primum. Et ex hoc sequitur quod nihil potest sibi accidere quod pertinet ad istam primitatem. Et ulterius, cum intellectio distincta omnium causabilium pertineat ad primitatem exemplantis omnia, et efficientis omnia per cognitionem, sequitur quod intellectio illa primi non potest esse accidens illi essentiae; ergo intellectio primi est sua essentia. Similiter, cum volitio omnium finibilium pertineat ad aliquid primum finiens omnia, sequitur quod volitio omnium non sit accidens primo fini. . . .

[3. Responsio ad tertiam quaestionem]

Tertio quaeritur, utrum ens simpliciter primum respectu omnium posteriorum sit actu infinitum intensive. . . .

[*Significatio nominis*] In ista quaestione omnes tenent eandem conclusionem, scilicet quod Deus est infinitus non secundum durationem tantum, sed etiam intensive. Primo ergo ponenda est significatio nominis. Voco autem hic infinitum quod quodcumque ens finitum datum vel possibile dari, excedit secundum omnem determinatam proportionem, acceptam vel acceptibilem. Quod autem intellexerint sic philosophi, patet I *Physicorum*,[9] ubi primo principio attribuit infinitatem. . . .

[*Quatuor probationes*] Teneo autem conclusionem cum aliis, et ostendo propositum, scilicet infinitatem eius actualem, ex quadruplici primitate praemissa.

[*Prima via*] Ex primitate efficientiae probo sic: primum efficiens movet tempore infinito, VIII *Physicorum*;[10] ergo habet virtutem infinitam et est infinitum movens. Sed dices quod antecedens falsum est. Respondeo: Antecedens est necessarium de possibili, licet non de inesse. Si enim causa potest causare, potest causare effectum; licet non causet, non propter hoc minus perfectior, quia habet virtutem causativam; ergo aeque sequitur perfectio virtutis.

Consequentia probatur sic: causa habens a se in virtute sua activa effectum infinitum est infinita; sed causa potens movere motu infinito habet a se in virtute sua activa effectum infinitum; ergo etc. —Minor est plana. Maior probatur: quia omnis effectus vel est formaliter in causa vel eminentius, sive eminentius est in causa quam in se, vel saltem aeque nobiliter; ergo

---

9. Aristotle, *Physics* 3.6.207a7–8.
10. Ibid., 8.10.266a10–24; 266b6–20; 267b17–26.

essences, and then nothing one would be first. From this it follows that nothing pertaining to this primacy can be connected to it only accidentally. And what is more, since to be the first exemplar cause of all things and the sort of efficient cause that knows what it is doing requires that it has a distinct understanding of all possible effects, it follows that this knowledge of the first being is one with its essence. Similarly, since the volition of all that can be directed to an end pertains to what is the end of all, it follows that this volition of all things is not an accident of the first end. . . .

| [3. Reply to the third question]

Third, it is asked: Is a being that is simply first with regard to all posterior things actually infinite intensively? . . .

[*Meaning of "infinite"*] In this question, all hold the same conclusion, namely, that God is infinite not only in duration but also intensively. Therefore, we must first set forth the meaning of the word. What I call "infinite" here is what excels any actual or possible finite being to a degree beyond any determinate measure you take or could take. That the philosophers understood it in this sense is clear from book 1 of the *Physics,* which attributes infinity to the first principle.

[*Four proofs for infinity*] I hold this conclusion along with the others, and I establish my thesis about God's actual infinity on the basis of his aforesaid fourfold primacy. . . .

[*The first way*] I prove it from the primacy of efficiency thus: The first efficient cause moves for an infinite time, according to book 8 of the *Physics;* therefore, it has infinite power and is an infinite mover. You may object, however, that the antecedent is false. I respond: The antecedent is necessary as regards what is possible, though not as regards the actual. For if a cause is able to cause, then it can cause an effect even though it does not actually do so, and it is not less perfect on this score, for it still possesses the causal power. Hence the perfection of such power follows equally from the possible as from the actual.

The validity of the implication is proved thus: A cause having of itself by virtue of its active power an infinite effect is itself infinite. But a cause that is able to move by a movement that is infinite has of itself by virtue of its active power an infinite effect. Therefore, etc. The minor premise is clear. The major is proved because every effect is in its cause either formally or in a more excellent way—in other words, it is present there in a more excellent way than in itself, or at least an equally noble way. Therefore,

effectus qui natus est esse infinitus in se formaliter, erit in sua causa formaliter infinitus eodem modo vel eminentius; sed non est ibi formaliter et eodem modo, quia tunc successive essent omnes in infinitum in causa, sicut successive omnes sunt in effectu; ergo virtualiter et modo eminentiori, et per consequens simul et per consequens infinita intensive.

Secundo probatur eadem consequentia sic: agens qui potest ex se in motum infinitum, potest in effectus infinitos productibiles per motum; primum est huiusmodi, ut probabitur, et quantum est ex parte sui, simul potest in omnes; sed quod potest a se in effectus infinitos in infinitum intensive; ergo etc. Probatio minoris: quia si sit perfectionis in unum effectum, posse in plures effectus est maioris perfectionis; ergo posse in infinitos arguit virtutem infinitam et potentiam infinitam intensive.

Item, causa quae potest simul quantum est ex se infinitos effectus, est infinita intensive; sed si primum movens formaliter haberet causalitates omnium causarum secundarum, quantum est ex se posset in effectus infinitos simul, sicut si illae causalitates essent simul; ergo si primum movens causalitates omnium causarum haberet formaliter, esset infinitum; sed primum nunc perfectius continet causalitates omnium causarum quam si haberet simul formaliter causalitates omnium, quia eminentius nunc omnes continet; ergo nunc est virtualiter infinitum. —Probatio maioris: ubicumque pluralitas includit maiorem perfectionem quam paucitas, ibi infinitas concludit infinitam perfectionem, ut patet etiam in pluralitate aliquorum eiusdem speciei: si facere decem sit maioris perfectiones quam facere quinque, facere infinita est infinitae perfectionis; ergo cum posse in plures effectus simul sit maioris perfectionis quam posse in pauciores, posse in infinitos effectus simul est posse in infinitum intensive.

Quarto probatur eadem consequentia sic: causa efficiens prior cui secunda causa nihil addit perfectionis in agendo est virtutis infinitae intensive, quia si esset virtutis finitae in agendo, secunda causa adderet sibi aliquam perfectionem, sicut sol, non potens immediate producere entia perfectiora nisi mediantibus secundis agentibus, quae addunt perfectionem soli, est virtutis finitae. Sed primum efficiens est huiusmodi, cui nullum agens addit aliquid perfectionis. Probo, quia quando

an effect that is apt by nature to be formally infinite in itself will be formally infinite in its cause either in the same way or in a more excellent fashion. But it is not there formally or in the same way, for then all the effects would be there as an infinite succession, just as they exist in actuality. Therefore, they are there only virtually and in a more excellent way, and hence simultaneously, and as a consequence the power that can produce them is intensively infinite.

This same implication is proved in a second way. An agent that of itself has the power of infinite motion has power over the infinity of effects that can be produced by motion. But the first is this sort of agent, as will be proved. And, so far as it is concerned, it possesses this power over them all simultaneously. But whatever has power of itself over an infinity of effects is intensively infinite. Therefore, etc.

Also, a cause that simultaneously on its part can produce an infinity of effects is intensively infinite. But if the first moving cause would have the causalities of all secondary causes formally, then so far as it goes, it would have power simultaneously over an infinity of effects, just as it would if these causalities existed simultaneously. Therefore, if the first moving cause possessed formally the causality of all causes, it would be infinite. But the first cause now possesses even more perfectly the causalities of all causes than it would if it simultaneously had them all formally, for now it contains all in a more excellent manner. Therefore, it is now virtually infinite. Proof of the major: Wherever plurality implies greater perfection than paucity, there an infinity implies infinite perfection, as is clear also in the case of a plurality of things of the same species. If making ten would be a matter of greater perfection than making five, then making an infinity would be a matter of infinite perfection. Therefore, since to have simultaneously a capacity for several effects is of greater perfection than to have a capacity for fewer effects, the simultaneous capacity for an infinity of effects is a capacity that is intensively infinite.

The same implication is proved in a fourth way thus: A prior efficient cause to which a second cause adds nothing of perfection in acting is of intensively infinite power. For if it were only of finite power in acting, the secondary cause would add something of perfection to its causation, as happens in the case of the sun. Being unable immediately to produce the higher forms of life without the help of secondary agents that add to its perfection, the sun is of finite power. The first efficient cause, however, is such that secondary causes can add nothing to the perfection of

causa secunda addit perfectionem in agendo, quanto plures causae secundae concurrunt cum prima causa, tanto effectus est perfectior; ergo si prima causa perfectius ageret cum causa secunda quam per se, quanto plures causae secundae concurrerent, tanto effectus eius esset perfectior, quod falsum est, quia primus effectus qui immediatius causatur ab eo est perfectior quam remotior.

[*Secunda via*] Ex secunda via, scilicet ex primitate exemplantis, arguitur sic: intellectio infinitorum distincte est infinita, quia intellectio plurium est perfectior quam paucorum; ergo infinitorum infinita. Sed intellectio primi exemplantis est infinitorum distincte, quia est omnium factorum et possibilium fieri; sed cum intellectio sua sit sua essentia, ergo sua essentia erit infinita. Ex hoc infero quod erit actu infinita, quia quaecumque sunt infinita in accipiendo alterum post alterum, ubi sunt simul actu, sunt actu infinita, quia si sunt finita in accipiendo, ergo accipiendo alterum post alterum tandem erit status et ita non sunt infinita in accipiendo successive hoc post hoc. Sed factibilia sunt infinita in potentia accipiendo alterum post alterum successive; ergo ubi simul sunt, sunt actu infinita. Sunt autem simul in cognitione divina a qua omnia factibilia et exemplabilia exemplantur; ergo etc.

Item, quod nihil addit in cognoscibilitate, nec in entitate, II *Metaphysicae;*[11] sed omne exemplabile nihil addit primo exemplanti in cognoscibilitate, ergo nec in entitate, quia si sic non posset ita perfecte cognosci per solam essentiam primi exemplantis sicut si ipsummet concurreret in movendo intellectum divinum. Exemplum: si nigredo aliquid addit in cognoscibilitate coloris ipsi albedini, non potest ita perfecte cognosci nigredo per albedinem sicut si ipsamet concurreret ad sui cognitionem. Nunc autem per solam essentiam divinam et non per aliquid additum cognoscitur distincte quidquid ab eo cognoscitur, ex corollario primo quaestionis praecedentis.

---

11. Ibid., 2.1.993b30–31.

its causation. I prove this, for when secondary causes add to the perfection of the causation, the more secondary concurrent causes there are, the more perfect their effect is. Therefore, if the first cause acted more perfectly with the second cause than when it acted alone, the more secondary causes would concur, the more perfect its effect would be—which is false, because the first effect caused by it immediately [e.g., a pure spirit or something of this sort] is more perfect than the remoter effect [e.g., a material organism].

[*The second way*] The argument from the second way, namely, from the primacy of exemplarity, goes like this: To know an infinity of things distinctly is an infinite intellection, because the intellection of several things is more perfect than that of only a few; therefore knowing an infinity is an infinite intellection. But the intellection of the first exemplar cause is the distinct grasp of an infinity of things, because it has to do with all that is made or can come to be. But since its intellection is its essence, its essence will be infinite as well. And from this I infer that the first exemplar cause will be actually infinite, for whenever one thing after another totals up to an infinity, then, if all are actual simultaneously, they are actually infinite. If one thing after another only added up to something finite, then, taking one item after another, one would eventually come to an end, and thus the items taken successively would not be infinite. But things that can be made one after another are potentially infinite; therefore, where they occur all at once, they are actually infinite. Now they do occur simultaneously in the divine cognition, where all things that can be made or modeled are exemplified; therefore, etc.

Likewise, that to which nothing thinkable can be added cannot be increased in entity, according to book 2 of the *Metaphysics*. But nothing that can be made from an exemplar adds anything thinkable to the first exemplar cause, hence it adds nothing to it in entity, for if it did, then the first exemplar cause could not be known as perfectly through its essence alone as it could if the thing modeled were to concur with the essence in moving the divine intellect. For example, if blackness adds something to whiteness as concerns the knowledge of color, then blackness could not be known as perfectly through whiteness as it could if blackness concurred in the acquisition of the knowledge of itself. According to the first corollary of the preceding question, however, the divine essence knows distinctly whatever it knows solely by reason of itself and not by virtue of anything added to it.

[*Tertia via*] Ex tertia via, scilicet eminentiae arguitur sic: eminentissimo aliquid repugnat esse eminentius; sed finito non repugnat aliquid esse eminentius eo; ergo primum eminens est infinitum. Probatio minoris: infinitum non repugnat enti; quia si sic, hoc est vel quia suum oppositum per se includitur in conceptu essentiali entis, quod non convenit, quia tunc non posset intelligens ens nisi intelligatur finitum, vel quia eius oppositum est passio convertibilis cum ente; nec hoc convenit, quia cognito subiecto statim passio eius fit in intellectu nota; sed cognito ente, non statim occurit intellectui finitas; ergo, etc.

Aliter etiam probatur eadem minor: potentiae sensitivae quae sunt minus cognitivae quam intellectus statim percipiunt disconvenientiam in suo obiecto; patet de auditu respectu soni disconvenientis. Ergo si infinitum repugnat enti statim intellectus istam disconvenientiam et repugnantiam percipiet; et tunc non posset apprehendere ens infinitum pro obiecto, sicut nec repugnantia, ut hominem esse irrationalem, potest habere pro obiecto, quia obiectum includit repugnantiam, cuius oppositum quilibet experitur, quia numquam quietatur in ente finito.

Hoc autem probatur per rationem Anselmi:[12] quo maius cogitari non potest, est infinitum, ergo infinitum est. —Minor probata est supra. Probatio maioris: illud dicitur cogitari quod potest intelligi sine contradictione; unde quod homo sit irrationalis est incogitabile. Unde sicut in rebus nihil est unum nisi sit simplex vel compositum ex potentia et actu, ita et in conceptibus. Contradictoria autem nihil faciunt unum nec simplex nec compositum; ergo non erit unus conceptus cogitabilis.

Redeo ergo ad propositum et arguo quod summum cogitabile est, quia summum cogitabile est cogitabile sine contradictione; sed tale possibile est in effectu, ergo potest cogitari in effectu esse. Sed non erit in effectu quod sit ab alio, quia adhuc maius cogitari potest, scilicet quod est a se. Si potest cogitari esse a se; ergo summum cogitabile necessario est a se. Sed quo

---

12. Anselm, *Proslogion*, c. 5.

[*The third way*] The argument from the third way, namely, from the primacy of excellence, proceeds thus: It is impossible that anything should excel what is most excellent. But it is not impossible that something should excel what is finite. Therefore, the most excellent is not finite but infinite. Proof of the minor: to be infinite is not repugnant to being, for if it were, this would be because its opposite [i.e., to be finite] is either included in the essential concept of being, which is not a convenient solution, because then one could not grasp the notion of being unless one conceived of it as finite; or it is a coextensive attribute of being. But this also is not a happy solution, because once a subject is known, its proper attribute would immediately come to mind; but finitude does not immediately come to mind once being is known. Therefore, etc.

The same minor is proved in another way: The sense faculties, which are less perfect cognitive powers than the intellect, immediately perceive any lack of harmony in their object, as is clear from the case of auditory perception of dissonance. Therefore, if "infinite" were repugnant to "being," the intellect would immediately perceive this repugnance and lack of harmony; then, because of the repugnance, it could not grasp "infinite being" as its object, just as it could not have something contradictory, such as "man is irrational," as its object. But everyone experiences the opposite, since the intellect never rests with finite being.

This is also proved by Anselm's argument: "That is infinite than which nothing greater can be thought; therefore, the infinite exists." The minor premise [i.e., that the most excellent, or that than which nothing greater can be thought, exists] was proved above. Proof of the major: By definition, what can be thought of is what can be understood without contradiction. Hence, that man [i.e., a rational animal] is irrational is something inconceivable. Just as in the real order nothing is one unless it be simple or composed of potency and act, so, too, with concepts. But contradictories do not form any unity, neither simple nor composite. Therefore, they will not form one conceivable concept.

I return then to my original proposal and argue that the highest thing that one can think of exists, because the highest thing that one can think of is conceivable without contradiction; but it is possible for such to exist in actuality, and therefore it can be thought to exist in actuality. But it cannot exist in actuality if it is from another, because one could still think of something greater, namely, something that exists of itself. If it can be conceived to exist of itself, then the highest thing one can think of exists necessarily of itself. But, as was proved above, a thing

maius cogitari non potest, est infinitum actu, ut supra probatum est; ergo est aliquid actu infinitum. Et sic intelligo auctoritatem Anselmi, quando dicit quod Deus est quo maius cogitari non potest.

Sed contra hoc dicitur, scilicet, quod contradictoria possunt cogitari et impossibilia, ut chimera vel mons aureus, et tamen non sunt possibilia fieri vel esse in effectu.

Respondeo: si idem cogitabile esset in intellectu et in effectu, non propter hoc magis cogitabile intensive, licet esset cogitabile pluribus modis; sic ex parte ista si iste intellectus quo cogito montem aureum, etc. Sed si aliquid summum cogitabile est in intellectu, sequitur: ergo potest esse in effectu, et si potest esse, est, quia si non, non est summum cogitabile.

[*Quarta via*] Ex quarta via, scilicet ex primitate finis, arguitur sic: sicut intellectus potest intelligere maximum verum et citra non quietatur in aliquo vero cognito, sic voluntas potest appetere maximum et ultimum bonum sed quiquid est citra illud non est maximum bonum, sed est finitum; ergo ratio ultimi quietativi non est nisi in infinito bono . . .

[Secunda Pars: De Unitate Dei]

Secunda parte principali huius distinctionis secundae, quae est de unitate Dei, quaerendum est unum tantum: utrum primum ens sit tantum unicum numero. . . .

[*Ex parte intellectus*] Et credo quod conclusio ista potest demonstrari, scilicet quod sit unicum ens primum unitate numerali, et primo ex parte intellectus. Probatum enim est quod primum efficiens est primum exemplans, quia distincte intelligens omnia et infinita intelligibilia, et intellectus et intellectum in ipso sunt infinita. Sicut intellectus finitus potest intelligere omne finitum intellectum, sic intellectus infinitus potest intelligere quodcumque intelligibile perfectissime. Si igitur sunt duo primi intellectus infiniti a et b, sequitur quod a intelliget b perfectissime; ergo a per essentiam suam intelliget

greater than which nothing can be thought is actually infinite; therefore, there is something actually infinite. And it is in this way that I understand Anselm's statement when he says that God is that greater than which nothing can be thought.

But against this it is objected that contradictories as well as absurdities, such as a chimera or a gold mountain, can be thought of and yet cannot come to be or actually exist.

I reply: If the same conceivable thing would be in the mind and in the world of actual existence, it would not on that account be any more conceivable intensively, although it would be conceivable in several ways [namely, abstractly and intuitively, for what can exist can be intuited]. And so things that we can think of, such as a gold mountain [or a chimera, etc.], would not on their part be conceivably greater insofar as existence is concerned [because an "actual gold mountain" or "existing chimera" is an absurdity and hence does not represent something conceivable without contradiction]. But if something that is the highest thing conceivable is in the intellect, it follows that it could exist in actuality; and if it could exist, it does exist; for if it were unable to exist, it would not be the highest thing conceivable.

[*The fourth way*] The argument from the fourth way, namely, from the primacy of the end, is constructed thus: Just as the intellect can understand the maximal truth and will not rest in any truth short of this, so also the will can seek the maximal and ultimate good. But anything short of this is not the maximal good but rather is finite. Therefore, the ultimate satisfaction of the will lies only in a good that is infinite. . . .

[Part Two: The Unicity of God]

The second main part of this second distinction, which is about the unicity of God, poses but one question: Is there numerically but one first being? . . .

[*Proof from the nature of God's intellect*] I believe this conclusion can be demonstrated, namely, that there is a unique first being that is one numerically, and the first proof is derived from the intellect. For it has been proved that the first efficient cause is also the first exemplar cause. Inasmuch as it knows distinctly all things and an infinity of intelligibles, both its intellect and what is known are infinite. Now just as a finite intellect can understand every finite thing known, so an infinite intellect can understand any intelligible most perfectly. If, then, there were two first infinite intellects—say, a and b—it would follow that a would understand b most perfectly. Therefore, a would under-

b—vel per essentiam ipsius *b* vel per essentiam ipsius *a*. Si per essentiam *b*, tunc intellectus *a* dependet a *b*, quia actus differens ab obiecto dependet ab eo, et per consequens si intellectio *a* dependet a *b*, et essentia ab essentia; et sic *a* non est Deus. Si per essentiam *a* intelligit *b*, hoc est dupliciter: vel per communem rationem quidditatis *a* et *b*, et hoc non potest esse, quia intelligens praecise aliquod per simile, non intelligit illud in se perfectissime; vel in se intelligit *b*, et hoc non est ita, quia una essentia non potest esse ratio perfectissime intelligendi aliam, eo quod quaelibet in se est intelligibilis per essentiam suam.

Praeterea, una non includit aliam virtualiter in se, quia si *a* includeret virtualiter in se essentiam *b*, tunc *b* non esset Deus. Sic igitur haec intellectio duorum non posset esse nisi per rationem universalis et communis essentiae, et sic imperfecte. —Dices quod per rationem deitatis *a* intelligit *b*. —Contra: ista ratio est universalis; ergo imperfecta cognitio.

Praeterea, unica intellectio non potest habere plura obiecta adaequata; sed *a* habet pro obiecto adaequato essentiam suam; ergo non habet essentiam *b* pro obiecto adaequato.

[*Ex parte voluntatis*] Item, ex parte voluntatis: voluntas enim infinita est recta, ergo diligit omne diligibile quantum ipsum diligibile est; sed *a* et *b* est infinite diligibilis; ergo *a* diligit *b* infinite. Sed quod hoc sit impossibile, probo. Omnis voluntas naturalis plus diligit bonum sui suppositi quam alterius cuius nihil est, nec pars nec aliquid tale; sed *a* nihil est ipsius *b;* ergo voluntas recta conformis naturali plus diligit *a* quam *b*, quia plus diligibile, —et per consequens non diligit *b* infinite.

Item, *a* aut fruitur *b* aut utitur; si utitur, est voluntas perversa; si fruitur, ergo erit beatus in *b* et beatus in *a;* ergo bis beatus in obiectis adaequatis. —Probatio: si fruitur *b*, igitur circumscripto *a*, nihilominus erit beatus se circumscripto; ergo non in se erit beatus, quod est impossibile; erit enim beatus et non beatus.

stand b through the essence—either through the essence of b itself or through the essence of a itself. If it were through the essence of b, then a would depend upon b, because an act different from its object depends upon it, and hence if a's intellection depends upon b, then its essence also depends upon the other's essence, and thus a is not God. If a understands b through its own essence, this would occur in one of two ways: either by virtue of the common character of the quiddity of a and b, and this could not be, because to understand something just through some similarity is not to understand that thing perfectly in itself; or it understands b in itself, and this is not so, either, because the one essence cannot be the reason for understanding the other perfectly, because each in itself is intelligible through its own essence.

Furthermore, one does not include the other virtually in itself, because if a in itself were to include virtually the essence of b, then b would not be God. And so this intellection of the two could only be through some common and universal notion, and thus it would be imperfect. You may say that a understands b through the aspect of deity. I say against this: This notion is universal; therefore the cognition is imperfect.

Furthermore, one intellection could not have several adequate objects; but a has its own essence as its adequate object; therefore it does not have b's essence as its adequate object.

[*Proof from the nature of God's will*] Also, there is a proof from the will. For an infinite will is upright, therefore it loves every lovable object to the extent that it is lovable. But a and b are each infinitely lovable; therefore, a loves b infinitely. But I prove that this is impossible. Every natural will loves its own individual good more than that of another of which it is nothing, neither a part nor any such thing. But a is not something of b itself; therefore, its upright will, being conformable to what is natural, loves a more than b, because it is more lovable—and consequently it does not love b infinitely.

Also, a either loves b for its own sake or uses it. If a uses it, then a's will is perverse; if it loves b for its own sake, then a's capacity for happiness will be satisfied fully by b and also fully satisfied by its love for itself. Therefore, a will achieve its perfect happiness twice in objects, each of which satisfies exhaustively its capacity for happiness. Proof: If a loves b for its own sake, then apart from loving itself, a would be perfectly happy; therefore, it will not be made happy by itself—which is impossible. For then it will be made happy and not made happy.

[*Ex ratione primitatis*] Item, ex ratione primitatis probo sic. Unum omnino unius rationis se habens ad plura unius rationis non determinatur ad illam pluralitatem, sive ad determinationem certam illorum; nec est instantia in natura respectu suppositorum nec causa respectu causatorum nisi instes in proposito. Sed deitas est una unius rationis, et—per te—se habet ad plura unius rationis supposita, ergo ex se non determinatur ad certam pluralitatem singularium, nec potest determinari ad unum, quia repugnat; ergo deitas est in suppositis infinitis.

Ista ratio fundatur in hoc quod primitas de se est determinata. —Si dicas quod non concludit, quia pari ratione deitas non erit in tribus personis, responsio distinctione quinta.

[*Ex necesse esse*] Similiter probari potest propositum de necesse esse sicut Avicenna[13] probat, et de voluntate.

[*Ex omnipotentia*] De omnipotentia autem probat Richardus I *De Trinitate,* cap. 17:[14] Facile efficere poterit, quisquis omnipotens fuerit, quod omne aliud nihil possit. Si ergo sunt plures omnipotentes, quilibet possit facere omnipotentes aliquod nihil potentes et eos destruere.

Sed insto, quia omnipotentia non respicit nisi obiecta possibilia: sed si alius Deus sit omnipotens, non esset possibile, eo quod est necesse esse. —Responsio: concedo in isto intellectu sicut, si Pater non faceret filium et ita non faceret eum omnipotentem, destrueret omnia producta ab illo omnipotente, quia sicut suo velle potest omnia velle et ea producere, ita suo velle potest impedire omnia volita a se et ab alio. Et hoc intendit Richardus. Unde dicit omnipotentem facere non ut non sit, sed ut nihil possit.

Sed dices quod concordarent ambo in voluntate et sic quod vellet unus, et alter. —Contra: sicut voluntas unius contingenter se haberet ad omnia, sic et voluntas alterius; nec voluntas unius potest determinari a voluntate alterius, quia tunc nullus

---

13. Avicenna, *Metaphysica* 8.1, 5.f 97rb–va, 99rb–vb.
14. Richard St. Victor, *De trinitate* 1.25.

[*From the nature of God's primacies*] I prove unicity from the primacy thus: One thing of a given kind is not related to others of its kind in such a way that it is limited to just this plurality or to a certain number of such things. There is nothing in the nature itself that requires that there be just so many individuals or in a cause that says there must be only so many things caused, unless you insist on what we seek to prove [namely, that the nature is such that it is found in but one individual]. But deity is one thing of a given kind and, according to you, is found in more than one individual of its kind. Therefore, deity of itself is not limited to any fixed number of individuals, nor can it be restricted to one [by anything else], for this would be repugnant [to it as first]; therefore, deity exists in an infinity of individual subjects. This argument is based on the fact that primacy by its very nature has to be somehow restricted. And if you object that this does not follow because it would rule out the possibility of deity being shared by three persons, look up what I have said in distinction five.

[*From the nature of "necessary existence"*] Our thesis can be proved from the nature of "necessary existence," as Avicenna does, and as the proof from the nature of the will does.

[*From the nature of omnipotence*] In chapter 17 of his *De trinitate,* however, Richard [of St. Victor] uses a proof from omnipotence. Anyone who would have been omnipotent could easily bring it about that every other agent could do nothing, and therefore, if there were several omnipotent beings, each could destroy the other "omnipotents" and render them incapable of doing anything.

But to this formulation I raise the objection that omnipotence only has to do with possible objects. If another God were omnipotent, however, that God would not be just possible but a necessary being. To this I reply: If one understands this in the sense [of two omnipotent persons, as we say with Augustine]: "If the Father would not generate a Son equal to himself and thus not make him omnipotent . . . ," then I concede that one omnipotent could still destroy all that was produced by the other omnipotent. For just as he could will all things and produce them by his volition, so, too, he could impede all things willed by himself and by another. And this is what Richard had in mind. Hence he does not say that each omnipotent makes the other nonexistent but rather impotent.

But you may say that both could agree voluntarily and thus what one wills the other does also. I say against this: Just as the will of one is related to all things contingently, so, too, is the will of the other. Neither can one's will be determined by the other,

esset deus. —Item, pono quod concordent; tunc arguo sic: unus omnipotens volens possibile esse producit illud in esse ut causa totalis, et alius omnipotens volens illud possibile esse, producit illud in esse ut causa totalis; sed impossibile est plures causas totales esse respectu eiusdem effectus; ergo impossibile est plures omnipotentes esse. Sed haec ratio non est evidenter necessaria, quia omnipotentia in Deo non est evidenter scita, sed credita; et licet aliqui ponerent Deum infinitum intensive, non tamen omnipotentem respectu omnium non includentium contradictionem, sicut nos intelligimus omnipotentem.

because then neither would be God. Also, if I assume that they do agree, then I argue thus: One omnipotent, by willing some possible, produces it in existence as its total cause; and the other omnipotent, by willing the selfsame thing, produces it in existence as its total cause. But it is impossible that there be more than one total cause with respect to the same effect. Therefore, it is impossible that more than one omnipotent exists. This is not an evidently necessary argument, however, because omnipotence in God is not something known evidently but is something believed. And although some might assume that God is intensively infinite, they would not think that he was omnipotent with regard to whatever does not include a contradiction, as we understand omnipotence. . . .

Chapter Three

Commentary

Introduction

The argument for the existence of God is an end point for Scotistic metaphysics. From the subjective side of the knower, metaphysical knowledge—what we described earlier as the *habitus* ordered to the transcendentals as such—reaches in its proof of a first principle a kind of fulfillment. Because of the predominant place that he gives to the will in his anthropology and because of his faith in a fuller beatitude in the afterlife, Scotus does not go so far as to assert that life's ultimate happiness consists in the metaphysical knowledge of God. Nevertheless, he does see this knowledge of God as a preeminent achievement of natural reason and makes the compelling claim that it is a deeply fulfilling personal achievement.[1]

Looked at objectively, from the standpoint of the science itself, one can also see God as the end of Scotus's metaphysics. In this sense, God becomes the "interpreter's key" that makes ultimate sense of the basic vocabulary of metaphysics. The first objects of metaphysics—being as such, the coextensive and disjunctive transcendental attributes, and the pure perfections—display their most complete significance when they are configured in the whole that is Scotus's argument for the existence of an infinite being. This means that the infinite being lies at the metaphysical center of things. Wherever one finds coherence, intelligibility, or worth in things, there one encounters evidence pointing to the first principle. The existence of finite things signifies something beyond themselves and their kind. It points to a source in which things in their multiplicity and partiality share great commonness, and from which, paradoxically, they suffer the greatest distance. In other words, the God of Scotus's metaphysics is a kind of logical lodestone that draws to itself other, more primitive metaphysical concepts and then forms them into an intelligible pattern in which they find their more complete meaning. If, as we explained in chapter 2, metaphysics begins with those terms that are maximally knowable in the sense of being both foundational and most certain, the fact that it ends with God means that our knowledge of God somehow secures and certifies all our knowledge.

As we turn to the argument itself, we shall first comment on the text and its historical context, then give a brief outline of its complex structure, and finally present a series of explanatory remarks on selected philosophical issues vital to various stages of the proof.

The Text

Our text comes from distinction 2 of book 1 of Scotus's *Reportatio* I A. There he raises questions concerning three broad issues: the existence of God, his unicity, and the trinity of persons in God. With respect to the first two issues, he asks four questions that he subsequently develops in an integrated fashion, and which the text at hand presents. As mentioned in chapter 1, a *reportatio* is the record of a lecture by a scribe or student; in the case of *Rep.* I A, the report has the added authority of having been examined and authorized by Scotus himself as faithfully representing his teaching.

Rep. I A's proof of the existence of God is one of at least four versions of the same. We know that the *lectura* version is the earliest, followed by the *ordinatio*. Where *Rep.* I A fits in is not altogether clear due to our imperfect knowledge of Scotus's career and the fate of his works. There is evidence that he produced two *ordinationes*. He may well have completed—or virtually so—a finished version of his Oxford lectures before lecturing again in Paris. In the composition of the *Ordinatio*, which is based on the Paris lectures, important manuscripts show that Scotus was simply repeating parts of his earlier work with which he was still satisfied. Accordingly, the Paris *reportatio* would be transitional to the two *ordinationes*— which were synthesized into a single edition by an early-fourteenth-century editor of the Assisi manuscript, a strategy followed by the contemporary editors of the Scotus Commission in their publication of the *Ordinatio*. We also possess Scotus's *De primo principio,* which is a philosophical inquiry into the existence and nature of God. It depends heavily upon the *ordinatio* texts for the substance of the last two of its four books. The *De primo*, which is developed out of his transcendental metaphysics, takes its point of departure from the metaphysical attribute of order. We can learn much about the development of Scotus's thought by comparing the different versions. For our purposes, it will suffice to note that they all proceed in the same distinctive way. What we have in *Rep.* I A is, in its basic architecture and in many of its details, identical with the other proofs.

The argument of the excerpt under discussion is developed in a text that fuses several modes of investigation. It is really a misnomer to call the works that derived from these lectures on the *Sentences* commentaries. At one time, the Schoolmen did comment literally on the actual text of Peter. By the second half of the thirteenth century, however, it had become customary to use the themes of Peter's chapters as occasions to pose questions of current theological interest. Probably in the years 1223–27, Alexander of Hales grouped the many chapters of Peter's four books into a much smaller number of "distinctions," a structure that shaped the nature of theological education well into the fourteenth century.[2] For instance, Alexander ordered Peter's 210 chapters of his book 1 into 48 distinctions. The distinctions then provided the topical framework in which the bachelors posed the sequence of questions to be developed in the familiar Scholastic *quaestio* style, which one finds exemplified with an elegant simplicity in Bonaventure and Aquinas. The element of literal commentary, of dealing with the actual content of Peter's text, had disappeared by the middle of the thirteenth century. Peter's influence continued primarily through the fact that the student theologians worked within his topical framework, mediated by Alexander's distinctions. At times it is hard to find any intrinsic conceptual link between a question posed by a bachelor and the chapter that occasioned it.

If it is not a commentary in any ordinary sense, then what do we have? We have a set of questions posed by inquiring minds in response to some aspect of Peter's text. In time, and probably because these commentaries were an obligatory stage in the education of the theology bachelors, some sorts of questions became customary; they represented the vexing issues of the day. Indeed, from a functional point of view, Alexander's "distinction" came to mean more a range of topics on which the student or master could pose timely research questions than a collection of chapters representing Peter's opinion on theological issues. In effect, the commentary was transformed by the *quaestio*.

Two more points need to be made. First of all, the *quaestio* was put to the service of *scientia*. From the second half of the thirteenth century and continuing into Scotus's day in the fourteenth, theologians aimed at theological *science,* at scientific knowledge in the Aristotelian sense.[3] The *quaestio* format supported the presentation of demonstrative arguments. It also framed these responses within a sic-et-non dialectic. Scotus is almost intemperate in his development of this aspect of the *quaestio;* on a given issue, the views of others are presented, together with objections and replies, often enough followed by follow-up objections and replies. Nested somewhere within all this is his own reasoned position.

Argument 1: Triple Primacy

The complex argument develops around a sequence of four conclusions. Scotus first argues for the existence of an entity that is both preeminent in the hierarchy of natures and first with respect to efficient and final causality. He then proves that the attribute of "simple firstness" belongs to only one kind of entity. Third, he demonstrates that a simply first being is infinite in an unqualified sense. Finally, he shows that there can be only a single infinite being. In other words, the attribute of being single in number follows on the attribute of being infinite in modality, which in turn follows upon the sui generis attribute of an entity that is simply first with respect to causality and eminence.

Before beginning, Scotus makes a preliminary remark on his methodology. In accordance with the canons of Aristotelian science, he is not content to discover the simple truth of these propositions, the mere fact, as it were. Rather, the intent is to grasp these truths as necessities, as reflective of the unalterable order of reality. From a methodological point of view, this means that the predicate must be seen to inhere necessarily in the subject. In this context, Scotus tells us that the subsequent conclusions will have the status of being *quia* demonstrations—or, as we translate it, demonstrations of the simple fact. The issue deals with a typology of necessary propositions, distinguished according to the grounds for asserting the inherence of the predicate to the subject. A necessary proposition is either self-evident (*per se notum*) or demonstrated. If some valid concept of God contained the notion of his existence, then the proposition with such a concept as its subject and the predicate asserting existence of such a being would be per se. But as he says in the text, in this life we have no such concept of God. The propositions must then be demonstrated conclusions, which can be either of the reasoned fact (*propter quid*) or of the simple fact (*quia*). The former is a syllogistic proof in which the middle term gives the cause or the reason why the predicate of the conclusion is asserted of the subject. For instance, if I know that an opaque body is intervening between a light source and a surface that it shines on, then I can infer that a shadow falls on the surface. My inference is based upon the knowledge of the cause (opaque body intervening between light source and surface) of the effect (a shadow cast). In dealing with the properties of divine existence, such as primacy, infinity, and unicity, however, the requisite middle term would have to be God's essence, which is unknown to us in this life. Therefore, our necessary knowledge of God is by *quia* demonstration.

In the proof of a simple fact, we argue from the effect to the nature of its cause. If such an effect exists, then its cause must also exist. In such an argument, we do not know why or how the cause exists but only the simple fact that it does. The proof that Scotus sets up will proceed from some existential fact and show that the adequate cause required to explain it will enjoy a triple primacy: it is an efficient cause that is uncaused, and it is first in the orders of excellence and finality. These relative properties of God—so called because they express God's relationship to the world as its creator—Scotus declares, are more readily knowable to us than his absolute properties, such as the fact that he possesses intellect and free will and is infinitely perfect. Although this process does not yield us knowledge of the divine essence, it is a systematic inquiry that continually reveals always more central attributes of God.

The conclusion to the first phase of the argument—that there is a being that is simply first in the orders of efficiency, eminence, and finality—is really the summation of three conclusions and a corollary. Scotus argues first that there is a first efficient cause, second that there is preeminent nature, and third that there is a first final cause. He then explains how being the first efficient cause is equivalent to being the first exemplar cause. Our subsequent remarks will center first on the significance of the architecture of the argument, and then turn to a variety of principles at work in his proof of a first efficient cause.

❙ Significance of the Three Primacies

"Prior" and "posterior" are terms that name the mutual relation of order obtaining between two terms compared with respect to some common *ratio* or idea. One thing can be prior to another with respect to a variety of properties, such as time (e.g., older), place (e.g., higher or nearer), motion (e.g., faster), power (e.g., stronger), or knowledge (e.g., more learned). Scotus will predicate "first" with respect to the concepts of efficient causality, excellence of nature, and final causality. The salient feature of causality and excellence is that whatever is first with respect to either of them need suffer no limitation. That is to say, the analysis of "preeminent nature" or "first efficient cause" entails no essentially imperfect conceptual component. By contrast, for example, the quality of being quick-witted, even if enjoyed in a surpassing degree, implies an essentially limited subject, namely, one that has to move from ignorance to understanding. Accordingly, if one were to know that an entity is a first efficient cause, then it would be entirely possible to come to realize that it enjoys the fullness of perfection. As such, it provides an ideal subject or minor term in a demonstration that concludes to an infinite being.

Scotus seems to have discovered the significance of this threefold approach to God from his study of Henry of Ghent, one of the guiding lights among the theologians at Paris in the last decades of the thirteenth century.[4] In his *Summa quaestionum ordinariarum* (art. 22, q. 4), Henry collects and categorizes the variety of demonstrative and dialectical proofs for the existence of God.[5] He divides demonstrative proofs into those of causality and eminence. The former he further divides into those based on efficient, formal or exemplar, and final causality. Scotus, as we see in his remarks preliminary to his first proof, reduces exemplarity to efficiency. Although Henry had shown a kind of necessity to his division of demonstrations of God's existence, he still presented the four kinds as independent categories, each with its own list of different proofs. For instance, under the way of efficient causality, he presents three independent arguments, and there is no reason that the list could not be extended considerably. By contrast, Scotus is interested in integrating the varieties into a single whole. His single argument based on efficiency provides the foundation for the single argument based on eminence, which in turn becomes the groundwork for the single argument based on finality.[6] The result is a single subject, the triple primacy, which then becomes the subject for further attributes, most notably infinitude and unicity. The logical structure of Scotus's extended argument shows a clearly articulated architecture that escapes much of the random and occasional character that the commentary/*quaestio* genre typically encouraged.

❙ First Efficient Cause

Stripped to the bare bones, the proof of the existence of first efficient cause consists of a brief argument, two objections, and their respective responses. Scotus devotes the bulk of his discussion, more than one-half of the text, to his reply to the first objection. We begin with the argument:

1. Some being is an effect, because some being is produced.
2. Whatever is produced is produced by nothing, by itself, or by another.
3. It cannot be produced by nothing, for nothing is the cause of nothing.
4. It cannot be produced by itself, for nothing begets itself.

5. Therefore, it is produced by another.
6. With respect to this other, it is produced by nothing, itself, or another.
7. Let the process continue indefinitely.
8. The process must come to a stop with something that is unproduced and that produces by its own power and not in virtue of any other. (This I call the first.)

The substance of the two follow-up objections and replies provides sufficient commentary, although we will do well at the outset to draw out the meaning of "first." It describes a cause in its relationship to another cause or other causes. We are asked to envision a sequence of causes in relationship to a common effect. If a cause is first, then it is itself unproduced, and furthermore, in exercising its causal influence, it produces its effect by its own power and in independence from any other causes in the sequence devoted to producing the effect. By contrast, a cause that has productive responsibility for the effect is said to be posterior or secondary either if it itself is produced, or if in producing its effect, it is only instrumental because it uses the power of another cause, or if in using its own power, it is dependent upon another cause.

The first objection targets the eighth proposition for its denial of an infinite regress of caused causes. The second objection raises a methodological difficulty that calls into question the probative value of the argument. We shall look at the second concern first.

From Existence to Possibility to Necessity

The question is whether we have a demonstration or not. It can be argued that we do not because a demonstration requires premises that are necessary propositions. But Scotus's argument starts with a proposition that is contingent: "some being is an effect." Although true and evidently so, it is a truth that need not have been or could still be otherwise. What follows from it is likewise contingent. One might agree that there is a cause, and even, let us say, a first cause, but our knowledge of its reality is only as secure as our knowledge of its initial supporting premise. As it now stands, there is no reason to think that there need not have been or soon may not be a first cause. The main point of a demonstration, however, is to have scientific knowledge, and such knowledge is a grasp of things in their necessities. In his response, Scotus accepts the standard of demonstrative necessity but thinks that his argument implicitly meets it or at least would manifestly satisfy it with the slightest adjustment.

His point is that behind the contingent fact of an existing effect and its producing cause lies the deeper reality of their possibilities. In accordance with the axiom "ab esse ad posse valet illatio" (the inference from existence of a thing to its possibility is valid), one can infer from propositions 1–5:

A. It is possible that some nature comes to be, i.e., it is effectible or producible, because some nature is able to effect or produce it.

Proposition 1 has the advantage of being evidently true, clearly supported by experience. Proposition A transposes it from the mode of contingency to that of possibility. And the possibilities of things are necessary features of the world. God might never have produced an entity that now exists, but the fact that it exists, even if contingently, is sufficient evidence of its possibility. That possibility is part of the unalterable order of things. Moreover, the possibilities of caused beings are coextensive with the necessary existence of the first cause in a way that contingent existents are not.

In shifting his premise to the mode of possibility, Scotus makes an important philosophical move. Not only has he reestablished the demonstrative character of his *quia* demonstration; he has also brought out the ontological weight of the possibilities inherent in contingent realities. They belong to the essence of things; they are part of the quiddity of an entity. Such possibilities are not "merely logical," but have existential significance because they tell us something of the way the world has to be.[7]

Nevertheless, one might imagine that this modal transposition puts us permanently in the realm of possibilities and thus precludes our drawing any existential conclusion. Indeed, it is sometimes alleged that Scotus makes the illicit inference from the conceptual to the actual order of extramental existence. Accordingly, he ends his response by explaining how one goes from the possibility of a first efficient cause to its actual existence.

9. If it is repugnant to the very notion of something that it is from another, then if it can exist, it can exist of itself.
10. That the first efficient cause stems from another is repugnant to the very idea of its being "first."
11. We have proved the possibility of a first efficient cause.
12. Therefore, the first efficient cause actually exists of itself.

Three elements are key to the argument. First, Scotus means by "being" or "thing" that which actually exists or can exist extramentally. So when he talks about the possibility of something, he means some extramental actuality that is either now existing or that could be brought into existence. Second, he has already demonstrated the possibility of the first efficient cause. And finally, that it is uncausable is implicit in its primacy. Having proved that it can exist extramentally and that it cannot be caused, then it must exist actually. Usually the transition from real possibility to existent entity is due to the causal influence of another. But where this is ruled out, then either the thing exists necessarily or one is forced into the philosophical absurdity of nonexistents just popping into reality with no reason to it.[8] The inference to actual existence from "can exist of itself" is immediate.

| Essentially Ordered Causes

Targeting proposition 8, the first objection insists that there is nothing incongruous about productions of the same sort continuing indefinitely. In effect, it says that there is nothing illogical about an infinite regress of caused causes. Sons come from fathers, and this process can be unending. If the objection holds, then it prevents the inference to a first efficient cause. Scotus's extended response consists of a set of distinctions, five separate arguments denying an infinite regress of caused causes, a rejoinder to the response, and a final reply to the rejoinder.

Order among cooperatively operating causes is the central philosophical issue taken up in the distinctions. The issue is raised by the fact that more than one cause is needed to explain the existence of an effect. Both Scotus and his adversary admit that an effect (E) is produced by a cause (A), and that A is itself caused by another cause (B). The purpose of Scotus's first remark is to keep one focused on the proper issue. He distinguishes two causal relationships. When speaking of the one-to-one relationship of a cause to its effect (i.e., of A to E), the relationship can be either essential (per se) or accidental (per accidens), depending upon whether the cause causing the effect operates with respect to it in terms of what is essential to the cause. For instance, a book bringing about learning or entertainment can be causing essentially, but if it is holding down papers or propping open a window, the effect is accidental to the nature of the cause. To take a second example, if a patient is healed by a doctor, it is because of the doctor's medical art, not because she happens to be female and educated at Johns Hopkins University. Important as the distinction between essential and accidental causes may be, it is not the one currently at issue, however. Rather, what concerns us is the many-to-one relationship of a sequence of coordinated causes responsible for a common effect (i.e., of A to B, with respect to their common relationship to E). Such causes are either essentially or accidentally ordered, depending upon the basis of their cooperative relationship to the effect for which they are jointly responsible.

If two causes (A and B) are essentially ordered, they meet three criteria: dependency, priority, and simultaneity. In causing E, A depends upon B in its very act of causing; for example, in order to propel air, the mechanical energy of a fan blade is dependent upon electrical energy; or to take a second example, in the genesis of a zygote, the causality of the male sperm is dependent on the causality of the female egg. By contrast, when accidentally ordered causes are involved, although A may be dependent upon B for its original existence, B subsequently acts independently of A in its relationship to E. To use Scotus's example, although a son is begotten by his father, his own procreative act proceeds independently of his father's.

Because each cause causes by virtue of what is essential to it, the fact that A depends on B means that B in some sense is superior or more perfect. Scotus seems to have in mind here a kind of Neoplotinian hierarchy of essences.[9] The core idea, however, is that the coordination of causes is required because one is deficient in a way that renders it unable to act independently; and insofar as this is so, it is subordinated to another cause that enjoys the perfection that the other lacks. Moreover, the difference between the two causes distinguishes their essences or natures. For instance, one mule may not have sufficient strength to tow a barge down a canal, but what is needed is more of the same, an additional mule or two. In this case, the difference is accidental, a matter of quantity, for it does not point to the need for a different sort of thing. However, if one were breeding dogs, then—as with the case of the barge to be towed—one needs more than one dog, but here each has to be of a different sort, one male and the other female. In this case, the male and female co-causes meet the second criterion for essentially ordered causes, priority.

In their relationship to the common effect, essentially ordered causes operate simultaneously. They must exercise their causality with respect to the effect synchronically. The whole point is that, although A is a real cause of E, its essential deficiency keeps it from being the adequate or total cause. Therefore, since only part of a cause effectively amounts to no causal act, the existence of the effect means that in the act of causing, A was cooperating with B. With his theory of essentially ordered causes, Scotus unites partial causes in a synchronic totality. He insists there is no room in such a totality for an infinite number of causes and gives five arguments to that effect.

Given an understanding of essentially ordered causes, Scotus's arguments are for the most part self-explanatory. Rehearsing the first argument will help draw out the basic philosophical insight behind the position. Imagine a sequence of causes responsible for the existence of a single, common effect. The elements of the sequence are such that each one depends for its causing upon the one just prior to it. For instance, A depends on B, and B in turn depends on C, and so on. What are we to say about the sequence A, B, C, . . . ? As a totality it is supposed to be responsible for E. But can it be an independent causal totality if its principle of composition is that each member depends on a prior for its causing? Scotus says that, given its principle of collection, the sequence is a dependent being: "the whole collection of dependents depends." It must, therefore, depend "upon something that is not part of that totality." The cause upon which the infinite sequence depends is the first efficient cause.

Note that Scotus allows for two different lines of causal sequences. There is the indefinitely long line of dependent causes—what we might call a horizontal train of caused causes. But the fact is that increasing the membership in the sequence does not overcome the systematic dependency of the set and of each member in it. To use an analogy, it would be like fighting one's state of indebtedness by taking out further loans. Or like trying to keep a chain suspended by the expedient of adding additional links to the end of the chain, when in fact one must hook the last of the dependent links to something of a different sort, such as a ceiling beam. With the introduction of the ceiling beam, one is dealing with a different sort of causal chain, what we shall call a vertical sequence. The important point is that the vertical sequence consists of members that are different in nature. This gives us essentially ordered causes. Perhaps a horizontal line can have an infinite number of dependent causes (e.g., indefinitely add new links; or take out new loans); Scotus allows it for the sake of argument. But a vertical chain requires a first (e.g., the line of dependency consisting of links and the ceiling beam stops at the beam or at whatever it is that supports the beam), otherwise there would be no actual effect.

Scotus's arguments presuppose an essential order, that is, they start with a cause that is dependent upon another for its causing. But, one might object, this is not the case with all causal sequences, such as the case of fathers and sons. The prior cause (the father) has no bearing upon the causal act of the posterior (the son's begetting). There is no reason that the succession of such caused causes cannot be infinite. In reply, Scotus will grant the possibility of an infinite number of causes in the sequence, but he insists that analysis of the causal power involved shows that the individual progenitor is not as independent as the objection assumes. The objection assumes a set of agents, each one existing at a time when that upon which it depended for existence is no longer existing, and such that each agent in the series acts in a manner like all the others previous to it in the sequence. In other words, there is uniformity among nonconcurrent agents. It envisions as a totality an infinite sequence of uniform changes. With regard to such a concatenation, Scotus invokes the principle that no sequence of changes with respect to a form is perpetuated save by virtue of something that is not part of the sequence ("nulla difformitas perpetuatur nisi in virtute alicuius uniformis quod non est aliquid illius successionis").[10] What he sees is that each thing in the assumed infinite series represents a momentary appearance in a continuum that itself manifests a permanent pattern. But no member can be responsible for the persistent uniformity, for by definition each belongs only to a transient moment in the enduring whole. Consequently, there must be a permanent entity, or one that perdures at least as long as the sequence continues, to account for the uniformity of form in the infinite series. Regarding this explanatory factor, then, Scotus holds that it must be essentially prior to the continuum of causes that it sustains. Hence, where there is an accidentally ordered series in causes (as in the example of fathers begetting sons), the sequence itself is a dependent entity that rests upon a cause to which it is essentially ordered.

First in Excellence

The second primacy pertains to the order of eminence. Two entities are said to be prior or posterior in the order of eminence depending upon whether the essence of one excels or is excelled by the essence of the other. The basic idea is that one can judge of different essences that X is better than Y.[11] In adopting this idea, Scotus means it, of course, not to be simply a reflection of the subjective condition of the one judging but rather a judgment corresponding to the objective order of a hierarchy of value that obtains among the natures of things.

His argument for a preeminent being is very brief and seems to bear the marks of being an unfinished thought typical of a lecture. The main idea, however, is quite clear. It trades upon the idea of equivocal causality. A general principle of causality is that every cause brings about in its effect something similar. The big question becomes, To what degree of likeness? The Schoolmen typically taught that the likeness can be present in cause and effect either univocally or equivocally. In cases like organisms regenerating themselves or billiard balls hitting one another, what is communicated to the effect by the cause is of the same kind in both cause and effect. This relationship is univocal. In some instances, however, what is present in the effect as communicated by the cause is present more perfectly in the cause. For instance, the intelligence evident in an artifact only imperfectly and analogously reflects the greater intelligence of its maker. Such a cause causes equivocally. As Scotus puts it, "An equivocal cause . . . is always nobler than its effect . . . it can be neither less perfect nor only equal in perfection with its effect."

Given the concept of equivocal causality, it is easy to see how Scotus argues from the existence of a first efficient cause to the existence of a preeminent being.

1. In an essential order of causes, the cause is always equivocal with respect to its effect.
2. An equivocal cause is nobler than its effect.
3. There exists an efficient cause that is simply first in an essential order of efficient causes.
4. Therefore, the first efficient cause is nobler than any of its effects.
5. Hence, some being is simply unexcelled in excellence of being.

There is a profound philosophical implication to the basic principle motivating this argument. It comes out best in Scotus's remark that if the higher efficient cause were not also nobler in essence, then "every other more perfect organism could be produced by a fly." Scotus's doctrine conflicts with reductive evolutionary theories of the origins of life and its species. Either they would deny the substantial or essential integrity of higher, more complex beings, or one would have to say that somehow something comes from nothing, the higher emerges from the lower. According to his principles, however, Scotus would have no difficulty appropriating a theory of the emergent development of the forms or essences of things, so long as the causality of the lower forms, under whatever dynamical principles are proper to them, cooperates with the first efficient cause and preeminent being.

First Final Cause

With his argument for the first final cause, Scotus completes his proof for the existence of a triple primacy. What he shows is that the first efficient cause necessarily acts for the sake of an end, but that end must be the most excellent of beings, and therefore is identical with itself. The argument grows out of the fundamental teleological position developed by Aristotle in book 2 of the *Physics*. For our purposes, the central point is that efficient causality only makes sense in the context of an intelligent order of things whereby incomplete or potential beings achieve a measure of perfection through the action of agents. By definition, then, the end is that for the sake of which the agent acts. Action is therefore always tied to the specific causality of the end. Agency requires motivation, direction, a measure of achievement. This ordination of an agent to the end is something either built into the agent's nature or chosen on the basis of intelligent deliberation. In other words, per se efficient causes divide into what Aristotle calls agents that act by nature and those that act by choice, or what Scotus calls natures and wills.

In the last phase of the argument, Scotus identifies the first efficient cause with the ultimate end. The point here is that if the first agent were to act for the sake of an entity other than itself, then it could not itself be the noblest being, for it is the good of the end that governs the agent's action. But the previous demonstration has already established that the first efficient cause is the preeminent being. Consequently, all action of the first efficient cause is ordered to its own self as the ultimate final cause.

At this point Scotus has concluded the substance of his proof of the existence of a being that is simply first.[12] That is, there is an entity that is the same subject of each sort of primacy. It remains to prove that the same subject is unique in kind and number and that it is infinitely perfect.

Argument 2: Sui Generis

The next part of the argument considers whether a being that is simply first is a unique sort of entity, or whether there are different natures or essences that enjoy a triple primacy. As he explains in a corollary to the thesis, all the previous argument establishes is that for a particular sequence of causes, there is a first to that sequence. But because there are a multitude of coordinated causes, each responsible for its different effect, there is no prima facie reason why there cannot be a multitude of firsts, one for each coordination. Scotus's task in this part of the argument is to link the simply first being to the totality of the world. Indeed, its uniqueness as a type lies precisely in the unique relationship that it bears to the whole of being. Each of the proofs brings this out in its own way. The three proofs correspond respectively to the properties of efficient causality, final causality, and excellence of nature.

The first argument tests the hypothesis of two efficient causes, each first in an unqualified way and exemplifying a different essence.

1. If there were two such causes, then they would be responsible either for the same effect or for different effects.

Scotus rules out the former possibility.

2. But if the same effect cannot have two efficient causes of the same kind that are each totally responsible for it, then much less could it have as total causes two agents that are essentially different.
3. Now the antecedent of (2) is true: consider a and b each total efficient causes of the effect; if one were to posit a and to completely write off b, the effect would still exist, and hence b is not necessary to account for the existence of the effect. Yet by hypothesis b is its total cause, and the effect should be dependent upon it. The effect, therefore, both is and is not dependent upon b.
4. Moreover, the consequence of (2) is true: two causes of different sorts would differ by a difference that would be either relevant or irrelevant to its causal relation to the effect. If it is irrelevant, then for practical purposes we have causes of the same sort. If it is relevant, then it equips one cause to be better disposed to the one effect, and therefore the sufficiency of the worse-disposed cause to account for the effect points up the absurdity of two total causes.

He then rules out the latter possibility in (1).

5. If there are two effects, then they are either of the same or of different species.
6. If they are of the same species, they can stem from the same cause, and then there is no basis for affirming specifically different causes.
7. If the effects belong to different species, then they are essentially ordered to one another and can therefore be traced back to a single principle upon which they depend. With the rejec-

tion of both alternatives in the consequent of (1), the conclusion follows: There cannot be two first efficient causes.

Much of the argument rests upon the principle of parsimony. Where one explanatory factor suffices, there is no rational justification for positing another. Admitting one exhausts the rational grounds needed to assert another.

The remote source for Scotus's second argument is Aristotle's *Metaphysics* 12.10. There Aristotle explains the two ways that the universe contains the good. Much as the good of an army is to be found first in its leader and then in the order of its ranks, so it is with the whole of being. All things are interconnected, despite their diversities, by being ordered toward one end. The end, of course, is the first being. Christian thinkers found this idea particularly adaptable to their notions of God as creator. Scotus, for instance, can speak of the divine being as the first exemplar cause, which models all things in its mind and immediately orders them to itself as its ultimate end. It is clear to Aristotle—and Scotus follows him exactly in this—that the goodness of the universe is expressed in the mutual interconnections among things, which make possible the existence of each limited thing. Moreover, that immanent coordination, which defines the universe as an existent, intelligible whole, rests upon a single independent, extrinsic principle. After his refutation of the traditional authorities who try to explain cosmic order by a multiplicity of first principles, Aristotle concludes (1076a5) by quoting Odysseus, who set about to rouse the Achaean troops to Agamemnon's leadership as they were about to abandon the cause and retreat from Troy: "The rule of many is not good; one ruler let there be" (*Iliad* 2.204). The difference between the body politic and the world is that "the world refuses to be governed badly" (*Metaphysics* 2.10.1076a4). Accordingly, Scotus concludes that "those who postulate several first principles, each with a distinct but coordinate group of effects, 'dismember the substance of the universe,' as the Philosopher says." Order in the complex world we experience comes from a subordination to one kind of an end. One vision, one purpose, coordinate the dynamic multiplicity into a single cosmos.

The last, very brief argument makes assumptions that would require a great deal of interpretation in order to render the proof plausible. Despite the technical deficiencies, however, it rests upon an important philosophical principle that deserves serious consideration. The argument begins with the claim that in each genus or category of being, there is one nature that is the measure of all the others. Aristotle had developed the idea at some length in

Metaphysics 10.1–2. Numbers provide the paradigm case, for all numbers, considered as distinct essences, are measured by "one." Aristotle then extends this doctrine analogically to different kinds or genera as diverse as colors, sounds, figures, movements, perception, knowledge, and even substance, finding in each category one member that is the measure of all the rest. Indeed, for him the primary meaning of "one" is "to be the first measure of a kind" (1052b18). As much as possible, one selects as the measure something that is one, indivisible, and simple and that has mensurable constancy due to the difficulty of increasing or diminishing its value. Aristotle has in mind, for example, the quarter tone in music, the phoneme in speech, letters in writing, white in colors, and the cycle of the constellations in natural change.

Scotus extends Aristotle's analysis by treating the whole of being as a category and then applying the principle that it must have some simply first nature that is the measure of all beings ("naturam simpliciter primam quae est ratio et mensura omnium entium"). There are two difficulties in following Scotus. First of all, the extension must be understood analogically, for being is not a genus or category in the sense that Aristotle used. Scotus himself considers being a transcendental concept, and so it is not clear how Aristotle's analysis applies in the case of the totality of being. The second difficulty leads us to a more interesting question. The problem is that in the obvious cases—such as numbers, writing, and music—the "one," the measure and *ratio* of all others in the category, can be thought of as the member of the genus that is the basic unit in the genus. But Scotus clearly has in mind as the "one" of all beings that which is the fullness of being, the most complete or perfect entity, the summation of all that any being is or can be. In other words, he seems to employ a different concept of "measure." His idea would be that the preeminent nature is the *ratio* of all other entities in the way that the perfect is the measure of the imperfect. Measure is here being used in the sense of the ideal. When Scotus subsequently demonstrates that the first being is actually infinite, he in fact provides the justification for considering the preeminent being the measure of all beings.

▌Argument 3: Infinity

This part of the argument presents the third of three questions devoted to the topic of God's existence. It is followed by one question on the unicity of God: whether a being that is simply first with regard to all posterior things is actually infinite intensively. The adverb "intensively" will be defined contextually as we proceed through the argument. The reader will find a direct account of the idea in chapter 4's discussion of infinity. At the outset, however, it suffices to say that Scotus understands divine infinity to be a measure of the intrinsic perfection of the divine being. Up to this point, God has been described in relative terms. He is the first efficient cause, the ultimate final cause, the preeminent nature. Each of these attributes expresses a relationship to creatures. If there were no creatures, it would make no sense to speak of God possessing these properties. The relationships would disappear with the elimination of the created term of the relation. When we turn to the issue of divine infinity, however, we deal with a different sort of attribute, one that is absolute, that names a perfection of God irrespective of the existence of creatures. When we speak of God's attributes in this way, whether relative or absolute, it bears emphasizing that we are considering the ontological status of the properties and not the epistemological conditions of our concepts about them. With respect to the latter, it should be clear from Scotus's methodology that all our concepts of God are derived from experience. Exactly how this is so will be the topic of chapter 4.

Scotus begins his answer to the question with a definition of "infinite"; he then follows it with four proofs, corresponding to the primacies of efficiency, exemplarity, eminence, and finality.

For philosophers, infinity is one of the most attractive and elusive concepts. It resolutely resists the human mind's attempt to possess it, yet it invariably invites us to make the effort. Our minds can be capable of the most beautiful and powerful of constructions, but like Icarus's wings, they fail us as we approach the infinite. Philosophers respond to this failure in different ways: some find wisdom in the silence that is left when reason has come to its limit, while others take the failure to satisfy the intellect's longing as proof of the philosopher's foolishness. Thomas Hobbes, one of the latter group, thought that the concept of infinity was devoid of descriptive content and could only signify emotively.[13] Scotus, who thought the term possessed clear intelligible content, considered "infinite being" to be the most perfect or simple concept we could naturally possess of God in this life. We shall defer an extended commentary on Scotus's analysis of the term to the next chapter. Here it will suffice to stipulate the meaning and let its deeper significance unfold by usage in the subsequent arguments.

"I call 'infinite' . . . what excels any actual or possible finite being to a degree beyond any determinate measure you take or could take." In a context where one can speak of a kind of number that measures the excellence of the being of things, "infinite" is the number that names the degree of excellence pertaining to that entity whose excellence is incommensurately greater than the excellence of any actual or possible finite entity. Two core notions one must accept in order to follow Scotus are that being is a concept whose content can be qualified by greater or lesser degrees of excellence; and that one can extrapolate from a scale whose measurements represent proportioned numbers a number that is incommensurately greater than any number you could possibly situate on the scale. If these ideas can be pulled together in a coherent fashion, then infinite being will signify that entity possessed of the fullness of being. It will be the plenitude of a perfection so complete that with respect to the whole composed by it and others, the excellence of the whole will not be increased or diminished by addition or subtraction of the others. It goes without saying that, along with the Christian thinkers in general, Scotus elevates infinity from the Greek idea of an imperfect state of something with insufficient definition to the status of a pure perfection.[14]

∎ Efficiency

The way to prove God's infinity that was most familiar to the medievals built on Aristotle's argument in *Physics* 8.10. The basic idea was that since the first mover moves secondary realities for an infinitely long duration, it must possess infinite power. Although Scotus did not believe in the eternity of the world, he did not think that this difference would much affect the soundness of the basic line of argument, since what Aristotle took to be actual could be transposed into the mode of possibility.[15] Even if God has not been moving the world for an infinite time, it would be possible for him to do so. The fact that this effect of infinite duration has not materialized in no way tells against the power to do so. As Scotus puts it, "the perfection of such power follows equally from the possible as from the actual." Reformulated, the argument reads: The first efficient cause can cause the effect of infinite motion; therefore, it has infinite power and is an infinite mover.

It is not easy to see, however, how one can legitimately infer infinite perfection in a causal power from the fact that the cause is responsible for an infinite number of effects. For example, if I saw one carpenter pound two nails into a board and later saw another carpenter pound ten, I could not reasonably infer that the second one was five times more powerful. It could well be that it takes the same limited amount of strength for nailing one as for a thousand. How, then, does Scotus discover in the possibility of producing infinitely many effects sufficient grounds for inferring an efficient cause with infinite power?

The first three proofs share common features. First of all, they begin with the possibility of an infinite number of effects taken distributively, as it were, one after the other in succession. Second, this succession or sequence is then considered as a whole retaining its infinite measure. Next, Scotus argues that the perfection of the effect indicates a like perfection in the cause, which is either formally the same or possessed in an even more excellent manner. Perhaps the first and third steps can be granted as relatively uncontroversial; the second, however, provides substantial philosophical difficulty. Somehow the infinite multitude of the effect must be telescoped so that its distributed infinitude—the sequence of effects whose number is always increased by yet another—can signify a corresponding infinitude enjoyed holistically. In other words, what is enjoyed successively in the effect (really a sequence of effects) has to be "gathered" in such a way as to provide grounds for attributing to the responsible causal power the "same" property. Notice that "infinite" will be predicated three times, and each time with a somewhat different meaning: first, the number of effects in the sequence will be infinite; then we call the sequence considered holistically infinite; and finally, the cause of the infinite totality is called infinite. The commentary to chapter 4 will develop in some detail the epistemological justification for such cognitive moves. Right now, we simply observe that Scotus finds the infinite perfection of the first being signified by the infinite multiplicity of created beings. As he puts it in the midst of his third proof, "Wherever plurality implies greater perfection than paucity, there an infinity implies infinite perfection." The problem is deciding when one is dealing with such a plurality.

The fourth proof is considerably different. Here we begin with a concatenation of essentially ordered causes in which the causal action flows from the integrated sequence as a whole. In some cases, each posterior cause in the chain adds something missing in the contribution of the prior causes, such as acts of generation among plants and animals. According to common ancient and medieval theory, the sun was a prior cause with which adult members of the species cooperated in their diverse generative acts. The seasonal rhythms of nature provide abundant evidence that in their reproductive behavior plants and animals are influenced by the movement of the heavens. According to that theory, it was also clear that the specific individuals contributed something to the effect over and above the sun's causal influence. In general, where secondary causes contribute additional perfections, the greater the number of such posterior causes concurring in the causal action, the more perfect the effect will be. Yet not all chains of cooperating causes have this sort of structure. In some, the posterior cause adds nothing of perfection to the prior in its acting. Indeed, the most perfect of created effects seem to flow from causal action where the influence of secondary causes is minimal. The pure spirit that God creates immediately far excels the rose bush, which is generated by a host of posterior causes cooperating with the first efficient cause. Within the context of these considerations, Scotus argues as follows:

1. A prior efficient cause to which a second cause adds nothing of perfection in acting is of intensively infinite power.
2. The first efficient cause is such that secondary causes can add nothing to the perfection of its causation.
3. Therefore, the first efficient cause is of infinite power.

To accept the major premise, one must understand that secondary causes are not merely instrumental in an occasionalist sense; rather, they are to be considered essential causes. Each is possessed of its own specific nature, the perfection of which is transmitted through its causal action and is thus reflected in the effect. Hence, if it contributes nothing to the causal perfection of the integrated whole, which includes the prior cause, it could only be because the prior cause is of infinite power. Were it of finite measure, then the addition of more, however small, would make more. Addition of a finite measure, however large, to what is already the fullness of perfection does not increase the totality. To put it simply, the infinite plus or minus any finite measure is still infinite. It remains to show that the first efficient cause has this endless causal reservoir.

If the first efficient cause were of finite power, then the most excellent created things would derive from the most complex causal concatenations, since the greater the number of causes integrated in the totality, the greater the perfection of the whole cause would be. Scotus appeals to certain common Christian, Neoplotinian convictions to prove that the opposite is the case. The more excellent creations, such as pure spirits, are the immediate effects of the first cause, whereas the lesser species derive from causal sequences with a host of essential causes intermediate between them and the first efficient cause. Justification of the minor premise does seem to require an appeal to spiritual, nonmaterial effects. The reason is that greater complexity appears to be a condition of higher material entities. More advanced entities absorb the features of lower types of being in a higher, integrated fashion. Physical, chemical, biological, even social realities provide ample evidence of the phenomenon.

Exemplarity

Scotus's first two proofs based on exemplarity are the clearest and perhaps the best he offers for infinity. He himself seems to have thought so, if we can judge by the fact that he placed their analogues as the first and second of the seven demonstrations of divine infinity in his *De primo principio* (4.48–55). His argument concerning divine exemplarity introduces the idea that God enjoys both intellect and will as pure perfections. Scotus presents these ideas as a consequence of the already established threefold primacy of the first being. In order to preserve divine simplicity, God's intellect and will, as well as his intellections and volitions, must prove identical with the divine essence, as he explains in the second corollary at the end of question two. In all of his other works, divine simplicity, intellectuality, and free will occasion substantial treatment preliminary to his proof of infinity. The compression of these issues in his use of exemplarity in *Rep.* I A represents considerable refinement in Scotus's proof schema.

Although the divine exemplars have provided a fertile field for speculation and dispute among Christian thinkers over the centuries,[16] we can skirt the controversial issues and stick to the generally accepted common ground. The governing idea is that insofar as God is the creator of all things, he acts like an inventive artist, who models his effects after the ideas he holds in his mind in a kind of prevision. Prior to every created effect, therefore, there lies the Divine Maker's distinct understanding of that individual creature.[17] Therefore, since the number of created effects is, if not actually, then at least potentially, infinite, the exemplar cause has in one act of knowledge the vision of an infinity of diverse, unique entities. The entity of God's knowledge of his creation must be infinitely perfect. What could it lack? If divine knowledge is identical with the divine essence, then the first being is infinite.

A few points in the argument merit comment. We have little difficulty accepting the idea that knowledge is a perfection of which one can have more or less. The nature of knowledge—the mind's appropriation of the intelligibility of things, to the point where the philosopher can say that in knowing, the knower becomes the known—makes it particularly suitable as a subject for discussing infinity. The things that are or can be made by the Creator one after the other is potentially infinite. If they were taken all at one time, their number would be actually infinite. It does not seem farfetched, once we have gotten as far along the path of metaphysics as we now find ourselves, to think that this is exactly what God does in his knowledge of the exemplars. He knows all things simultaneously in one act. Even so, the transition from a sum of finite goods to an infinite good calls for some attention.

The truth of any finite thing corresponds to its mode of being and is therefore finite. The sum of any finite sequence, however indefinitely long, will at any stage be finite. "At any stage" signifies that we are working from within or along the line of created effects unfolding one after another. What if one were to stand outside of the sequence and take it as a finished whole? The measure of the new whole would be incommensurate with that of any part or sum of parts taken within the original collection. In this way, the potential infinity of creatures is transformed into the intensive infinity of divine knowledge. Taking the vantage point of the intellect in order to assume this holistic integration of the potentially infinite seems an ideal choice in that we all have experience of intellectual insight pulling together many disparate truths into a single, more comprehensive understanding. Moreover, we know that the excellence of our synthetic insight cannot be reduced simply to the summary worth of the parts. Something new and greater has been added. The Creator does something similar on a far grander scale.

The second argument from exemplarity closely parallels, mutatis mutandis, the fourth proof from efficiency, which we commented on above. Scotus brings out here that God's being or perfection is not amplified by his knowledge of creatures in his divine art. In familiar, ordinary cases of understanding, the intellect and its object concur as partial agents. This means that the object—that is, the intelligibility of the thing to be known—contributes to the entity and the perfection of the knowledge that it causes. But because God knows all that he knows through the knowledge of his essence, it follows, as Scotus says in the text, that "nothing that can be made from an exemplar adds anything thinkable to the first exemplar cause, hence it adds nothing to it in entity." That is to say, then, that the first exemplar cause is intensively infinite; the Creator is the fullness of perfection, the plenitude of being. Were the infinite not the measure of this fullness, then the Divine Being would be augmented by his exemplar knowledge, and he could not know the things he knows by self-knowledge. Scotus's doctrine of God's intensive infinity allows him to affirm both the radical self-sufficiency of the Divine Being and the real being and intelligibility of finite entities.

| Eminence

In developing his argument based upon the primacy of excellence, Scotus explores fundamental issues concerning the ontological significance of our ideas. One of philosophy's great mysteries is that mind somehow reflects reality. Plato had his ideas and theory of recollection; Aristotle developed his complicated system of abstraction; Augustine appealed to his theory of illumination; Descartes discovered innate ideas; Locke registered and processed the effects of experience on the tabula rasa; Wittgenstein explored his language games. The human experience of knowledge is as universal as it is mysterious, and the variety of explanatory theories testifies to the depth of the mystery. At this stage, we should consider certain basic ideas of Scotus's theory of knowledge because he thinks that he can prove that the preeminent being is infinite by appealing to certain facts about the intellect's ability to know. There appear to be two proofs. The first is a simple syllogism with an obvious major and a minor premise, which he supports with two uncomplicated arguments. The second is a complex adaptation of Anselm's famous *Proslogion* argument.

First he argues it is impossible that anything should excel that which is most excellent, but it is not impossible that something should excel that which is finite; therefore, that which is most excellent is infinite. Since the form is valid and the major premise is true by definition, the soundness of the argument turns on the truth of the minor. It is not self-evident that something should excel that which is finite. The ancient Greeks considered finite form to be a defining property of perfection. Some forms are more excellent than others, to be sure, but in every case "to be" meant to have a definite, limited form. To think of the infinite was to descend into regions where finite form held imperfect mastery over what was indefinite, potential, material. For someone of this cast of mind, the minor premise is false; it would be impossible that a preeminent being should exceed a finite entity. Scotus establishes his counterposition by a phenomenological description of how bedrock metaphysical concepts cohere in the light of the intellect.

The first proof of the minor premise runs:

1. If "infinite" were repugnant to "being," it would be because "finite" is either essential to it or a coextensive attribute of it.

2. But our direct experience with conceiving being apart from finitude proves otherwise.

The argument rests on an appeal to the fact that we can adequately conceive being without discerning in that conception any necessary or essential reference to finitude. Our concept of being, therefore, is indifferent to being either finite or infinite. The experienced indifference is a telling one, because Scotus holds that concepts have their own intrinsic dynamics by which they attract or repel other ideas with varying degrees of necessity. As he puts it, "once a subject is known, its proper attribute would immediately come to mind."

What the proof does not demonstrate, however, is that infinitude corresponds to perfection. In part this is taken care of in the opening definition, and in part it is argued in the next proof, which is interesting for the teleological interpretation he gives to the "motions" of the intellect. The central part of the second proof holds:

1. If "infinite" were repugnant to "being," then the intellect would experience dissonance at the expression "infinite being."
2. Quite the contrary, however; we experience a restlessness with "finite being," signifying an attraction toward infinitude.

We spoke above of the teleology of the intellect, which is evident in its being unsatisfied with the intelligibility of finite being. The same point could be developed in terms of aesthetic notions. Because for Scotus ideas have built-in relationships to one another, truth would be for the intellect a kind of music whose beauty sounds when the right relationships are drawn upon. In the end, the proofs work to the degree to which one endows the intellect with the revelatory power that Scotus gives it.

Throughout his brief career, Scotus was fascinated with certain Anselmian strains of thought. This is evident in his ethics and theology as well as in his metaphysics. In the proofs for the existence of God in the *Ordinatio, De primo principio,* and *Rep.* I A, he found occasions to interpret Anselm's renowned *Proslogion* argument. Scotus never thought that Anselm gave us the so-called ontological argument, if by this we mean a proof that moves from the a priori world of ideas to the real world of existence. There is no reason to think that he would have been any more sympathetic to such an approach than was Immanuel Kant some five hundred years later.[18] Scotus sees in the Anselmian argument an anticipation of two of his own ideas: our intellectual experience with the natural proclivities of basic metaphysical concepts and the existential necessity of a possibility that is both real and uncausable.

The gist of the proof at hand is that infinitude is an attribute of "that than which nothing greater can be thought [quo maius cogitari non potest]." Scotus's operational definition of "infinite," we recall, is the property of "excel[ling] any actual or possible finite being to a degree beyond any determinate measure you take or could take." So the question becomes: Does that than which nothing greater can be thought excel any actual or possible being to a degree beyond any possible measure? It obviously does if the question is conceivable. Norman Malcolm has argued that Anselm's argument, at least the version found in chapter 3 of the *Proslogion,* holds true if the basic formula (that than which nothing greater can be thought) is meaningful.[19] This is precisely Scotus's opinion as well. For this reason he begins a gloss on "conceivability," explaining that "what can be thought of is what can be understood without contradiction." But in determining this, one has to appeal to the experience of the intellect.

Just as in the first proof, where Scotus proves conceivability by appealing to our experience of the intellect, so also here he describes how concepts align themselves within the intellect. We cannot think everything we can say. For instance, "that man is irrational is something inconceivable," because the formula conceals a contradiction. To understand "irrational man" requires making a coherent unity out of the contradictories rational/irrational. One can shift back and forth, thinking now one term and now the other, but the intellect cannot blend them into an integrated whole so as to think them simultaneously—as we do when we think both "animal" and "rational" in thinking "man." By contrast, and more to the point, the highest being that can be thought of (*summum cogitabile*) is conceivable without contradiction. This means that it is a possible being; and it is not merely an *ens rationis,* that is, a being whose possibility depends upon some mind actively thinking it. Accordingly, "it can be thought to exist in actuality." We therefore have reason to treat it differently from a pure fancy or imaginative construct.

Up to this point, we have been given leave, as it were, to think of the *summum cogitabile* as existing in reality, as part of the extramental world. The terms of its existence, however, are special. It has to be thought of as existing of itself, otherwise one would have to think of it as a dependent being, and therefore not as the *summum cogitabile.* In short, if it can be thought without contradiction, then it must exist necessarily.

As Scotus sees it, the trick to understanding Anselm is to avoid thinking that he puts into one pan of the balance a conceivable thing that only exists in the mind and into the other pan the same conceivable thing, this time existing in reality, then determines that the latter entity is more conceivable. Rather, what he thinks Anselm is saying is that the conceivable thing has as one of its quidditative features its possibility of actually existing. To affirm such a property requires supporting evidence, which Scotus gets by appealing to the attractions and repugnancies—the implicit coherencies or incoherencies—of basic metaphysical concepts that become apparent to the intellect. Like Kant, Scotus considers it absurd to think that "existing" enhances the conceivability of "chimera" or "gold mountain." Per impossibile, were a chimera to actually exist, then we could conceive of its actually existing. Such an a posteriori concept would have real possibility as one of its quidditative features evident to the intellect conceiving it, and the possibility of actual existence would therefore add to its conceivability. But there is nothing about fancies like chimeras or gold mountains that demands "existing extramentally" as one of their quidditative features. That is what makes them figments of the imagination. Like fanciful notions, Anselm's *summum cogitabile* is not derived from a direct encounter with the first nature; but unlike such figments, the consistent inner logic of Anselm's concept includes real possibility and uncausability. The noncontradictory character of this concept, however, is not self-justified; its consistency has to be argued. As Scotus points out elsewhere, even our simplest notions of God are argued constructions.[20] The basic ideas are transcendental concepts common to God and creatures that have been derived from our experience of creatures. The combinations among them devised to uniquely name God have to be argued.

▌Finality

The final proof rests on rudimentary observations of the operations of the intellect and the will. Both are active powers understood here as appetites whose operations are ordered to their proper objects of truth and the good, respectively. Arguing from analogy, Scotus holds that just as the intellect is not satisfied with the cognition of any truth that falls short of the greatest truth, so also the will is restless till it enjoys the maximal good. But the love of no finite good can bring complete rest to the will's desire. He therefore concludes that "the ultimate satisfaction of the will lies only in a good that is infinite." First of all, the argument endorses a teleological interpretation of natural powers. They are appetites with natural ends meant to be achieved in the ordinary course of things. Second, one must accept the implicit appeal to the universal experience that no finite good—nor any sum of such goods, however integrated—adequately satisfies the will's desire. At this point, one is left with two alternatives: either human existence is in the end a tale of unfulfilled desire, or at some point an infinite good saturates the will.

The place to begin a critical assessment is with the second premise. Aristotle, for instance, would say that we are humans, not gods, and should therefore seek a good proper to our limited station.[21] The life of virtue, both moral and intellectual, lived in good health and with friends, is a very good life indeed, rarely achieved, though satisfying beyond the expectations of most men and women. But for all its nobility, it is a finite good. In the prologue to the *Ordinatio,* Scotus shows that he is well aware of the difficulty of finding rational grounds for exceeding the Greek philosophical ideal of the mean (*meson*) or the limit (*peras*).[22] One might argue that the greatest barrier to human happiness is the denial of limits. "Good enough" sums up, in the simplest terms of human experience, an ideal that adequately answers to the deepest impulses of the human soul. Unfortunately, Scotus did not explore this issue directly, though it is not hard to surmise how he might have replied. It is clear from the foregoing arguments, and will become more evident in the next chapter, that Scotus thinks we have a naturally available concept of an infinitely perfect being. He also holds that there are rational grounds for not limiting the nature of the human intellectual soul to the terms of our material existence.[23] Both ideas contain resources perhaps sufficient for a philosophical anthropology that would overcome the objection introduced above.

Argument 4: Unicity

The burden of the prior three questions has been to demonstrate that among the totality of entities, there must be at least one infinitely perfect being. *Ens infinitum* exists and is sui generis, but how many individuals of this kind are there? Can we now show that there is at most one such being? Scotus offers five proofs. The second and third proofs are of particular interest and will be discussed in more detail below. The first proof, based on necessities of the divine intellect, is a straightforward reductio argument.

We have glossed its basic terms in our earlier comments on the second proof of infinity (from exemplarity). The fourth promises that a proof could be developed "from the nature of 'necessary existence,' as Avicenna does," but none follows.[24] For his fifth proof, he repeats an argument held by many, most notably by Richard of St. Victor, only to reject it as not demonstrative because he does not believe that apart from faith we can be certain of divine omnipotence.[25] In what follows, we shall comment on the two more interesting arguments and conclude with some summary remarks on the God of Scotus's metaphysics.

Scotus argues his proof from the will as follows:

1. Assume A and B are both infinite beings, and therefore both are infinitely lovable.
2. An upright will loves each lovable object to the extent that it is lovable.
3. Because A and B are upright, each will love the other infinitely.
4. But A cannot love B infinitely.

Premises 2 and 3 follow from the nature of the will, understood as an active power perfected in the love of the good, to which it is ordered. Because they are free, rational wills have the power of loving, in varying degrees of intensity, a variety of objects insofar as they are conceived as good. Scotus's analysis of the will involves two factors. First of all, it is distinguished as one of two species of active power by its nondeterministic mode of operation. Second, its freedom is not simply a matter of being nondetermined but is positively rooted in an intrinsic inclination to love rightly the just good. If (4) proves true, however, then it contradicts (3) and draws out the absurdity in the opening assumption. Two arguments are brought forward on behalf of (4).

The first defense rests upon the will's natural inclination to seek its own good above all. This egoism, if you will, is a defining aspect of the will's constitution and is altogether wholesome, so long as self-love does not interfere with just duties to others. In fact, Scotus would argue that every person has a duty in justice to meet the demands of self-love. On the basis of these ideas, the proof continues.

5. Every natural will loves its own individual good more than another, unless the entity of the other (beloved object) is bound up with the entity of the first (the agent).
6. But the entities of A and B are altogether independent of one another.

7. Therefore, A's upright will loves its own good more than B's good.

A second defense of the fourth premise proceeds from consideration of the will's inclination to the good of others. According to common medieval opinion, the good of another could be taken as an object of either use (*uti*) or fruition (*frui*), which is the love of something else for its own sake. In the love of use, the good of the other is subordinated to the good of self. By contrast, fruition-love offers the possibility of loving an object whose lovability is not derived from the good of one's own self. In such acts of love, one finds personal happiness in adhering to one's beloved for the sake of the beloved itself. Such an analysis of the dynamic of the will informs the second proof of the fourth premise:

8. A either loves B for its own sake or uses it.
9. If A uses it, then its will is perverse.
10. If A loves B for its own sake, then it would find in it an object that fully satisfies its capacity for happiness.
11. But A also necessarily achieves satisfaction in self-love.
12. A is thus completely satisfied twice, which is absurd because it makes unnecessary the necessary satisfaction of self-love.
13. Therefore, A and B cannot both be infinitely perfect beings.

Use-love of an infinite beloved perverts the will, as (9) insists, because it esteems itself over what is infinitely good. The use of an object makes an implicit judgment that the good of the used should be subordinated to the good of the user. In the case at hand, nothing could be rightly considered greater than what is infinitely perfect. The point of premises 10–12 is that a single infinite will cannot be satisfied twice. The proposal is nonsense. The reflexive nature of divine knowledge, together with the proper inclination of the will toward self-love, means that God's beatitude will be exhaustively complete in the love of his own Godhead. To find perfect satisfaction in another is either nonsensically redundant or an obstacle to the self-love required for happiness. The first case runs up against the principle of parsimony; the second entails the contradiction that God is both happy (love of B) and not happy (satisfaction of B precludes love of A).

The proof from God's primacy proceeds as a reductio of the assumption that there can be more than one individual instantiation of the divine nature. The guiding principle of eminence holds that where you have a nature that allows multiple individuals, there would be no reason intrinsic to the nature to explain why there is *this* number of them rather than *that* number. One must appeal to external reasons—for instance, that the power of the agent was depleted, or the matter was exhausted, or time and space were limited. Deity, or infinite being, as Scotus has developed the concept, is a specific nature, so if one allows that there are two individuals, this means that, save for externally imposed limitations, there is no reason that there could not be an infinity of divine beings. But by the very nature of divine infinity, there could be no external constraints. By implication, we are led to affirm an extreme form of polytheism. In Scotus's judgment, the absurdity of there necessarily being an infinite number of infinitely perfect first principles forces one to the conclusion that "primacy by its very nature [is] restricted."[26]

God at the End of Metaphysics

It is not insignificant that the question of unicity arises only after consideration of divine infinity. Having demonstrated the convergence of three different, fundamental lines of explanation (efficiency, finality, and eminence) in a unique kind of being, Scotus shows why we must conceive of the first principle as all in all, as a plenitude of being that creates and sustains all other beings, each with its distinctive measure of reality and intelligibility. Under his analysis, the extrinsic mathematical notion of infinity proper to finite collections is gradually transformed into an attribute describing the radical fullness of the first being. In the process, notions of God's self-sufficiency start to take shape. When the question next arises whether there could be two or more such individuals, the answer is to be found in the implications of God's infinity. Because it is the fullness of perfection or the plenitude of being, divine existence needs no explanation. Rather, only being insofar as it is limited requires explanation, precisely because it appears as caused or purposed or in some degree of excellence. In a similar way, the first philosophers knew that it was becoming and plurality that called for reasons. One begins to see that plurality makes no sense in regard to what is the fullness of being. To imagine more than one such individual is to drop the main conceit, for if there are two, then we legitimately should look for the efficient and final cause, or we rightly seek to rank their excellence. This is what Scotus meant by his remark that "primacy by its very nature has to be somehow restricted." In the simplest terms, he means that one cannot pluralize the "metaphysical first" without its losing its meaning. More precisely, he seems to be saying that when one comes to understand the metaphysical basis for affirming a first principle, those reasons also imply its uniqueness both in kind and number. "Restriction," therefore, is an unnecessarily pejorative way of referring to the implications of radical self-sufficiency.

At the end of his complex metaphysical argument, Scotus returns us to one of the founding insights of philosophy. In his own way, he agrees with Parmenides that being is one, complete, undivided, held together by the chains of necessity, which are nothing more than the identity of intelligibility with being itself. Understandably, his differences with Parmenides are many. But on this one count, these two minds, separated by seventeen centuries and several great cultural transformations, fall under the sway of a common insight.

NOTES

1. *Ordinatio* prol., p. 1, no. 75 (Vat. 1:45–46). Eng. trans. by Wolter, "Duns Scotus on the Necessity of Revealed Knowledge."
2. Ignatius Brady, "The Distinctions of Lombard's Book of Sentences and Alexander of Hales."
3. Scotus's own attempt to put his theology on a "scientific" footing is documented in Stephen Dumont, "Theology as a Science and Duns Scotus's Distinction between Intuitive and Abstractive Cognition" and "The *Propositio Famosa Scoti*: Duns Scotus and Ockham on the Possibility of a Science of Theology."
4. Henry of Ghent was a secular master at Paris from 1276 to 1292, the year before his death at Tournai. When Pope John XXI, who himself had been a master of theology at the University of Paris, requested from Parisian bishop Stephen Tempier an account of the status of radical Aristotelianism at the university, Tempier's investigation concluded in the famous condemnations of 1277. Henry served on the commission that drew up the list of 219 anathematized doctrines. Throughout his illustrious tenure as a theologian, Henry tried to incorporate the new Aristotelianism within an overarching Platonic or Augustinian framework. This conservative element brought him into frequent opposition to Godfrey of Fontaines (regent master 1285–c. 1304), the other great Parisian theologian in the final decades of the thirteenth century, whose Aristotelianism, however, was of a more rigorous form than Henry's.
5. For Henry's text, see *Medieval Philosophy: From St. Augustine to Nicholas of Cusa,* ed. John F. Wippel and Allan B. Wolter, 376–89.
6. The developed logical interconnection between the three kinds of proof appears to be something that only gradually occurred to Scotus. It is one of the distinctive features of the *Rep.* I A version, missing in the earlier *Lectura* and *Ordinatio* editions. It is also missing in his *De primo principio,* which, however, has the highly developed concept of essential order integrating the whole work.
7. Compare Wittgenstein: "It is essential to things that they should be possible constituents of states of affairs. . . . If a thing *can* occur in a

state of affairs, the possibility of the state of affairs must be written into the thing itself" (*Tractatus Logico-Philosophicus*, 2.011–2.012; see also Allan B. Wolter, "The Unspeakable Philosophy of the Late Wittgenstein," esp. 174–78).

8. See Wolter's remarks on the absurdity of the contingent existence of an entity that exists of itself in *A Treatise on God as a First Principle*, 240–41.

9. Ibid., 228–31.

10. Ibid., 232–34.

11. Ibid., 1.7; 2.41, 47. See also Henry in *Medieval Philosophy*, 384–85.

12. It is true that Scotus adds a fourth primacy, namely, that God is the first exemplar cause, but this is not an attribute different from God's efficiency. Scotus is well known for his rejection of exemplar causality as a distinct kind. It is clear from the discussion in *Rep.* I A that he simply affirms that the first efficient cause acts as an intelligent, free agent in its productions, that it "acts knowingly [and] orders its effects to the end that it has in mind.... Therefore, in modeling the thing in its mind, it immediately orders it to itself as ultimate end."

13. Thomas Hobbes, *Leviathan*, 99, 402–3.

14. Meldon C. Wass, *The Infinite God and the "Summa Fratris Alexandri,"* charts an early and influential thirteenth-century attempt to conceive of divine infinity.

15. The parallel text in *De primo principio* 4.67–72 takes greater pains to touch up unacceptable Aristotelian aspects of the argument. See Wolter's corresponding commentary, *Treatise*, 305–9.

16. The proximate state of the debate at Paris just prior to Scotus's arrival on the scene can be gathered in part from John Wippel's explication of three thirteenth-century Parisian masters—Aquinas (*magister regens* from 1256 to 1259 and from 1269 to 1272), Henry (from 1276 to c. 1292), and Godfrey (from 1285 to c. 1304)—in his "The Reality of Nonexisting Possibles according to Thomas Aquinas, Henry of Ghent, and Godfrey of Fontaines." James Ross criticizes Wippel's interpretation in a way that illuminates the critical philosophical issues in the doctrine of exemplarism; see Ross, "Aquinas's Exemplarism; Aquinas's Voluntarism."

17. The issue of whether God knows creatures distinctly was a challenging one for the Scholastics. In Scotus's case, he answers the difficulty with his doctrine of individuation, which affirms in the strongest terms the intelligibility of each creature in its uniqueness; see our treatment of individuation in chapter 5.

18. See Wolter, "Is Existence for Scotus a Perfection, Predicate, or What?" in *The Philosophical Theology of John Duns Scotus*, 278–84.

19. Norman Malcolm, "Anselm's Ontological Arguments."

20. See *Collatio* 13, no. 4 (Vivès 5:202).

21. *Nicomachean Ethics* 10.7

22. See Wolter, "Duns Scotus on the Natural Desire for the Supernatural," in *The Philosophical Theology of John Duns Scotus*, 125–47.

23. *Quodlibet* q. 14, nos. 11–12 (Vivès 26:39–47); Eng. trans. by Felix Alluntis and Allan B. Wolter, *God and Creatures: The Quodlibetal Questions*, 14.39–43, pp. 325–27.

24. What Scotus has in mind can be found in *Ordinatio* I, d. 2, nos. 71, 176–77 (Vat. 2:171–72, 232–34).

25. *Quodlibet* q. 7 ("Can it be demonstrated by natural and necessary reason that God is omnipotent?") provides a thorough account of Scotus's ideas on omnipotence (*God and Creatures,* 159–97).

26. At this point, someone who is theologically sophisticated might object that in insisting upon the self-containment of the divine nature, Scotus has effectively taken away the grounds for deity being shared by the three divine persons. Scotus refers the reader to his response in distinction 5, which deals with the generation of the Son, where he applies his formal distinction to a careful analysis of the concepts of essence and relation to solve the problem. See the parallel treatment in *Ordinatio* I, d. 5, nos. 106–41 (Vat. 4:65–80).

CHAPTER FOUR | Three Questions about Knowledge

Text

[1. De Natura Conceptus Nostri Dei]

[A. Conceptus quiditativus potest haberi de Deo]

Dico[1] ergo primo quod non tantum haberi potest conceptus naturaliter in quo quasi per accidens concipitur Deus, puta in aliquo attributo, sed etiam aliquis conceptus in quo per se et quiditative concipiatur Deus. —Probo, quia concipiendo "sapientem" concipitur proprietas, secundum eum, vel quasi proprietas, in actu secundo perficiens naturam; ergo intelligendo "sapientem" oportet praeintelligere aliquod "quid" cui intelligo istud quasi proprietatem inesse, et ita ante conceptus omnium passionum vel quasi passionum oportet quaerere conceptum quiditativum cui intelligantur ista attribui: et iste conceptus alius erit quiditativus de Deo, quia in nullo alio potest esse status.

[B. De conceptu univoco Deo et creaturae]

Secundo dico quod non tantum in conceptu analogo conceptui creaturae concipitur Deus, scilicet qui omnino sit alius ab illo qui de creatura dicitur, sed in conceptu aliquo univoco sibi et creaturae. —Et ne fiat contentio de nomine univocationis, univocum conceptum dico, qui ita est unus quod eius unitas sufficit ad contradictionem, affirmando et negando ipsum de eodem; sufficit etiam pro medio syllogistico, ut extrema unita in medio sic uno sine fallacia aequivocationis concludantur inter se uniri.

Et univocationem sic intellectam probo.... Primo sic: omnis intellectus certus de uno conceptu et dubius de diversis,

---

1. *Ordinatio* I, d. 3, nos. 25–30 (Vat. 3:16–20).

[1. The Nature of Our Concepts of God]

[A. We have naturally concepts by which we conceive God per se and quidditatively.]

I say to begin with, therefore, that it is naturally possible to have not only a concept in which God is known incidentally, for example, in some attribute, but also some concept in which he is conceived per se and quidditatively. I prove this, because in conceiving "wise," we conceive a property, according to him [Henry of Ghent], or a quasi-property, which perfects the nature as some further actuality. Hence in order to conceive "wise," it is necessary to think of some quiddity in which this quasi-property exists. And thus it is necessary to look beyond the ideas of all properties or quasi-properties to some quidditative concept to which we attribute these; and this concept will be a quidditative concept of God, because in no other sort will our quest cease.

[B. God is thought of in some concept univocal to himself and creatures.]

Second, I say that God is thought of not only in some concept analogous to that of a creature, that is, one entirely different from what is predicated of a creature, but also in some concept univocal to himself and to a creature. And lest there be any contention about the word "univocation," I call that concept univocal that has sufficient unity in itself that to affirm and deny it of the same subject suffices as a contradiction. It also suffices as a syllogistic middle term, so that where two terms are united in a middle term that is one in this fashion, they are inferred without a fallacy of equivocation to be united among themselves.

And understanding univocation in this sense, I prove it first thus: Every intellect that is certain about one concept and dubious about others has the concept about which it is certain as

habet conceptum de quo est certus alium a conceptibus de quibus est dubius; subiectum includit praedicatum. Sed intellectus viatoris potest esse certus de Deo quod sit ens, dubitando de ente finito vel infinito, creato vel increato; ergo conceptus entis de Deo est alius a conceptu isto et illo, et ita neuter ex se et in utroque illorum includitur; igitur univocus.

Probatio maioris, quia nullus idem conceptus est certus et dubius; ergo vel alius, quod est propositum, vel nullus—et tunc non erit certitudo de aliquo conceptu.

Probatio minoris: quilibet philosophus fuit certus, illud quod posuit primum principium, esse ens, —puta unus de igne et alius de aqua, certus erat quod erat ens; non autem fuit certus quod esset ens creatum vel increatum, primum vel non primum. Non enim erat certus quod erat primum, quia tunc fuisset certus de falso, et falsum non est scibile; nec quod erat ens non primum, quia tunc non posuissent oppositum. —Confirmatur etiam, nam aliquis videns philosophos discordare potuit esse certus de quocumque quod aliquis posuit primum principium, esse ens, et tamen propter contrarietatem opinionum eorum potuit dubitare utrum sit hoc ens vel illud. Et tali dubitanti si fieret demonstratio concludens vel destruens aliquem conceptum inferiorem, puta quod ignis non erit ens primum sed aliquod ens posterius primo ente, non destrueretur ille conceptus primus sibi certus, quem habuit de ente, sed salvaretur in illo conceptu particulari probato de igne, —et per hoc probatur propositio, supposita in ultima consequentia rationis, quae fuit quod ille conceptus certus, qui est ex se neuter dubiorum, in utroque istorum salvatur.

Quod si non cures de auctoritate illa accepta de diversitate opinionum philosophantium, sed dicas quod quilibet habet duos conceptus in intellectu suo, propinquos, qui propter propinquitatem analogiae videntur esse unus conceptus, —contra hoc videtur esse quod tunc ex ista evasione videretur destructa omnis via probandi unitatem alicuius conceptus univocam: si enim dicis hominem habere unum conceptum ad Socratem et Platonem, negabitur tibi, et dicetur quod sunt duo, sed "videntur unus" propter magnam similitudinem....

other than the dubious concepts. The subject [of this proposition] includes the predicate. But the intellect of a person in this life can be certain that God is a being while doubting whether this being is finite or infinite, created or uncreated; therefore the concept of God as a being is other than this or that concept; and although included in each of these, it is none of them of itself, and therefore it is univocal.

Proof of the major [premise]: A certain concept is not the same as a dubious concept, and therefore it is other (which is our proposal), or there is no concept, and then there will be no certitude about any concept.

Proof of the minor: Each philosopher was certain that what he proposed as a first principle was a being; for instance, one as regards fire, another as regards water—each was sure this was a being. But he was not certain that it was a created being or an uncreated one, or whether it was first or not first. He was not certain it was first, for then he would have been certain about something false, and what is false is not scientifically knowable. Nor was he certain it was not first, or he would not have claimed the opposite.

This reason is also confirmed, for someone, seeing that philosophers disagree, could have been certain that what someone had proposed as a first principle was a being, and still, because of the contrariety of their opinions, could be in doubt whether [the first principle] would be this being or that. And if, to such a doubter, a demonstration would either verify or destroy some one alternative—for example, that fire will not be the first being but something posterior to the first being—this would not destroy his first certain notion of it as a being; rather, that notion would survive in the particular conception proved about fire. And this proves the proposition proposed above in the final inference from reason, [namely], that this certain concept, which of itself is neither of the doubtful ones, is preserved in both of them.

Perhaps you do not accept the force of the argument based on the diversity of the opinions of the philosophers, but instead you say that each thinker has in his intellect two similar concepts that only appear to be one concept because of their analogous resemblance. One can argue against this objection in the following way. If you accept this evasion, then it appears to destroy every way of proving the unity of some univocal concept. So, for instance, if you say that "man" is one concept pertaining to Socrates and Plato, then it will be denied, and one can claim that there are two concepts that only seem to be one because of a great resemblance. . . .

Secundo principaliter arguo sic:[2] nullus conceptus realis causatur in intellectu viatoris naturaliter nisi ab his quae sunt naturaliter motiva intellectus nostri; sed illa sunt phantasma, vel obiectum relucens in phantasmate, et intellectus agens; ergo nullus conceptus simplex naturaliter fit in intellectu nostro modo nisi qui potest fieri virtute istorum. Sed conceptus qui non esset univocus obiecto relucenti in phantasmate, sed omnino alius, prior, ad quem ille habeat analogiam, non potest fieri virtute intellectus agentis et phantasmatis; ergo talis conceptus alius, analogus qui ponitur, naturaliter in intellectu viatoris numquam erit, —et ita non poterit haberi naturaliter aliquis conceptus de Deo, quod est falsum.

Probatio assumpti: obiectum quodcumque, sive relucens in phantasmate sive in specie intelligibili, cum intellectu agente vel possibili cooperante, secundum ultimum suae virtutis facit sicut effectum sibi adaequatum, conceptum suum proprium et conceptum omnium essentialiter vel virtualiter inclusorum in eo; sed ille alius conceptus qui ponitur analogus, non est essentialiter nec virtualiter inclusus in isto, nec etiam est iste; ergo iste non fiet ab aliquo tali movente.

Et confirmatur ratio, quia "obiectum"; praeter conceptum suum proprium adaequatum, et inclusum in ipso altero duorum modorum praedictorum, nihil potest cognosci ex isto obiecto nisi per discursum; sed discursus praesupponit cognitionem istius simplicis ad quod discurritur. Formetur igitur ratio sic, quia nullum obiectum facit conceptum simplicem proprium, in isto intellectu, conceptum simplicem proprium alterius obiecti, nisi contineat illud aliud obiectum essentialiter vel virtualiter; obiectum autem creatum non continet increatum essentialiter vel virtualiter, et hoc sub ea ratione sub qua sibi attribuitur, ut "posterius essentialiter" attribuitur "priori essentialiter," —quia contra rationem "posterioris essentialiter" est includere virtualiter suum prius, et patet quod obiectum creatum non essentialiter continet increatum secundum aliquid omnino sibi proprium et non commune; ergo non facit conceptum simplicem et proprium enti increato. . . .

---

2. *Ordinatio* I, d. 3, nos. 35–36 (Vat. 3:21–24).

My second principal argument runs thus. No real concept is caused naturally in the intellect in our present state except through those agents that naturally move our intellect. But the natural agents are the sense image—or the object revealed in the sense image—and the active intellect. Therefore, no simple concept naturally arises in our intellect unless it can come about by virtue of these causes. Now, the active intellect and the sense image cannot give rise to a concept that, with respect to the object revealed in the sense image, is not univocal but rather, in accordance with an analogical relationship, is altogether other and higher than the object. It follows that such an "other," analogous concept will never arise in the intellect in our present state. Also it would thus follow that one could not naturally have any concept of God—which is false.

The assumption is proved thus. At the limit of its causal power, any object, whether revealed in the sense image or in the intelligible species, cooperates with the causality of the passive or active intellect and brings about as its adequate effect either its own proper concept or a concept of all that is essentially or virtually included in it. But this "other" concept which is thought to be analogous is not included in the causal object either essentially or virtually—nor is it a proper concept of the object. Therefore, this analogous concept cannot be produced by such an efficient agent [namely, by the object revealed in the image or species].

This argument based on the role of the object is confirmed in the following way. With the exception of its own proper adequate concept and whatever is included in it in either of the aforementioned ways, the object can only be the source of knowing something else through discursive reasoning. But discursive reasoning presupposes a prior grasp of the simple things toward which one reasons. Based on this, a proof can be formulated thus. No object produces both a simple proper concept [of itself] and in the same intellect the simple proper concept of another object, unless the former object contains the latter essentially or virtually. However, no created object essentially or virtually contains an uncreated object, at least not under the formality by which what is essentially posterior is related to what is essentially prior. Indeed, it is contrary to the very idea of being essentially posterior that it virtually include what is prior to it. And with respect to something that is altogether proper to the uncreated and not just common to it, it is evident that a created object does not essentially contain the uncreated. Therefore, it does not produce a simple concept that is proper to the uncreated being.

[Etiam arguitur sic:][3] omnis inquisitio metaphysica de Deo sic procedit, considerando formalem rationem alicuius et auferendo ab illa ratione formali imperfectionem quam habet in creaturis, et reservando illam rationem formalem et attribuendo sibi omnino summam perfectionem, et sic attribuendo illud Deo. Exemplum de formali ratione sapientiae (vel intellectus) vel voluntatis: consideratur enim in se et secundum se; et ex hoc quod ista ratio non concludit formaliter imperfectionem aliquam nec limitationem, removentur ab ipsa imperfectiones quae concomitantur eam in creaturis, et reservata eadem ratione sapientiae et voluntatis attribuuntur ista Deo perfectissime. Ergo omnis inquisitio de Deo supponit intellectum habere conceptum eundem, univocum, quem accepit ex creaturis.

Quod si dicas, alia est formalis ratio eorum quae conveniunt Deo, —ex hoc sequitur inconveniens, quod ex nulla ratione propria eorum prout sunt in creaturis, possunt concludi de Deo, quia omnino alia et alia ratio illorum est et istorum; immo non magis concludetur quod Deus est sapiens formaliter, ex ratione sapientiae quam apprehendimus ex creaturis, quam quod Deus est formaliter lapis: potest enim conceptus aliquis, alius a conceptu lapidis creati, formari, ad quem conceptum lapidis ut est idea in Deo habet iste lapis attributionem, et ita formaliter diceretur "Deus est lapis," secundum istum conceptum analogum, sicut "sapiens," secundum illum conceptum analogum. . . .

[C. Deus non potest cognosci sub propria ratione]

Tertio[4] dico quod Deus non cognoscitur naturaliter a viatore in particulari et proprie, hoc est sub ratione huius essentiae ut haec et in se. Sed ratio illa posita ad hoc in praecedenti opinione non concludit. . . .

Est ergo alia ratio huius conclusionis, videlicet quod Deus ut haec essentia in se, non cognoscitur naturaliter a nobis, quia sub ratione talis cognoscibilis est obiectum voluntarium, non naturale, nisi respectu sui intellectus tantum. Et ideo a nullo intellectu creato potest sub ratione huius essentiae ut haec est naturaliter cognosci, nec aliqua essentia naturaliter cognoscibilis a nobis sufficienter ostendit hanc essentiam ut haec, nec

---

3. *Ordinatio* I, d. 3, nos. 39–40 (Vat. 3:26–27).
4. *Ordinatio* I, d. 3, nos. 56–57 (Vat. 3:38–39).

[It is also argued in this way:] The manner in which every metaphysical inquiry about God proceeds is by considering the formal notion of something and taking away from that formal notion the imperfection that it has in creatures while retaining that formal meaning and completely attributing to it the highest perfection, and thus ascribing it to God. For example, take the formal notion of wisdom (or of the intellect) or of the will: it may be considered in itself and without qualification; and from the fact that this notion implies no imperfection or limitation, the imperfections that accompany it in creatures are removed from it; and, keeping the same meaning of wisdom and of will, these are attributed to God in a most perfect way. Therefore, every inquiry about God presupposes that the intellect has the same univocal concept that it received from creatures.

And if you say that the formal notion is other as regards those things that pertain to God, a disconcerting consequence results, [namely], that from the proper notion of anything found in creatures nothing can be inferred about God, because the notion of what each has is entirely different; indeed, there is no more reason to conclude that God is formally wise from the notion of wisdom that we perceive in creatures than [there is to conclude] that God is formally a stone; for some concept other than the concept of a created stone can be formed that bears a relationship to the concept of a stone as an idea in God, and therefore one can say, "God is formally a stone," according to this analogous conception, just as he can be said to be "wise" according to that [other] analogous concept. . . .

[C. God is not known naturally in the present life in a particular, proper way.]

Thirdly, I say that God is not known naturally by one in the present life in a particular and proper way, that is, under the aspect of his [unique] essence as it is in itself and as it is just *this*. But the reason given for this in the preceding opinion [of Henry of Ghent] is not conclusive. . . .

Hence, there is another reason for this conclusion, namely, that God as "this essence" in itself is not known naturally by us, because under this aspect such a knowable thing is a voluntary object. Only for the divine intellect would it be a natural object. And therefore by no created intellect can it be naturally known under the aspect of this essence insofar as it is just *this*. Neither is there some essence naturally knowable to us that reveals this

per similitudinem univocationis nec imitationis. Univocatio enim non est nisi in generalibus rationibus; imitatio etiam deficit, quia imperfecta, quia creatura imperfecte eum imitatur....

[D. De conceptu entis infiniti]

Quarto[5] dico quod ad multos conceptus proprios Deo possumus pervenire, qui non conveniunt creaturis, —cuiusmodi sunt conceptus omnium perfectionum simpliciter, in summo. Et perfectissimus conceptus, in quo quasi in quadam descriptione perfectissime cognoscimus Deum, est concipiendo omnes perfectiones simpliciter et in summo. Tamen conceptus perfectior simul et simplicior, nobis possibilis, est conceptus entis infiniti. Iste enim est simplicior quam conceptus entis boni, entis veri, vel aliorum similium, quia "infinitum" non est quasi attributum vel passio entis, sive eius de quo dicitur, sed dicit modum intrinsecum illius entitatis, ita quod cum dico "infinitum ens," non habeo conceptum quasi per accidens, ex subiecto et passione, sed conceptum per se subiecti in certo gradu perfectionis, scilicet infinitatis, —sicut albedo intensa non dicit conceptum per accidens sicut albedo visibilis, immo intensio dicit gradum intrinsecum albedinis in se. Et ita patet simplicitas huius conceptus "ens infinitum."

Probatur perfectio istius conceptus, tum quia iste conceptus, inter omnes nobis conceptibiles conceptus, virtualiter plura includit—sicut enim ens includit virtualiter verum et bonum in se, ita ens infinitum includit verum infinitum et bonum infinitum, et omnem "perfectionem simpliciter" sub ratione infiniti, —tum quia demonstratione "quia" ultimo concluditur "esse" de ente infinito, sicut apparet ex quaestione prima secundae distinctionis;[6] illa autem sunt perfectiora quae ultimo cognoscuntur demonstratione "quia" ex creaturis, quia propter eorum remotionem a creaturis difficillimum est ea ex creaturis concludere.

Si dicis de summo bono vel summo ente, quod istud dicit modum intrinsecum entis et includit virtualiter alios conceptus, —respondeo quod si "summum" intelligatur comparative, sic dicit respectum ad extra; sed "infinitum" dicit conceptum ad se. Si autem intelligas absolute "summum," hoc est quod ex natura

---

5. *Ordinatio* I, d. 3, nos. 58–60 (Vat. 3:40–42).
6. *Ordinatio* I, d. 2, no. 40 (Vat. 2:148–49).

[unique] essence as just this, whether by reason of a likeness of univocation or of imitation. For only in general notions is there univocation; imitation also is deficient, because it is imperfect, since creatures imperfectly imitate him. . . .

[D. The concept "infinite being"]

Fourth, I say that we can arrive at many concepts that are proper to God because they do not apply to creatures. Such would be the concepts of all pure perfections taken in the highest degree. And the most perfect concept of all, by which we know God most perfectly, as it were, in a descriptive sort of way, is obtained by conceiving all the pure perfections and each in the highest degree. Now a less perfect but simpler concept is possible to us, namely, the concept of an infinite being. For this is simpler than the concept of "good being" or "true being" or other similar concepts, since infinite is not a quasi-attribute or property of "being" or of that of which it is predicated. Rather it signifies an intrinsic mode of that entity, so that when I say "infinite being," I do not have a concept composed accidentally, as it were, of a subject and its attribute. What I do have is a concept of what is essentially one, namely, of a subject with a certain grade of perfection—infinity. It is like "intense whiteness," which is not a notion that is accidentally composed, as "visible whiteness" would be, for the intensity is an intrinsic grade of whiteness itself. Thus the simplicity of this concept "infinite being" is evident.

The perfection of this concept is proved first from the fact that it virtually includes more than any other concept that we can conceive. As "being" includes virtually "true" and "good" in itself, so "infinite being" includes the "infinitely good," the "infinitely true," and all pure perfections under the aspect of infinity. It is also proved from this fact. With a demonstration of the simple fact, the existence of an infinite being or the fact that something has infinite being is the last conclusion to be established. This is clear from distinction 2, question 1. The more perfect, however, are the last to be established by a demonstration of fact that begins with creatures. For their remoteness from creatures makes knowledge of them from creatures most difficult to attain.

But if you say that "highest good" or "highest being" expresses an intrinsic mode of being and includes other concepts virtually, I reply that if "highest" is taken in a comparative sense, then it includes a relation to something extrinsic to being, whereas "infinite" is an absolute [or nonrelative] concept. But if "highest" is understood in an absolute sense—that is, as meaning that the very

rei non posset excedi perfectio illa, expressius concipitur in ratione infiniti entis. Non enim "summum bonum" indicat in se utrum sit infinitum vel finitum. . . .

[E. Deus per species creaturarum cognoscitur]

Quinto[7] dico quod ista quae cognoscuntur de Deo, cognoscuntur per species creaturarum, quia sive universalius et minus universale cognoscantur per eandem speciem minus universalis sive utrumque habeat speciem sui intelligibilem sibi propriam, saltem illud quod potest imprimere speciem minus universalis in intellectu, potest etiam causare speciem cuiuscumque universalioris: et ita creaturae, quae imprimunt proprias species in intellectu, possunt etiam imprimere species transcendentium quae communiter conveniunt eis et Deo, —et tunc intellectus propria virtute potest uti multis speciebus simul ad concipiendum illa simul quorum sunt istae species, puta specie boni et specie summi et specie actus ad concipiendum aliquid "summum bonum et actualissimum"; quod apparet per locum a minori: imaginativa enim potest uti speciebus diversorum sensibilium ad imaginandum compositum ex illis diversis, sicut apparet imaginando "montem aureum."

Ex hoc apparet improbatio illius quod dicitur in praecedenti opinione de illa suffossione, quia suffodiendo numquam illud quod non subest suffossioni invenitur per suffossionem; non autem subest conceptui creaturae aliquis conceptus vel species, repraesentans aliquid proprium Deo, quod sit omnino alterius rationis ab eo quod convenit creaturae, ut probatum est per secundam rationem in secundo articulo; ergo per suffossionem nullus talis conceptus invenitur. —Et quod adducitur simile de aestimativa, dico quod videtur adduci falsum ad confirmationem alterius falsi, quia si maneat ovis in eadem natura et in eodem affectu naturali ad agnum, mutaretur tamen—ut esset similis lupo—per miraculum in omnibus accidentibus sensibilibus, puta colore, figura et sono et ceteris huiusmodi, agnus fugeret ovem sic mutatam sicut fugeret lupum, et tamen in ove

---

7. *Ordinatio* I, d. 3, nos. 61–62 (Vat. 3:42–44).

nature of the thing is such that it cannot be exceeded—then this perfection is conceived even more expressly in the notion of an infinite being, because "highest good" as such does not indicate whether it is infinite or finite.

> [E. Those things we know of God are known from their likenesses in creatures.]

Fifth, I say that those things that are known of God are known from their likenesses [species] in creatures, for whether the more universal and less universal are known through the same species, or whether each has an intelligible species proper to itself, at least that which can impress a less universal species in the intellect can also cause a species of anything more general; and thus creatures, which impress in the intellect a likeness [species] proper to themselves, can also impress the species of the transcendentals, which are applicable commonly to themselves and to God; and then the intellect, by virtue of its own proper power, can make use of many species at the same time to conceive at once those things of which these are the species. For example, [it can use] the species of good and the species of highest and the species of act to conceive "the highest good that is most actual." This is apparent from the dialectical rule *a minori* ["What is true of the lesser is true of the greater"], for the imagination can use the species of different sense-perceptibles to imagine something composed of these diverse elements, as is apparent in imagining a gold mountain.

From this the refutation of the claim made [by Henry] in the preceding opinion about the intellect digging beneath the surface becomes apparent, because by such digging what was never buried cannot be unearthed. Beneath the concept of a creature, however, no concept or species exists that represents anything proper to God and that is of an entirely different nature than what pertains to a creature, as was proved by the second reason for the second assertion [on univocation]. Hence, no such concept is to be found by such digging. And [as for] the analogy about the estimative power [of the mind], I say that [Henry] seems to adduce one false example to confirm something else that is false. For if a sheep were to retain the same [essential] nature and the same natural affections for a lamb but by some miracle was changed in all its sense-perceptible appearances so as to resemble a wolf—for instance, in its color, its shape, its cries, and all such like—then the lamb would flee from the sheep that had been so altered

sic mutata non esset intentio nocivi, sed convenientis. Ergo aestimativa agni non suffoderet ad inveniendum intentionem convenientis, sub speciebus sensibilibus, sed praecise ita moveretur secundum appetitum sensitivum sicut accidentia sensibilia moverent. Si dicas quod ibi intentio convenientis non multiplicat se, quia non sunt talia accidentia convenientia tali intentioni, et intentio convenientis non multiplicatur sine accidentibus convenientibus, —hoc nihil est, quia si agnus fugeret lupum propter perceptionem nocivi conceptam ab aestimativa, et illa non multiplicatur cum accidentibus istis sensibilibus (quia non est cum eis, tento casu), ergo aut hic est suffossio agni ad intentionem nocivi quae nulla est, aut si hic non fugit propter suffossionem, ergo nec alias.

[2. Primum Objectum Intellectus: Ens]

[D]ico[8] . . . cum nihil possit esse communius ente et ens non possit esse commune univocum dictum in "quid" de omnibus per se intelligibilibus, quia non de differentiis ultimis nec de passionibus suis, —sequitur quod nihil est primum obiectum intellectus nostri propter communitatem ipsius in "quid" ad omne per se intelligibile. Et tamen hoc non obstante, dico quod primum obiectum intellectus nostri est ens, quia in ipso concurrit duplex primitas, scilicet communitatis et virtualitatis, nam omne per se intelligibile aut includit essentialiter rationem entis, vel continetur virtualiter vel essentialiter in includente essentialiter rationem entis: omnia enim genera et species et individua, et omnes partes essentiales generum, et ens increatum includunt ens quiditative; omnes autem differentiae ultimae includuntur in aliquibus istorum essentialiter, et omnes passiones entis includuntur in ente et in suis inferioribus virtualiter. Ergo illa quibus ens non est univocum dictum in "quid," includuntur in illis in quibus ens est sic univocum. —Et ita patet quod ens habet primitatem communitatis ad prima intelligibilia, hoc est ad conceptus quiditativos generum et specierum et individuorum, et partium essentialium omnium istorum, et entis increati, —et habet primitatem virtualitatis ad omnia intelligibilia inclusa in primis intelligibilibus, hoc est ad conceptus qualitativos differentiarum ultimarum et passionum propriarum.

---

8. *Ordinatio* I, d. 3, nos. 137–39 (Vat. 3:85–87).

as it would have fled from a wolf. And yet in the sheep thus changed there would be no harmful intent but only a felicitous one. Therefore, the estimative power would not burrow beneath the sense-perceptible species to discover the felicitous intent; rather it would be moved precisely in the way that sensible accidents would tend to move it. And if you say that this friendly intent is not transmitted sensibly here because the perceptible appearances do not accord with such an intent, and a felicitous intent does not betray itself where its sensible manifestations are missing, this is no solution. For if the lamb would flee the wolf because of the harmful perception conceived by the estimative power and this [intent] is not conveyed by such sensible accidents (because in the given case, [the reality of the wolf] is not present with its appearance), then there is here the unearthing of a harmful intention that does not exist. Or if the lamb does not flee because it has unearthed something, then it does not do so in other cases.

[2. Being: The First Object of the Intellect]

I say . . . since there can be nothing more common than being and that being cannot be predicated univocally *in quid* of all per se intelligibles, because it cannot be predicated of ultimate differences or of its attributes, it follows that nothing is the primary object of the intellect by reason of commonness *in quid* with respect to all per se intelligibles. And this not withstanding, I say that being is the first object of our intellect, because in it concurs a twofold primacy, namely, one of commonness and one of virtuality. For every per se intelligible either includes the notion of being or is contained virtually or essentially in something that does include the notion of being essentially. For every genus, species, and individual, and every essential part of a genus, and the uncreated being as well, include being quidditatively; but all ultimate differences are included in these essentially, and all attributes of being are included in being and in its inferiors virtually. Therefore those of which being is not a univocal predicate *in quid* are included in those in which being is univocal in this way. And so it is evident that being has a primacy of community to the first intelligibles—that is, to the quidditative concepts of genera, species, and individuals, and to all the essential parts of these—and to the concept of the uncreated being; and it has a primacy of virtuality to all intelligibles included in the first intelligibles—that is, to those qualitative concepts of ultimate differences and proper attributes.

Quod autem supposui communitatem entis dicti in "quid" ad omnes conceptus quiditativos praedictos, hoc probatur—de omnibus illis—duabus rationibus positis in prima quaestione huius distinctionis, ad probandum communitatem entis ad ens creatum et increatum. Quod ut pateat, pertracto eas aliqualiter.

Primam sic: de quocumque enim praedictorum conceptuum quiditativorum, contingit intellectum certum esse ipsum esse ens, dubitando de differentiis contrahentibus ens ad talem conceptum, —et ita conceptus entis ut convenit illi conceptui est alius a conceptibus illis inferioribus de quibus intellectus est dubius, et ita alius quod inclusus in utroque inferiore conceptu, nam differentiae illae contrahentes praesupponunt eundem conceptum entis communem, quem contrahunt.

Secundam rationem pertracto sic: sicut argutum est etiam quod Deus non est cognoscibilis a nobis naturaliter nisi ens sit univocum creato et increato, ita potest argui de substantia et accidente. Si enim substantia non immutat immediate intellectum nostrum ad aliquam intellectionem sui, sed tantum accidens sensibile, sequitur quod nullum conceptum quiditativum poterimus habere de illa nisi aliquis talis possit abstrahi a conceptu accidentis; sed nullus talis quiditativus abstrahibilis a conceptu accidentis est, nisi conceptus entis. . . .

Nullus[9] igitur conceptus quiditativus habetur naturaliter de substantia immediate causatus a substantia, sed tantum causatus vel abstractus primo ab accidente, —et illud non est nisi conceptus entis.

Per idem concluditur etiam propositum de partibus essentialibus substantiae. Si enim materia non immutat intellectum ad actum circa ipsam, nec forma substantialis, quaero quis conceptus simplex in intellectu habebitur de materia vel forma? Si dicas quod aliquis conceptus relativus (puta partis) vel conceptus "per accidens" (puta alicuius proprietatis materiae vel formae), quaero quis est conceptus quiditativus cui iste "per accidens" vel relativus attribuitur? Et si nullus quiditativus habetur, nihil erit cui attribuatur iste conceptus "per accidens." —Nullus autem quiditativus potest haberi nisi impressus vel abstractus ab illo quod movet intellectum, puta ab accidente, — et ille erit conceptus entis: et ita nihil cognoscetur de partibus essentialibus substantiae nisi ens sit commune univocum eis et accidentibus.

---

9. *Ordinatio* I, d. 3, nos. 145–47 (Vat. 3:90–91).

I have presumed, however, that being is predicated *in quid* of all the aforementioned quidditative concepts. This is proved of all of these by the same two reasons used in the first question of this distinction to show that being is common to both created and uncreated being. To make this clear, I run through them a bit.

The first [I explain] thus: For of each of the aforementioned concepts, the intellect can be certain that it is a being and still be in doubt as to the differences that restrict being to such a concept; and thus the concept of being that agrees with that concept is other than those that fall under it about which the intellect is dubious, and it is so distinct that it is included in each of the inferior concepts, for those restricting differences presuppose the same common concept of being that they restrict.

The second reason I explain thus: Just as it was argued that we cannot know God naturally unless being is univocal to the created and uncreated, so one can argue about substance and accident. For if substance does not act immediately upon our intellect to produce some intellectual awareness of itself, and rather it is only some sensible accident that does so, it follows that we will have no quidditative concept of substance except what can be abstracted from the concept of accident; but nothing quidditative of this sort can be abstracted from the concept of an accident other than the concept of being. . . .

Hence we have naturally no quidditative concept of substance that is caused immediately by substance itself but only something caused or abstracted from an accident—and this is nothing other than the concept of being.

By the same token, the conclusion that we propose holds good for the essential parts of substance as well. For if neither matter nor substantial form moves the intellect to an act of knowledge about it, I ask, Just what simple concept will there be in the intellect in regard to matter or to form? If you say that some relative concept (for example, that of a part) or some incidental concept (for example, of some property of matter or of form), then I ask, To what quidditative concept is this incidental or relational concept attributed? If no quidditative concept is to be had, there will be nothing to which the incidental concept may be attributed. But the only possible quidditative concept that one can have is abstracted from what impresses or moves the intellect, namely, an accident—and that will be the concept of being; and so nothing will be known of the essential parts of substance unless being is univocal to them and to accidents.

Istae rationes non includunt univocationem entis dicti in "quid" ad differentias ultimas et passiones. . . . [S]ed[10] non oportet quod insit utrique illorum in "quid"; sed vel sic, vel est univocus eis ut determinabilis ad determinantes vel ut denominabilis ad denominantes.

Unde[11] breviter: ens est univocum in omnibus, sed conceptibus non-simpliciter simplicibus est univocus in "quid" dictus de eis; simpliciter simplicibus est univocus, sed ut determinabilis vel ut denominabilis, —non autem ut dictum de eis in "quid," quia hoc includit contradictionem.

Ex his apparet quomodo in ente concurrat duplex primitas, videlicet primitas communitatis in "quid" ad omnes conceptus non-simpliciter simplices, et primitas virtualitatis—in se vel in suis inferioribus—ad omnes conceptus simpliciter simplices. Et quod ista duplex primitas concurrens sufficiat ad hoc quod ipsum sit primum obiectum intellectus, licet neutram habeat praecise ad omnia per se intelligibilia. . . . Igitur tunc non includeretur primum obiectum in omnibus per se obiectis, sed quodlibet per se obiectum vel includeret ipsum essentialiter, vel includeretur in aliquo essentialiter vel virtualiter includente ipsum: et ita in ipso concurreret duplex primitas, scilicet communitatis, ex parte sui, et primitas virtualitatis, in se vel in suis inferioribus, —et ista duplex sufficeret ad rationem primi obiecti talis potentiae.

[3. Certitudo Practica et Reprobatio Scepticismi]

[S]ciendum[12] est quod triplicia sunt cognoscibilia quorum indigemus certa cognitione: scibilia quae ex terminis cognoscuntur; et etiam scibilia quae cognoscuntur per experientiam; et actus et opera nostra, quia requiritur ut sciamus et cognoscamus actus et opera nostra, aliter non sciremus quid operaremur.

[A. De cognitione certa principiorum ex terminis]

De primo dico quod veritas principiorum sic acquiritur in nobis: quando enim propositio est per se nota, intellectus noster non

---

10. *Ordinatio* I, d. 3, no. 149 (Vat. 3:92).
11. *Ordinatio* I, d. 3, nos. 150–51 (Vat. 3:92–94).
12. *Lectura* I, d. 3, nos. 172–81 (Vat. 16:292–97).

These reasons do not imply the univocation of being *in quid* with respect to the ultimate differences and attributes. . . . It is not necessary that being be present in all of these concepts *in quid;* but it suffices if it is either so or is univocal to them as the determinable is to the determinant or as what can be denominated to what denominates.

Briefly, then, being is univocal for all, but of concepts that are not irreducibly simple, it is predicated univocally *in quid;* and of the determinable or denominable it is not predicated *in quid,* for this would include a contradiction.

From this it is clear how there belongs to being two primacies, namely, a primacy of commonness *in quid* as regards all concepts not irreducibly simple, and a primacy of virtuality—either in itself or in its inferiors—as to all concepts that are irreducibly simple. And the occurrence of this double primacy is sufficient for it to be the case that [being] is the primary object of the intellect, although neither primacy extends to all that is intelligible per se. . . . The first object then would not be included in all per se objects, but every per se object would include it essentially or would be included in something that did include being either essentially of virtually; and so in [being] this double primacy will concur, namely, of community on its part, or a primacy of virtuality either in itself or in its inferiors, and this twofold [primacy] will suffice as the notion of the first object of such a potency.

[3. Practical Certitude and Refutation of Skepticism]

You must realize that among those things that can be known there are three of which we need certain knowledge: those propositions that can be known from the analysis of their terms; those things that we know from experience; and our own actions and works, for if we did not need to know these, we would not be aware of what we are doing.

[A. Regarding the certain knowledge of principles from their terms]

About the first I say that the truth of principles is acquired by us in this way: When a proposition is known through itself, our in-

potest eam componere nisi cognoscat terminos, termini autem sunt noti ipsi intellectui naturaliter; sed ipsi termini includunt conformitatem unionis terminorum ad ipsos terminos, igitur includunt veritatem talis unionis; cum igitur intellectus possit habere certam notitiam de terminis, igitur et certam veritatem de principio talium terminorum.

Probatio assumptae, quod termini includant conformitatem compositionis et unionis terminorum ad terminos <patet>. Ut de terminis istius propositionis loquamur, "omne totum est maius sua parte": si compositionis "maioris" cum "parte" et "toto" conformitas non includatur in toto et in maiore, igitur in intellectu concipiente terminos potest stare deformitas illius unionis, et sic stabunt simul apprehensio terminorum in intellectu et deformitas compositionis terminorum; sed in intellectu apprehendente terminos non potest stare quin "totum" includat "maioritatem," igitur ibi causaliter includitur conformitas unionis terminorum; si igitur cum apprehensione terminorum stet deformitas unionis, tunc in eodem intellectu erunt contrariae opiniones, una tamen formaliter et alia causaliter, — quod est inconveniens. Unde Philosophus IV *Metaphysicae*,[13] probans primum principium esse verum, dicit quod "si contingat simul aestimare idem esse et non esse, simul habebit contrarias opiniones qui de hoc mentitus est"; et ducit ad maius inconveniens isto modo, sicut ibi habet declarari.

Sed dices contra hoc quod sensus potest decipi circa naturam terminorum, puta visus potest iudicare aliquid esse "totum" quod non est, et aliquid esse "partem" alicuius quod non est pars; igitur cum cognitio intellectiva ortum habeat a sensu, intellectus poterit decipi circa cognitionem terminorum, et per consequens errare circa principia.

Dicendum quod in hoc cognitio intellectiva ortum habet a sensu, quia intelligit per abstractionem a sensibilibus quidquid intelligit, et non potest cognoscere intellectus aliquid nisi sibi phantasia phantasietur singulare illius. Verumtamen, licet omnes sensus decipiantur circa naturas sensibiles speciales, intellectus tamen abstrahendo speciem communem a sensibilibus in lumine naturali iudicat terminos communes primi principii sic se habere quod in uno includatur alius. Unde licet visus decipiatur circa "hoc totum" et "hanc partem," iudicando

---

13. Aristotle, *Metaphysics* 4.3.1005b 29–32.

tellect cannot put the terms together unless it knows what they mean; but the [basic or primitive] terms are known naturally by the intellect; but included in the terms themselves is the indication of their fitness to be united, and therefore they include the truth of such a union. Since the intellect could have certain knowledge of the terms, it can therefore have certain truth about the principle with such terms.

Proof of the assumption: It is evident that the terms include their fitness to be combined and united in a proposition. Let us speak, for example, of the terms of the proposition "Every whole is greater than its part." If the fitness of the combination of "greater than" with "part" and "whole" were not included in the terms "whole" and in "greater than," the unfitness of the union could exist in the intellect conceiving these terms, and thus an awareness of the terms and the unfitness of their union would exist together in the intellect; but in the intellect, apprehending the term "whole" could not but include "greater than," and hence the fitness of the union would be included there causally. Consequently, if the unfitness of the union would coexist with the apprehension of the terms, then contrary opinions would be present in the same intellect—one formally, the other causally—which is incongruous. Hence the Philosopher in book 4 of the *Metaphysics,* in proving that a first principle is true, says that "if one mistakenly could simultaneously think the same thing to be and not to be, one would have contrary opinions"; and in this way he deduces this greater incongruity that had to be made clear here.

But if you say against this that the senses could be deceived as to the nature of the terms—for instance, vision could judge something to be a whole that is not such and something to be a part of it that is not a part—then, since intellectual cognition has its origin in sense perception, the intellect could be deceived as regards the cognition of the terms and as a consequence could err as regards principles.

As to this we must admit that intellectual cognition has its origin in sense perception, because it is by abstraction from the sensible that it understands whatever it understands; and the intellect can only know something if the imagination produces an image of its singular. Nevertheless, even though all the senses could be deceived as to special sensible natures, nevertheless in abstracting a common species from the sensibles the intellect judges by its natural light the common terms of the first principle in such a way that one is included in the other. Hence, even though vision is deceived about "this whole" and "this part," judg-

illud quod non est totum esse totum, intellectus tamen per abstractionem totius et partis in lumine naturali videt quod de ratione totius est esse maius sua parte; quod si intellectus iudicaret "hoc" esse totum et "illud" esse maius "hac parte," deciperetur, —et hoc non est primum principium.

[B. De cognitione certa veritatis per experientiam]

De certitudine veritatis secundae cognitionis, acquisitae per experientiam, est sciendum quod per experientiam acquiritur certa cognitio veritatis tam de conclusione quam de principio.

De conclusione autem sic: nam primo habetur cognitio "quia est" de conclusione ex hoc quod videt frequenter talem effectum provenire, ut quando videt lunam eclipsari aut aliquam herbam frequenter sanare a tali infirmitate; cum isto autem experimento habet intellectus propositionem per se notam, istam scilicet quod "quidquid evenit ut in pluribus, est effectus naturalis et habet causam naturaliter ordinatam ad talem effectum"; et ex hoc concludit intellectus quod similiter est in omnibus singularibus talis effectus, ut quod omnis herba talis speciei sanat a tali infirmitate. Et ad habendam cognitionem "quia est" de ista conclusione, sufficit experimentum "ut in pluribus" cum tali propositione per se nota intellectui.

Ultra, intellectus habens cognitionem "quia est" de conclusione, et sciens quod eius est aliqua causa naturalis, inquirit tamen per modum divisionis et, removens illa quae non sunt causae nec esse possunt, concludit hanc esse determinatam causam illius: et sic habetur scientia et cognitio "propter quid." Sicut aliquis videns lunam eclipsari et non videns causam, inquirit eam; quam si videret, non inquireret, quia, sicut dicitur in II *Posteriorum*,[14] "si essemus super lunam et videremus terram obiectam inter solem et lunam, non quaereremus quare luna eclipsatur." Inquirit igitur intellectus quae est causa, per modum divisionis, ut luna eclipsatur: aut quia luna est corpus patiens defectum in se et variabile, aut quia capit lumen ab alio et ideo per obiectionem alterius patitur eclipsim; et sic ulterius removendo ea quae non possunt esse causa, concludit ultimo

---

14. Aristotle, *Posterior Analytics* 2.2.90a26–27.

ing what is not a whole to be a whole, nevertheless the intellect, through its abstraction of whole and part, by its natural light understands that it pertains to the meaning of "whole" for it to be greater than its part. It would be deceived if it were to judge "this" to be a whole and "that" to be greater than "this part"—but this is not a first principle.

[B. About certain truth from experience]

As for certitude about the truth of the second type of cognition acquired through experience, one must realize that certain knowledge of the truth about both the conclusion and the principle is acquired through experience.

About the conclusion it is acquired thus: One first has a knowledge of the simple fact that stems from perceiving that a certain effect occurs frequently—for instance, when one sees the moon is eclipsed or that some herb frequently cures some infirmity. With this experience, however, the intellect has a self-evident proposition: "Whatever happens in most cases is a natural effect, and there is a natural cause that produces such an effect." And the intellect concludes from this that it is the same way in all of these singular instances of such an effect—for instance, that every herb of this sort cures such an infirmity. And in order to have simple factual knowledge of such a conclusion, it suffices to have the experiential knowledge that it happens in most cases, together with the intellect's knowledge of such a self-evident proposition.

What is more, the intellect that has such simple knowledge of this conclusion and knows that there is some natural cause of this then proceeds to inquire by way of division and, eliminating those things that are not causes nor could be causes, concludes that this particular one is the cause of it; and thus it has knowledge of the reason why the fact is so. Just as someone who observes that the moon is eclipsed and does not see its cause inquires about it, which he would not do if he perceived the cause of it, as is said in book 2 of the *Posterior Analytics:* "If we were on the moon and we saw that the earth was interposed between the sun and the moon, we would not inquire why the moon is eclipsed." Hence the intellect inquires as to the reason why the moon is eclipsed by employing the method of division. Either it is because the moon is a body that is variable and subject to defects in itself, or it is because it receives its light from another and therefore is eclipsed when another intervenes; and thus by eliminating those things that cannot be the cause, the intellect eventually concludes the true cause

veram causam eclipsis. Et sic in geometria et astrologia habetur cognitio veritatis.

Sic igitur de conclusione per experientiam acquiritur certa cognitio veritatis, et sic etiam inquiritur causa istius quod omnis talis herba sanat a tali infirmitate, ut quia calida est aut frigida aut propter aliquam aliam causam.

Cognitio etiam principii per experimentum acquiritur hoc modo. Nam sensus aut vere "ut in pluribus" videt causam alicuius effectus, aut "ut in pluribus" decipitur. Si "ut in pluribus" vere apprehendat, intellectus concludit ex hoc quod est causa eius, cum propositione per se nota "quidquid producit aliquem effectum ut in pluribus, est causa naturalis eius." Si aliquis sensus decipiatur "ut in pluribus," alius "ut in pluribus" vere iudicet, —etiam si omnes deciperentur, intellectus per propositionem sibi per se notam iudicaret quis sensus esset verus et quis falsus; sicut, licet visus videns aliquid a remotis, iudicet aliquod "quantum," quod est aequale alteri, sibi esse inaequale, tamen intellectus per hoc principium quod "nullum quantum aequale alteri est maius eo," iudicat oppositum. Similiter, licet visus iudicet baculum in aqua fractum, tactus tamen, hoc sentiens, non decipitur, et tunc intellectus per propositionem sibi per se notam iudicat tactum esse verum et visum decipi; nam notum est intellectui quod nullum corpus molle frangit durum, et per hoc iudicat visum decipi, et ideo inquirit causam quare sic apparet, ut propter diaphaneitatem.

[C. De cognitione certa actuum nostrorum]

De tertio est considerandum quomodo potest haberi certa cognitio de actibus nostris, puta quomodo possumus scire nos intelligere, sentire, aut dormire, aut vigilare etc.

Dico quod, sicut supra dictum est in isto primo libro,[15] in genere propositionum contingentium sunt aliquae propositiones immediatae (alioquin in contingentibus esset procedere in infinitum, vel aliquod contingens verum immediate esset ab aliqua causa necessaria, sicut in genere propositionum necessariarum) et per se notae, et huiusmodi sunt propositiones factae de actibus nostris, ut "me dormire" et "me vigilare" (unde Philosophus IV *Metaphysicae*[16] dicit quod "dubitantes de primis principiis, quaerentes quis potest iudicare de actibus, habent

---

15. *Lectura* prolog. nos. 114–18 (Vat. 16.41–42).
16. Aristotle, *Metaphysics* 5.6.1011a 6–23.

of the eclipse. And thus we have knowledge of the truth in geometry and astronomy.

And certain knowledge of the truth is acquired in this fashion about conclusions based on experience. And in this way also one inquires about the cause of the fact that every herb of this kind cures a certain infirmity, and that this is because it is hot or cold or because of some other reason.

Also a knowledge about a principle is acquired by experience in this way: A sense either in most cases correctly perceives the cause of some effect, or it is deceived in most cases. And if in most cases it apprehends correctly, the intellect concludes from this that there is a cause of such by reason of the self-evident proposition that whatever produces an effect in most cases is a natural cause of that effect. If one sense is in most cases deceived, there is another that in most cases judges correctly; but even if all were deceived, the intellect through some self-evident proposition would judge which sense was true and which false. Although vision, when seeing something from afar, judges that something is equal in size to something not equal, the intellect can judge the opposite through this proposition "Nothing equal in size with another is greater than it." Similarly, although vision judges a stick partially immersed in water to be bent, touch, when one feels it, is not deceived; and then the intellect knows that no body that is soft bends a body that is hard and judges thereby that vision is deceived; and therefore it inquires as to the reason it appears to be so—for instance, because of transparency.

[C. Certain knowledge about our actions]

Third, we need to consider how there can be certain knowledge about our acts, for example, how we know that we understand, feel sensations, or are asleep or awake, and so on.

I say that, as was pointed out in book 1, in the class of contingent propositions there are some that are immediate (otherwise either one could trace contingent propositions back indefinitely, or some true contingent proposition would follow from some necessary cause and thus would fall into the class of necessary propositions) and [hence] self-evident, and such are the propositions that refer to our actions, such as "I sleep" and "I am awake." (Hence the Philosopher in book 4 of the *Metaphysics* says that "those who have doubts about first principles and who question who can make judgments about their acts have a similar doubt

similem dubitationem dubitationi qua quis dubitat utrum dormimus nunc aut vigilamus"; unde vult quod qui quaerit rationem de huiusmodi actibus, "quaerit rationem quorum non est ratio"); nec possunt nobis manifestari a priore, nam magis notum est nobis aliquem vigilare quam se reflectere supra actus suos, et similiter nobis magis notum est aliquem dormire quam se non posse reflecti supra actus suos (cum tamen aliqui volunt ostendere sic huiusmodi actus esse, et male: "Unde expertus sum me in somniis reflectere supra actum meum? quia somniavi me somniare"); et ideo non decipimur de actibus nostris qui sunt in potestate nostra, licet lateant nos actus nostri qui non sunt in potestate nostra, ut actus potentiae vegetativae. Unde licet visus videat quasdam reliquias postquam clauserit oculos suos, secundum Augustinum, non tamen decipitur sed vere videt, quia potentia visiva non est in pupilla ut in organo, sed est in concursu nervorum opticorum, et ideo speciem adhuc relucentem in pupilla visus potest videre. Et sic etiam est quando videtur quasi ignis excussus de oculo alicuius, sicut patet ex I *De sensu et sensato*.[17]

---

17. Aristotle, *De sensu et sensato* 2.437a 23–26: "When the eye is pressed, fire appears to flash from it."

about the doubting by which someone doubts whether we are now sleeping or awake." Hence, he means that whoever asks about such acts "seeks a reason for things that have no reason.") Such cannot be made manifest a priori, for it is better known to us that someone is awake than that he is reflecting upon his actions, and likewise it is better known to us that someone is sleeping than that he cannot reflect upon his acts. (Inasmuch as some wish to show that such acts exist, however, they do so badly. For who is it that experiences that I am reflecting upon my acts in my dreams, because I have dreamt I am dreaming?) Therefore we are not deceived about those acts that are in our power, although those acts not under our control are hidden to us, such as those of our vegetative ability. Even though, according to Augustine, we may see certain afterimages when the eyes are closed, vision is not deceived; rather we do truly see because our visual power is not in the pupil as its organ but in the bunch of optic nerves, and therefore vision can still see the likeness that is still in the pupil. And it is like this, too, when one's eye is pressed and something like a flash of fire is seen, as is clear from book 1 of *De sensu et sensato*.

Commentary

Introduction

Only after presenting his argument for the existence of an infinite being did Scotus have an opportunity to analyze the logical structure of concepts that he had used in his metaphysical proof. This was due to the topical arrangement in book 1 of Peter's *Sentences,* which located the topic of God's existence in distinction 2 and that of his knowability in distinction 3. In his answers to the three questions in this distinction, we discover the underlying principles of Scotus's philosophical theory of knowledge. The first question asks whether God is naturally knowable to a person in the present life. It is here that Scotus discusses the nature of our concepts of God and introduces his important but controversial theory of univocity. The second asks whether God should be called the primary or adequate object of the intellect. The third asks whether we can have true and certain knowledge naturally, without some special illumination by the divine archetypal ideas. It is here that we find Scotus's refutation of skepticism and his explanation of how we arrive at practical certitude.

To realize why these specific questions were even raised or were of interest to a theologian like Scotus, we need to say a word about an important transformation in the psychological way that Scholastics during the last half of the thirteenth century came to think about human knowledge and the manner in which our mind functions, particularly when we think about God. Scotus's solution, however, is of wider interest than this particular theological application, for it explains how we can rationally explain our knowledge of things that we are convinced are real yet are not known as objects directly experienced.

The Nature of Our Concepts of God

Scotus's proof for God's existence, we recall, begins with common notions used to describe familiar objects of immediate experience. It ends with a concept of God as uniquely singular, unlimited in being and perfection, however—quite unlike anything characteristic of the world about us. This disparity between what deity seems to be and what we daily encounter led philosophers to stress the analogical nature of any of our concepts of God that were borrowed from creatures. So entrenched was this tradition that when Aristotle's philosophy became fully known to the Scholastics in the mid-thirteenth century, theologians made every attempt to integrate his theory of knowledge with the Christian version of Neoplatonism of Augustine, which had so colored their thinking up to this point. The process, however, was gradual, and each of the major thinkers developed his own unique theological theory of knowledge in which Aristotelian and Neoplatonic elements drawn from both Christian and Islamic thinkers were blended. In the following sections, we shall trace the stages in this progressive transformation that led up to the form in which Henry presented his version of the illumination theory.

Illumination Theory

Earlier Christian Platonists had located the archetypal ideas of Plato in the mind of God, whereas Aristotelians identified them with the common form that the mind discovers in creatures. In creating the human intellect with something of his own perfection, God gave it the power to rethink something of his own thoughts. But the two schools differed in their account of how God accomplished this. The Scholastics who followed Augustine, such as Bonaventure, opted for some special illumination through the exemplar ideas in the divine intellect. These were not perceived directly, as the blessed would see them in the afterlife, however; it was rather the way the eye, unable to gaze upon the sun directly, sees colored objects, which are made visible through diffused and reflected light whose original source is the sun. The eye of the mind, they claimed, is enlightened in a similar way. It perceives the forms and intelligible features of things, which bear the marks of their creator. This would explain how our mind, gazing upward as *ratio superior,* forms ideas of God that transcend anything that the mind, looking downward as *ratio inferior,* could abstract from the sense-perceptible world about it.[1]

On the other hand, Aristotle himself also spoke of a "light" (*phos*) that illuminates the intellect (*nous*) in the process that gives it its information. Later Aristotelians, such as Alexander of Aphrodisias (fl. 200 A.D.), contrasted this active agent with the receptive portion of the mind, calling the latter the passive intellect (*nous patetikos*) and the other, the agent intellect (*nous poietikos*). He and subsequent interpreters of Aristotle's work on the soul, however, had widely different opinions as to whether the agent intellect was a part of the human mind or a distinct spiritual being. Was it to be identified with the spiritual soul or with one of the bodiless intelligences that moved the celestial spheres or even with God?[2] In either case, its function was largely the same. The agent intellect worked upon the imagination to form a likeness, or intelligible species, representing the form of the object known, which could be impressed upon the passive or possible intellect. Thus by being informed, the passive intellect passed from a purely passive state of potency, or potential knowledge, to one of actual information.

Though the Islamic philosophers believed that they were following Aristotle, their interpretation was significantly colored by Alexander of Aphrodisias and the influential spurious *Theology of Aristotle* as well as other Neoplatonic works. These works affected their interpretation of Aristotle's *Physics* and *Metaphysics* and their conceptions of the human soul and its relationship to the agent and possible intellects.[3] While Avicenna's assessment can be reconciled with some form of illuminationism,[4] that of Averroes led to the radical Aristotelianism of Siger of Brabant, which provoked condemnations at both Paris and Oxford. The condemnations of 1277 are, as Etienne Gilson points out, "a landmark in the history of medieval philosophy and theology."[5] Though the brief Neoaugustinian movement that they initiated could not impede theologians' eventual acceptance of a moderate interpretation of Aristotelian abstraction before the turn of the century, these condemnations on both sides of the English Channel throw light on why the theory of illumination survived as long as it did.

The secular master at Paris most affected by the condemnations of 1277 was perhaps Henry.[6] Understandably, his views were well known and defended by a number of Franciscans at Oxford when Scotus began his theological studies.[7] Thus Scotus often used Henry's teaching as the starting point of his own treatment of any theological topic. Scotus's proof for God's existence in distinction 2 begins with Henry's summary account of all the arguments for the existence of God that he considered either demonstrable or probable. In distinction 3, Scotus presents his own answers in contrast to those given by Henry to the three questions about our natural knowledge of God. Though Henry's answers were based on an acceptance of Augustine's theory of illumination, he did not simply substitute this for Aristotle's theory of abstraction. Rather, he combined the two views to explain how our knowledge of mutable creatures could be true and certain. But "unless our concepts are formed in us with the assistance of the eternal light," he insisted, "they remain without form, neither do they contain truth in an unqualified and undiluted fashion." It is only because "the natural light of reason ascends to the eternal light itself" that it can form an irreducibly simple concept proper to God—one that is only analogous to the concept that we abstract from creatures.[8] It is this aspect of theological discourse that most concerned Scotus when he analyzed the nature of our concepts of God. Scotus believed that this radical conception of analogy, unless implemented by the illumination theory, placed an unbridgeable logical chasm between ordinary language and meaningful talk about God. He was convinced that if our concepts begin with what we can abstract from creatures and from sense perception—as Aristotle held—then some univocal notions are needed as an intermediate step to arrive at any proper concept of God. If our intellect is a tabula rasa at birth, as Aristotle claimed, then God, in creating it, gave it the potentiality to form whatever concepts we need to know, including a natural knowledge of the divine itself. No special additional illumination, which Henry insisted on, is required. If Aristotle's view is substantially correct, three other philosophical theories as to the origin of our ideas of God can be eliminated as well: that of Plato, who postulated a previous state of existence in which our soul enjoyed a vision of these exemplar ideas; that of Avicenna and other Islamic philosophers, who claimed that these transcendental ideas that can be applied to God—such as "being," "one," and "necessary being"—are the first to be impressed upon the mind from above; and that of some Scholastics—and later Descartes and other philosophers—who maintained that such ideas, and others that apply properly to God, are innate or congenital.

The natural creativity of the human mind, Scotus insisted, can explain how we bridge the logical gap between our notions based on actual experience and our analogous notion of theoretical entities—prime matter, substance, or God, for example—provided we admit the validity of some primitive univocal notions, such as being (*ens*) or thing (*res*) as the metaphysician understands these terms.

Scotus thus represents a significant turning point in the history of metaphysics. Like Aquinas, he rejected the Neoplatonic illumination theory, whether it be in the Bonaventurian form or that of Avicenna,[9] and insisted that our conceptions of God must be formed from the universal notions that we abstract from the world about us. By showing that this required some theory of univocity, however, Scotus accomplished what Aquinas failed to do. He was thus able to explain that the way we construct notions of God was not significantly different from the way that Aristotle had constructed his notions of matter and form and of the substantial underpinnings of phenomena.[10]

Henry, the last holdout for some vestige of a special divine illumination, presented this theory in a particularly vulnerable form, since it included the Aristotelian theory of abstraction as well. Consequently, Scotus's devastating critique of Henry had the practical effect of eliminating the Augustinian as a distinct alternative to the Aristotelian theory of abstraction from that time onward.[11]

Augustinian Abstraction

It is useful to consider in some detail precisely how Henry understood what we might call an Augustinian theory of abstraction. Henry's interpretation of Augustine's explanation of how we can form a natural but proper idea of God indicates how he could reconcile some form of illumination with a natural abstraction theory, which required no special illumination of this sort.

In *On the Trinity*, Augustine claims that we come to know God as the supreme good first by discovering the various forms of goodness that exist all around us. Then he asks us to abstract from particularity and consider what is common to all of these good things:

> "This good" and "that good"; take away "this" and "that," and see good itself if you can; so you will see God who is good not by another good, but is the good of every good. For in all these good things, either those which I have enumerated, or any others which are seen or thought, we would be unable to call one better than the other, if we judge in accordance with the truth, if the idea of the good itself had not been impressed upon us, according to which we approve of something as good, and also prefer one good to another.[12]

The special process that Augustine is describing in his injunction—"'Bonum hoc' et 'bonum illud,' tolle 'hoc' et 'illud,' et vide ipsum bonum, si potes"—is what we have referred to as an Augustinian abstraction.[13] The single quotation marks indicate that this is not the usual abstractive process that it seems at first sight to be; and it is certainly far different from the Aristotelian theory of abstraction, which we shall refer to shortly.

The command "tolle 'hoc' et 'illud'" (Take away "this" and "that") appears to be calling for a straightforward abstraction in taking "good" away from "this good" and "that good." Yet Augustine requires you to do something more, "if you can" (si potes). You must look at the abstracted content "good" in a totally new way: "vide ipsum bonum" (see good itself). This concept is only remotely similar in meaning to the limited notion of "goodness" that one can abstract from creatures. At the abstractive level, we have not yet made that further step of seeing the familiar in an unfamiliar fashion. We are still considering "good" as a common attribute of much of what God has created rather than in the exclusive sense applicable to divinity as the fullness of goodness. There are two different ways of "seeing": "We form images of bodies in our mind in one way," says Augustine, "but we comprehend in a different way the types and the ineffably beautiful art of such forms as are above the eye of the mind, by simple intelligence."[14]

We might note that at the visual level, such a switch in what we see is referred to by psychologists as a Gestalt-shift. Ambiguous perceptual data can be interpreted in more than one meaningful way. But the same process occurs at the intellectual level. To see something old and familiar in a new and unfamiliar way is the way a revolutionary scientific discovery often comes about.[15] Philosophers and scientists speak of such as a flash of insight or as an inspired guess. This birth of a new idea differs from the slow process of deduction or logical inference or from the recognition based on memory. Like the reorganization of perceptual data, it involves understanding old conceptions in an unprecedented and pioneering way. The insight appears instantaneously before the eye of the mind, as the visual form does to the bodily eye. Augustine also conceives it as an illumination.

Where Augustine differs from the Gestalt-psychologist, however, is in viewing the cause of this information or illumination as stemming from some special influx or action on the part of divine ideas: "The idea of the good in itself," he says, is "impressed upon us." As a Neoplatonist, he is thinking of "good" with a capital G, a Platonic idea, or as a Christian Platonist, of "good" as an exemplar idea in the mind of God, the unparticipated good.[16]

This theory of illumination from the divine exemplars themselves, Henry maintained, can be philosophically defended. Augustine's explanation is not unlike Avicenna's interpretation as to how ideas such as "one," "being," and "necessary being"—the last is Avicenna's definition of God—are impressed upon us from above.[17] Where Avicenna and Henry differed, however, was in their interpretations of the agent intellect.[18] This special illumination is "natural" only in the sense that it pertains to the natural order that we find in the world; like all that a creature possesses, it is a gift from one's creator. It is given to the evil man or woman as well as to the good and God-loving individual. It is quite distinct from the supernatural vision that the apostle Paul describes or that we find granted to the prophets in the Bible.

As psychologists have indicated, to perceive a particular form is not an inevitable or necessary response; not everyone is able to see the data under some recognizable shape. Augustine says the same of this conceptual shift in meaning: "See good itself if you can." Indeed, this is something that we can and often do. From the abstract notion of good, our mind not only can but may well jump to a positive notion of the good itself. Augustine insists we must view these two distinct conceptual meanings according to the ontological relationship that exists between them. The good itself is not a participated good: it "is good not by another good." Furthermore, it "is the good of every good."

Finally, Augustine argues that "we would be unable to call one better than the other or approve of something as good and also prefer one good to another" if we did not have some vague knowledge of what is perfect. To judge one thing as less than perfect presupposes some knowledge of what is perfect. Even though we may never have previously experienced such perfection, we still are dissatisfied with what is imperfect. The sinner, Augustine declares, discerns his or her lack of perfection,[19] and the artist instinctively recognizes what is wanting in beauty.[20] This implies that in some subtle way, our mind knows what is required of any particular kind of thing to make it a perfect or true specimen. But such generic or specific creature-perfection exists primarily in the mind of the divine artist, who first conceived of it.

One can extend Augustine's analysis of the good to the concept of being that Avicenna regarded as the subject of metaphysics. And that is precisely what Henry did, as we shall see when Scotus explains the different ways in which he and Henry regard the nature of the concepts that we have of God. It is the first of three areas where Scotus contrasts his theory of knowledge with Henry's. The question reads: "Is God naturally knowable by the intellect of the pilgrim in this life?"

Scotus and Henry both agreed that God is naturally knowable by the human intellect. By reason of their different theories of knowledge, however, they understood the nature of those concepts that we have of God to be formed in radically different ways.

❙ Henry's Theory of Knowledge

Scotus begins with a synoptic account of Henry's theory:

> A certain teacher[21] answers the question in this way. Speaking of the knowledge of anything, one can distinguish on the part of the object known a knowledge that stems from the thing itself or from something incidental to it and knowledge in particular and in general.

> In reality God is not known through anything incidental, since whatever is known of him is himself. Nevertheless, in knowing some attribute of his, we know what God is in a quasi-incidental way. Hence Damascene says that the attributes do not assert the nature of God but things about his nature.[22]

Henry's first distinction is not unlike the distinction between knowledge by acquaintance and knowledge by description, which was used by Bertrand Russell. We know persons we have met or anything we directly experience in the first way, but those persons or events we read of or hear about from others are known only by description. Like most theologians in his day, Henry believed that although Moses or the prophets may have known God by acquaintance, the ordinary Christian can have such face-to-face knowledge of God only in the afterlife. Why does Henry call the descriptive knowledge we have of God only incidental or quasi-incidental? Is it, perhaps, because the descriptions we have of God are based upon what we know of him through his creation and this relationship to creation is not necessarily connected with his essence? Or is it rather because of the logical way in which we invest God with the best of what we find in creation? Henry seems to have the latter aspect in mind. He claims that any terms we use to describe God never refer to his intrinsic nature or essence but seem rather to encircle that nature, to lie round about it, as it were. Attributes logically lie outside their subject, in this case the divine nature in which they inhere. In that respect they resemble the accidents that inhere in a substance. They differ from mere accidents, however, in that they are proper to their subject and hence are necessarily connected with it, though they do not enter into its essential definition.

Regarding the second distinction, Henry declares that this quasi-incidental knowledge does not give us any particular knowledge of God but only varying degrees of general knowledge. As Scotus describes Henry's theory,

> In particular he is not known from creatures, since a creature bears a remote likeness to him, for it resembles him only in those attributes that do not constitute this nature in particular. Therefore, since nothing leads to the knowledge of something else save by reason of a similar characteristic, it follows [that God is not known in particular through creatures].[23]

Henry does admit, however, that the attributes that we ascribe to God do give us at least a general knowledge of him:

> God is known also in general, for example, in a universal attribute. Not indeed that any universal according to predication

is affirmed of him, in whom nothing is universal, for that quiddity is singular of itself, but in a universal that is only analogically common to himself and a creature; nevertheless we conceive this as if it were one, because of the close resemblance of the concepts [contained], although they are diverse concepts.[24]

Note that Henry admits that somehow God is known in the general concept—for example, as "good" or "being"—which we abstract from created things. But in this process of abstraction, the universal concept that is predicable univocally of creatures is only analogically a concept of God. It does not apply properly to him at all, because his goodness and his being are unique to himself and transcend anything we find in creatures. However, as Scotus indicates, Henry is not using a straightforward Aristotelian conception of abstraction. Rather, he is interjecting his interpretation of what happens if we follow Augustine's injunction "'Bonum hoc' et 'bonum illud,' tolle 'hoc' et 'illud.'" For, Henry argues, if one looks long and hard at the abstract concept of "good," the mind eventually discovers the twofold interpretation that can be given to it. Thus the seemingly simple concept, whether it be that of "good" or "being," is really not simple at all in terms of what it may mean. Each word has a twofold sense. This becomes apparent, however, only after we reflect upon diverse objects to which the word refers. Here we have the double entendre, the indeterminate meaning akin to those ambiguous illustrations—such as the duck-rabbit or the young wife and old mother-in-law—that Gestalt psychologists prove can be visualized in at least two distinct ways.

This becomes clearer when Scotus explains the five steps that Henry claims mind goes through in coming to a more precise and distinct knowledge of God. The first three, which he calls "most general," replay the scenario described by Augustine ("'Bonum hoc' et 'bonum illud,' tolle 'hoc' et 'illud,' et vide ipsum bonum"). Only instead of "bonum" (good), says Scotus, Henry uses the attribute of being.

> The most general way has three degrees. For to know anything as "this being" is to conceive [God] most indistinctly, for being is conceived as a quasi-part of the concept; this is the first degree. The second degree consists in removing "this" and conceiving just "being"; for already in conceiving this as a concept rather than a part, one is conceiving a common analogue to God and to a creature.[25]

Scotus then goes on to explain the third degree. Here we see the Augustinian abstraction in operation:

> If the concept of "being" that pertains to God (for instance, conceiving "negatively indeterminate being," that is, not determinable) is distinguished from the concept of "being" that pertains analogically, which is "privatively indeterminate being," then this is already the third degree. In the first concept, "undetermined" is abstracted, as a form is from all matter, as something subsistent in itself and able to be shared. In the second concept, "indeterminate" is a universal abstracted from particulars, and actually shared in them.[26]

Here the two meanings that one can give to "indeterminate" are made explicit. As Scotus explains, Henry regards the two meanings as diverse concepts—that is, they are both simple concepts, having nothing conceptually in common. Here is the radical difference between Henry's view and the more logical view that Scotus insists upon. There must be more than the common word "indeterminate" that these two analogical concepts of privative and negative indeterminacy have in common; there must also be a common concept or meaning associated with the common term. The basic difference between Scotus and Henry, then, is that Henry believes that the mind is deceived about the diversity of the concept that applies to God, since the two meanings of "good" and of "being" are so close that the mind considers them as if they were one.

Henry begins with what looks like a form of Aristotelian abstraction, but alongside the concept of being that is minimal in comprehension and maximal in extension, he slips in another concept that is minimal in extension and maximal in comprehension. Like Augustine's "good itself" ("ipsum bonum"), Henry claims we have a similar notion of "being itself" ("ens ipsum"), which is anything but universal in its extension, since it applies uniquely to God, who is being without qualification or limitation. What we have here implicitly is the fullness of being that Scotus equates with "Ens infinitum," the Infinite Being. Henry is suggesting that in the natural process of abstracting from creatures general terms that seem to be applicable in some way to God, the mind sees this pair of concepts in the way that the eye views a distant pair of objects as one. Like the eye of the body, the eye of the mind has a limited power of resolution. It cannot distinguish two meanings so similar as to trick the mind into perceiving them as one. This is the famous analogical concept of being, as Henry understands that phrase. He attributes to the concept "being" the same ambiguity that one can ascribe to the word "being," whereas Scotus insists that only the latter is ambiguous, or equivocal, not the concept when the term is used substantively, that is, as referring to a real subject. The concept "being" means simply "that to which 'to be' is not repugnant."[27]

Besides these three most general degrees of knowing God, Henry admits that we can know him in a less general way by ascribing such qualifications as "maximal" or "most eminent" to whatever universal quality we wish to attribute to God. Thus instead of saying God is good, we say he is the greatest good; or rather than declaring that God is wise, powerful, and loving, we say that God is omniscient, almighty, and all-loving. In other words, instead of simply using the affirmative way, we turn to the way of eminence, the *via eminentiae*.

The fifth and most precise—but still general—way of knowing God is to regard any or all of these attributes as being identified, by reason of God's simplicity,[28] with his primary attribute of being (*esse*).

Critique of Henry's Theory of Knowledge

Scotus's account depends upon and reveals in great part Henry's theory of knowledge. Though it was born of Henry's reaction to the condemnations of 1277 and the brief Neoaugustinian revival that they inspired, it was retained substantially unchanged during his long teaching career. This ended in 1292, a year after Scotus's ordination to the priesthood and during his theological course of studies. By that time, Scholastics had become comfortable with Aristotle's basic description as to how the intellect abstracts concepts from the sense image (*phantasma*) retained in the imagination—the internal sense—which correlates and records the data received through the eye, ear, touch, and other external senses. There were minor differences, of course, and we might review briefly how Scotus interprets Aristotle.

Our spiritual soul has a twofold intellectual potency, one active, the other passive. The active aspect is what is known as the agent intellect. Its function is to interact with the sense image, or phantasm, and produce an intelligible likeness of the object. This "intelligible species" (*species intelligibilis*) is distinct in nature from the sensible likeness or species impressed upon or created in the sense organs. Like the intellectual ideas habitually retained by the mind, these intelligible species substitute for the object and leave their impression or form on the passive, or possible, intellect. Unlike other Scholastics' interpretations of Aristotle, Scotus believed that the possible intellect is not purely passive when it understands the meaning of something and forms an idea or conception of the object within itself. Rather, it plays a creative role together with the intelligible species in producing actual thought, just as the agent intellect and the sense image were co-causes of the intelligible species. Though he interprets the cognitive process in a radically different way from Augustine, Scotus is willing to accept Augustine's statement that knowledge is born or begotten of both the knower and the object known ("Ab utroque enim pariter notitia cognoscente et cognito").[29]

Henry has to modify this Aristotelian theory of agent intellect and intelligible species substantially when he seeks to integrate it with something of Augustine's illumination theory. There is obviously no intelligible species that could do justice to anything that is proper to God. The simple concepts that we form of God, Henry claims, are radically different from anything we conceive of or find exemplified in creatures. Yet the two sets of concepts resemble each other analogically. What is more, initially both have their origin in something that the mind abstracts from what it discovers in creatures, perceived through the senses and pictured by one's imagination. God is simple, and thus there is no way to know only a part of what he is, Henry argues. How, then, does the intellect get this simple notion of being as negatively undetermined and indeterminable that is proper to God? Scotus explains Henry's solution this way: "Since nothing is simpler than God, he is known not through a species proper to him but in a manner reminiscent of the estimative power through a species alien to him, derived from creatures."[30]

The human intellect, according to Henry, has the capacity to dig beneath appearances to unearth something quite different from any likeness (*species*) in the imagination.[31] The process, Henry claims, is similar to the way in which the estimative power in a lamb, for example, digs beneath sense appearances to discover instinctively whether another animal is friendly or dangerous. The representation of the sensible object conveys neither the friendliness of the ewe nor the malevolence of the hungry wolf. Like a picture—for example, that of Hercules—the species does not depict the real thing—that is, Hercules himself. The intellect, Henry argues, also digs beneath pictorial images when it discovers intelligible and noncorporeal realities, such as mathematical entities and the essences of substance, matter, and substantial form. Why, then, can it not do the same in regard to God, discovering not only what is common to creatures but something quite alien to a creature, namely, a concept that applies uniquely to God?

Scotus rejects this account as contrary to the Aristotelian theory of knowledge commonly accepted in his day. The species is the sole bearer of meaning and information from the object to the mind, through the senses. As the intellect judges on the basis of the intelligible species, so does the estimative power in animals judge on the basis of sensible species. If one could put Henry's wolf in sheep's clothing, so that all the sensory input from the animal would be the same as if it were from a sheep, Scotus argues that a lamb would not flee from that wolf any more than it would from a ewe.

It is from this basically Aristotelian theory of knowledge, then, that Scotus criticizes Henry's affirmative answer to his original question. He rewords the first question slightly to stress the crux of his difference with Henry: "Is it possible by natural means for the human intellect in the present life to have a simple concept in which God is grasped?"[32]

The stress here is upon the idea of a simple concept. Henry's initial concept is only apparently simple; actually, it contains two radically divergent concepts, as we discover when we follow Augustine's injunction. Each of these diverse concepts, however, is simple; unlike differences, concepts that are diverse have nothing in common. In one such concept, the mind grasps what is common to creatures—that is, goodness or being as a universal that is predicable of many finite or limited things. In the other concept, the intellect grasps what is proper to God, namely, being in the sense of something that is in no way limited or determinable. As Henry insists, in the fifth stage of knowledge, God's being includes all of the divine attributes, since God's nature is simple.

Scotus's Theory about Natural Knowledge of God

Scotus says that his answer to the question is different, and it will contradict Henry's view on five points.

First, our notions of God must start with a concept that is substantive, one that expresses some essential or defining characteristic. Such a concept indicates something that exists or subsists in itself and does not merely inhere in another. Scotus calls such knowledge quidditative, because it represents a reply to the question "Quid est?" ("What is it?"). This is a purely logical requirement: incidentals or accidents require a substance, and attributes need to be anchored in some subject. Hence, Henry is wrong when he claims that all our knowledge of God is quasi-incidental and tells us nothing of what deity itself is. A quidditative concept is expressed grammatically as a noun rather than an adjective or participle. In Latin such a concept is said to be predicated of its subject *in quid*, rather than *in quale* or *in quantum*, which are answers to the questions "Of what sort?" or "How much?" respectively.

Scotus's second point is that not all of the notions we predicate of God are analogous to those applicable to our everyday world. We need at least some core concepts that can be predicated in an unambiguous and straightforward way. Such concepts are univocal, in contrast to those that are equivocal, or only partially true. The most important and basic of these univocal concepts is that which serves as the subject of further predications. According to the Aristotelians, this is the metaphysical notion of a "being" or "thing."[33] The Latin term is *ens*, which is a participial form of the verb *esse* ("to be" or "to exist"). When used as a noun, this word indicates any real thing (*res*) that actually exists or at least can exist outside the mind or imagination.[34] It is in regard to the meaning of this term that Scotus introduces his controversial theory of univocity.

Scotus seems to be a pioneer as regards his belief that the term "being" (*ens*) can have a univocal meaning when predicated of God and creatures. The Vatican edition of the text, which is based exclusively on Codex A, however, may obscure this fact. In place of the categorical assertion *dico* ("I say") of the Vatican edition, most of the manuscripts have the much more cautious expression "Non asserendo, quia non consonat opinioni communi, dici potest [Not as an apodictic assertion, for it does not accord with the common opinion, it can be said]." Apparently Scotus first introduced his idea tentatively, but over the course of time, he became more and more convinced of the correctness of his view. In what may be the final version in Codex A, he proposed it apodictically. He was convinced that his contemporaries, who had abandoned the illumination theory in favor of that of Aristotle, were not yet aware of how this affected their theory of analogy. Unwittingly they were already making use of univocal concepts. As he put it in his earliest Oxford lecture, "All the masters and theologians seem to use a concept common to God and creatures, although they contradict this in word when they refer to it, for in this all agree that they accept metaphysical concepts and remove from them what is imperfect in creatures and attribute to God what is a matter of perfection, such as goodness, truth, wisdom."[35] He asserted the same charge categorically, however, in his revised Oxford lectures and in his later Paris lectures: "The masters also, in treating of God or of those things we know of God and creatures, observe univocation of being in their doctrine or the way they speak, as is clear, although they contradict this in word."[36] Scotus showed that this is so particularly in his second argument for univocation. Every metaphysical inquiry of God begins with a univocal affirmation of something that God has in common with creatures. Through negation and eminence, it fashions from this core concept one that is unique and proper to God.

Of the many arguments Scotus felt he could cite to prove univocation, the one he considered the most cogent is the first of the two we have given here.[37] Defenders of the radical theory of analogy argued that when one predicates any common term of God and creatures, it has either one or the other of two contradictory senses—for example, finite or infinite, created or uncreated, caused or uncaused. One or the other of these intrinsic modes must be associated with the very meaning of the term before it can be truly predicated of either God or of creatures.

Scotus argued that there is a very simple test we can use to discover whether or not our common notions of "being"—or any other pure perfection, such as "wise," "powerful," and "good"—have been completely divorced from their intrinsic modes. Apply to the concept in question contradictory predicates. If "being," for instance, implicitly includes in its very concept the mode of infinity when applied to God, then the meaning of the word "being" as applied to God and the meaning of the term "infinite being" are formally identical. Hence I cannot simultaneously affirm contradictory predicates of either of these two terms. But how can one be certain and doubtful about one and the same formal notion? As Scotus argued, I can be certain that God is a being and still be in doubt whether he is infinite or not. I may know that he is wise, without knowing that he is infinite, self-subsistent wisdom. I may define God as the cause of the visible universe and yet be uncertain whether he is an uncaused cause. A child at her mother's knee may learn that God is good, but we cannot say that the content of her childish concept includes even implicitly some modality proper to God.

Scotus applied this same argument later to the question of whether being is predicated univocally of substance and accident. We are certain, he declared, that light is a being, but we may still doubt whether it is a substance in its own right or an accidental modification of some translucent medium. Scotus's example might have come from a textbook on theoretical physics: modern physicists treat light both as an electromagnetic wave and as a particle with the characteristics of a substance.

Henry maintained that "being" is a term with two meanings that are so closely related and similar that we cannot separate them, even in concept. If this is so, said Scotus, we might as well admit that all univocal knowledge is impossible. We certainly have no more cogent way of demonstrating the unity of a concept than the principle of contradiction. And if univocal knowledge is impossible, then we can never construct a logically valid argument about anything, and hence sheer skepticism will result. It was for this reason that Scotus defined univocation the way he did:

> And lest there be any contention about the word "univocation," I call that concept univocal that has sufficient unity in itself that to affirm and deny it of the same subject suffices as a contradiction. It also suffices as a syllogistic middle term, so that where two terms are united in a middle term that is one in this fashion, they are inferred without a fallacy of equivocation to be united among themselves.

Scotus's second argument involves an analysis of the famous three ways of knowing God attributed to Pseudo-Dionysius:[38] the affirmative way—that is, saying what he is; the way of negation—denying what he is not; and the way of eminence—ascribing the most perfect or maximal degree to whatever property is asserted of him. As Scotus explained it, every metaphysical inquiry about God begins with a consideration of some formal perfection he possesses. From this formal notion we remove any imperfection associated with it in creatures. Finally to this formal notion we add the mode of infinite perfection and attribute this properly to God. Consider the idea of wisdom, intelligence, or free will. Any imperfection linked with these perfections as they exist in creatures is removed, as, for example, the idea of discursive or step-by-step reasoning, which is characteristic of the human intellect, or the fact that wisdom is accidental in us and can be gained or lost. We retain, however, the sheer formal notion of wisdom or intelligence, which as such says nothing as to whether it is finite or infinite. To this formal notion we add the idea of unlimited perfection and thus arrive at a concept inapplicable to any creature but proper to God. But the whole procedure is invalid unless the formal notion can be validly predicated of God apart from the mode of infinity.

The third point of Scotus's refutation of Henry argues that we have no natural knowledge of God as a "this" or as an individual. That is to say, we know him not by personal acquaintance but by description, to use Russell's distinction. Only in the afterlife can we expect to meet God face-to-face, according to the apostle Paul. But Scotus gives another reason why God is not a natural object that we could be directly acquainted with. All of God's relationships to anything other than himself are contingent, since they depend upon his will. Scotus thus distinguishes between an object that naturally motivates the intellect by reason of its nature and by the simple fact that it is present to the intellect, and a "voluntary object," such as the divine essence, which requires the direct intervention of God's will to be knowable in all its uniqueness.[39] The reason that God is only contingently related to the world is because the creation of the world was a voluntary act on God's part, not a necessary emanation or consequence of his own existence and nature. This radical contingency on the part of anything created is the logical corollary of the absolute independence and necessary being or existence of the first principle or divine being.

Scotus admitted that we can naturally have a descriptive knowledge of God, such as he proposed on the basis of his argument for an infinite being. How a descriptive phrase can be formed that applies exclusively to what we mean by God as distinct from creatures is explained in the Scotus's two final points against Henry.

There are two ways in which we can form concepts of God that are not applicable to creatures. One is by attributing to him those properties that do not seem to contain limitations in their defining characteristics—for example, notions such as "wisdom" or "knowledge" that is not restricted to any specific area. Technically these are pure or unqualified perfections (*perfectio simpliciter*). Though such perfections are found in creatures in various limited degrees, we see no reason why the perfections as such should be limited. To attribute them to God in this maximal sense —using the *via eminentiae*—is to ascribe something proper or unique to divinity; by combining all such predications of specific pure perfections to God, we form our most perfect concept of him, his nature, and his properties.

But Scotus claimed that we can form a single, simpler conception when we understand the meaning of the term "infinite being" (*ens infinitum*). When we attribute "being" in an unlimited and unrestricted way, this has the equivalent or virtual meaning of the cluster concept, which globally enumerates all such pure perfections. "Infinite being" has the same extramental referent as the global or cluster concept, since it means that God is a being or thing in which every pure perfection is to be found and is present in a maximal degree. This concept is simpler even than a concept such as "good being" or "true being," since "truth" and "goodness" have a meaning of their own and can stand as the subject of a sentence or proposition. But "infinite" and "finite" are essentially modalities and express degrees of being. Hence, Scotus speaks of "infinite" as an intrinsic mode, inseparable either conceptually or in reality from the subject that it modifies. This simpler concept of "infinite being" represents the culmination of Scotus's previous proof for the existence of God.

This holistic concept of God is achieved by the same type of shift we spoke of earlier with regard to Augustinian abstraction. But Scotus did not attribute this shift to any special influence of divine ideas, as illuminationists do, nor did he regard it as something impressed upon our mind from above or as something innate or congenital. He indicated the psychological steps that one can take to lead up to the final state, but he regarded the flash of insight as an act of simple intelligence.

It is interesting to note that in his early lectures, Scotus apparently did not regard "infinite being" as an exceptional sort of construct. It seems to be simply the result of a double negation. The first negation imposes a limit to being, while the second negates that limit. We conceive this double negation as something positive. Aristotle questioned its existential character: "Nothing infinite can exist," he claimed, "and if it did, at least the notion of infinity is not infinite." Rather, he regarded the concept as constructed from the finite by finitistic methods. When Scotus came to revise his Oxford lectures, however, he believed we could move beyond this construct to a holistic grasp of its positive meaning. In his late *Quodlibet*, he described the steps that lead psychologically to this move from the notion of "highest" to that of "infinite." He begins with the definition of Aristotle:

> For the Philosopher "the infinite is that whose quantity is such that no matter how much one removes from it, there is always more for the taking." The reason is that the infinite in quantity, of which the Philosopher speaks, can have being only potentially, if we take one after another. For this reason, no matter how much is removed, what one takes will still be finite and will represent only a certain part of the infinite potential whole. More of it will always remain for the taking. From this he infers that since the infinite in quantity has only being in the making or potentially, it does not fulfill the notion of a whole, for a whole has nothing outside itself. But there is always something outside this sort of infinite, that is, outside that which of itself has being in potency. It is never perfect, for the perfect lacks no perfection, whereas this always lacks something.[40]

Note at this point that Scotus recognized that we are differentiating between the imperfect, which is abstracted, and something that lies beyond the definite and lacks this imperfection. Aristotle recognized this as a peculiar type of experience that is felt by everyone: "Not only number but also mathematical magnitudes and what is outside the heavens are thought to be infinite because they never give out in our thought."[41] This makes us think that what lies beyond is something positive rather than simply another negation. This demarcation divides the world of experience into two segments: the "definite world of real distinct entities" and the "what-lies-beyond," which seems to have no limit in thought. Augustine used this fact of introspection to argue that we judge by rules or norms impressed upon us from above as to what is perfect; and by comparing this to what we see here as imperfect, we recognize the difference between them, something we would not do if all we experienced were the finite and imperfect. As Augustine put it, "We comprehend in a different way [i.e., from abstraction from the world about us] the types and ineffably beautiful art of such forms, as are above the eye of the mind, by simple intelligence."[42]

Scotus goes on to explain the next step:

> For our purposes, let us change the notion of the potentially infinite in quantity, if possible, to that of the quantitatively infinite in act. For just as it is necessary [in the case of the potentially infinite] that the quantity of the infinite should always grow by receiving one part after another, so we might imagine that all the parts that could be taken were taken at once or that they remained in existence simultaneously. If this could be done, we would have in actuality an infinite quantity, because it would be as great in actuality as it was potentially. And all those parts which in infinite succession would be actualized and would have being one after the other would be conceived as actualized all at once. Such an infinite in act would indeed be a whole and in truth a perfect whole, since there would indeed be nothing outside it, and it would be perfect since it lacks nothing. What is more, nothing in the way of quantity could be added to it, for then it could be exceeded.[43]

As he explained it, one moves from the potential to the actual infinite, while still dealing with *quantity*. Scotus's next step was to push his analogical model a stage higher. Some sort of special insight seems involved, whereby one substitutes for discrete or distinct numbers the notion of pure perfections, each of which is formally distinct from every other, just as the concept of one number is distinct from that of any other. Thus he went on to say:

From this, we argue further: If we think of something among beings that is actually infinite in entity, we must think along the lines of the actual infinite in quantity we imagined, namely as an infinite being that cannot be exceeded in entity by any other being. It will truly have the character of something whole and perfect. It will indeed be whole and complete. While something actually infinite in quantity would not be missing any of its parts or lacking any part of quantity, still each of its parts would lie outside the other and consequently the whole would be made up of imperfect elements. A being infinite in entity, however, would not have any entity outside itself in this way. Neither would its totality depend upon elements which are themselves imperfect in entity, for it exists in such a way that it has no extrinsic part; otherwise it would not be entirely whole. As for its being perfect, the situation is similar. Although something actually infinite in quantity would be perfect as to quantity, because as a whole it would lack no quantity, nevertheless each part of it would lack the quantity of the other parts. That is to say, an infinite of this sort would not be quantitatively perfect [as a whole] unless each of its parts were not imperfect. An infinite being, however, is perfect in such a way that neither it nor any of its parts is missing anything.[44]

Scotus summed up the steps he had taken so far in this way:

From the notion of the infinite in the *Physics*,[45] then, applied imaginatively to something infinite in quantity, were that possible and applied further to something actually infinite in entity, were it possible, we can form some sort of idea of how to conceive a being intensively infinite in perfection and power.[46]

Scotus went on to explain how we can describe such a maximally perfect being, which excludes only such entities as are by definition intrinsically imperfect. Pure perfections, by contrast, do not exclude one another in the way that those that are not sometimes do.

This enables us to describe a being infinite in entity as a being which lacks no entity in the way that one single being is able to possess it. The qualification "in the way, etc." is added because a single being cannot possess every entity whatsoever formally and by a real identity.[47]

Another way of describing this extended sense of "more to less," which applies to pure perfection, is to use the term "degrees of difference" in a new and extended sense. Mineralogists, for instance, use Mohs's scale of hardness, which ranges over ten degrees from talc, the softest, to diamond, the hardest. "Harder" is described simply as what can scratch that which is softer. It does not mean, for instance, that topaz, which is eighth on this scale, is mathematically twice as hard as fluorite, which is fourth on the scale. Here "degrees of difference" are not extensive or additive properties (as mathematicians use the term) but are rather intensive or nonadditive differences. Scotus used such a scale when he said that "infinite being"

> can also be described in terms of how it exceeds any other being in this fashion. Consider whiteness, for instance. It is exceeded triply by another entity, knowledge, or ten times by the intellective soul, or a hundredfold by the most perfect angel. No matter how high you go among beings, there will always be some finite measure according to which the highest exceeds the lowest. Not that there is any proportion or relative measure, properly speaking, as mathematicians use it, because the angel, being simpler, is not constituted by some lesser entity to which something has been added. It must rather be understood as the relative measure of perfection or power in the way one species is superior to another. In this fashion, by contrast, the infinite exceeds the finite in entity beyond any relative measure or proportion that could be assigned.[48]

He continued with an explanation of why he considered "infinity" to be an intrinsic mode rather than a simple property:

> From this it follows that intensive infinity is not related to the being that is said to be infinite as a kind of attribute that accrues to it extrinsically. Neither should it be thought of as an attribute or property of being in the way "good" and "true" are. Indeed, intensive infinity expresses an intrinsic mode of that entity. It is so intrinsic that if we abstract from all its properties or quasi-properties, we have still not excluded infinity, but it remains integrally included in that one single entity itself. Hence if we consider that entity most precisely, namely, without any property, it will be true to say it has a measure of intrinsic excellence all its own which is not finite, since any limitation of degree is repugnant to it. Therefore it is infinite. That which is infinite, considered most precisely, and not under the aspect of some attributable property such as wisdom or goodness, can also be aligned according to an essential order with something it excels, but its superiority will not be measurable in any definite degree, for then it would be finite. Therefore, the intrinsic mode of anything intensively infinite is infinity itself, which intrinsically expresses a being or essence which lacks nothing and which exceeds everything finite beyond any determinable degree.[49]

Scotus appealed to John Damascene's analogy of a limitless "sea of substance":

Damascene confirms this corollary when he says that the essence is an infinite and limitless sea of substance. Substance, then, insofar as it represents what is absolutely first in the divine, he calls a sea, and as such it is infinite and boundless. But substance in this sense does not include [in its formal concept] either truth, or goodness, or any other attributable property. Therefore, infinity as such is a mode of essence more intrinsic than any attribute it [actually] has [in reality].[50]

In the final two passages, which we have taken from his *Quodlibet,* Scotus dealt with the important issue of how the attribute "infinite" belongs to its subject, "being." In contrast to the two commonly recognized kinds of distinction—namely, the real distinction, which holds between separable entities that can actually be taken apart, and a purely conceptual distinction, which holds when notions are indifferent or noninclusive of one another—he introduced the modal distinction to characterize the unity of "infinite being." "Infinite" and "finite" are intrinsic modes of the subjects they modify. As such, the mode is really and conceptually inseparable from its subject.

The essential point to be gained from this extended excursus on Scotus's explanation of how we form our concept of the Infinite Being is to see in some concrete detail his deepest reason for rejecting Henry's doctrine of illumination. By walking us through the transformation which began with Aristotle's potentially infinite quantity and ended with infinity as an intrinsic mode of being, he has demonstrated the irrelevancy of Henry's sort of divine illumination. For if Scotus is right, then the remarkable but natural power of the human intellect suffices to give us some concepts of the transcendent God.

Scotus's fifth and final point refuting Henry is that in our encounter with the world of experience we are able to think of, as well as classify, things according to various degrees of generality. An orange, for instance, can be conceived of as a sphere, or one can regard its circumference as a circle, its composition as material, or itself as something real. Scotus had in mind this ability of one thing to give rise to a variety of concepts when he wrote:

> I say that those things which are known of God are known from their likeness [*species*] in creatures. For whether the more universal and less universal are known through the same species, or whether each has an intelligible species proper to itself, at least that which can impress a less universal species in the intellect can also cause a species of anything more general, and thus creatures, which impress a likeness [*species*]

proper to themselves, can also impress the species of the transcendentals, which are applicable commonly to themselves and to God.

Just as our imagination can create images constructed from perceptual elements, so our mind can creatively assemble conceptual elements to form ideas that are proper to various things that we have reason to believe exist. Scotus claimed that although we can abstract no simple concepts that are proper to God, as Henry believed we could, we can construct proper concepts, such as first cause, unmoved mover, and infinite being. Before such notions can be called real, however, we must have reasons or arguments to prove that the two or more simple concepts coexist in the same subject. In other words, we must be able to establish such conclusions as "some cause is first," "some mover is unmoved," and "some being is not finite and hence is infinite." All our proper concepts of God are arrived at by way of inference, or as Scotus put it, they are "concepts inferred by way of a proposition."[51] The more universal intelligible species, according to Scotus, can be abstracted from the less universal. The notion of a living being and of an animal are contained in the less universal notion of a human being. Our proper notions of God are built up of simple affirmations and negations of intelligible characteristics discoverable in creatures. These simple affirmative features are univocally common to God and creatures. Such, for example, would be "being," "good," "wise," or other pure perfections. These simple transcendental notions are pieced together to form a mosaic, a complete concept of God. While the concept may be a composite, the reality that it represents and to which it refers is simple, not composed.

The Adequate Object of the Intellect

Another question that Scotus raised in regard to God's knowability is this: "Is God the primary object that is naturally adequate to the intellect of the pilgrim in this life?" ("Utrum Deus sit primum obiectum naturale adaequatum respectu intellectus viatoris?").[52]

The adequate object of a cognitive power or faculty is known as its first, or primary, object. "Adequate" means properly proportioned or commensurate to the power in question. It implies, first of all, that the object is able to motivate or elicit from the faculty an awareness of itself both as to its formal meaning and its virtual implications. And second, it must be either formally or virtually coextensive with whatever can be known by the particular power under consideration, so that by knowing that object fully, everything is known that can be known.

An object is said to be adequate or commensurate to a respective faculty in the sense that it enjoys either a *primacy of virtuality* or a *primacy of commonness* in regard to what can be known. An example of the first would be God's essence in reference to his divine intellect. His essence alone is capable of motivating his intellect, yet he knows not only his own essence but also creatures, which are distinct from him. Thus his essence has a primacy of virtuality, for it has the power or virtue (*virtus*) of producing a knowledge of all that can be known. An example of a primacy of commonness would be color in reference to the faculty of sight. In the primacy of commonness, the object is not a particular physical entity but rather a common feature or characteristic that can be predicated of all the physical objects capable of motivating the faculty.

In his *Ordinatio* Scotus criticized two current opinions. The first could be called Aristotelian, and it was voiced by Aquinas; it declares the quiddity, or essence of a material—that is, sense-perceptible being—to be the proper object of the human intellect. The second is the form of Augustinian illuminationism championed by Henry, which makes God the proper and adequate object of the intellect.

The Aristotelian Theory

Scotus rejected the first opinion because it attributes too little to our intellect. It cannot suffice for a theologian, who believes that our intellect can continue to function in the afterlife when our intellectual soul is no longer joined to a body or works in conjunction with the bodily senses. Although Scotus was primarily concerned with determining the adequate object of the intellect in its present state of existence, in discussing Aquinas's position, he could not ignore its possible theological implications. The notion of adequate object contains at least two distinct requirements. First, the adequate object must be able to motivate the intellect. Second, it must be formally or virtually coextensive with whatever the intellect is able to know. Reason alone cannot tell us a great deal about what motivates the intellect apart from the body, but it can tell us something about whether the object reputed to be adequate is coextensive with what we are able to know already in this life.

At first sight, Aristotle might seem to be correct, since, in this life at least, only material quiddities seem to have the power to motivate our intellect. Yet it is quite clear that material quiddities cannot be the adequate object of the intellect in the same sense that color is the adequate object of vision. While color can be predicated of whatever can be seen, sensible quiddity cannot be predicated of everything that can be known. We have a very real notion of God and substance. We are able to form a concept that is more universal than sense-perceptible quiddities and is predicable of things that cannot be experienced by the senses at all. The very fact that we possess a science of metaphysics—a science that transcends the sensible order and deals with being qua being—is proof that sensible or material quiddities are not commensurate to our intellect. In short, we are in the anomalous position of possessing a faculty that is able to transcend its starting point and arrive at a notion of things whose proper meaning is neither formally nor virtually contained in the simple apprehension of the sensible quiddity. The eye, however, never transcends color.[53] It never sees anything that is more common and universal than its proper object. Consequently, on the basis of reason alone, Scotus argued, we have grounds to question the Aristotelian hypothesis and to look for a broader or more universal notion than that of sensible quiddity as the adequate object of the intellect.

The Theory of Henry of Ghent

If the first theory attributes too little to the intellect, Henry's attributes too much to it, mainly because he claimed that we have an irreducible simple concept of God—for example, the good itself—that is only analogous to the common concepts that we abstract from creatures. Since Henry's interpretation of intellectual abstraction incorporated Augustine's theory of illumination, it is not surprising that he considered God to be the primary adequate object of our intellect. Virtually, the divine nature contains the good itself as well as the fullness of being. But, according to Augustine, God impresses upon the human intellect something of his exemplar ideas, so that everything we know contains some pure perfection that is found in its fullness in God. As Augustine pointed out, "in all these good things . . . , we would be unable to call one better than the other, if we judge in accordance with the truth, if the idea of the good itself had not been impressed upon us, according to which we approve of something as good, and also prefer one good to another."[54] Hence, Henry insisted that it is only by knowing its idealized essence as it exists in God that we know what any created thing really is.[55]

As Scotus pointed out in his third refutation of Henry above, God is a voluntary object, and hence his divinity is not the sort of nature that would naturally motivate the intellect. According to Henry, God is only known in a concept that is analogous to creatures and thus does not really fall under the concept of being as a subject of metaphysics. If one admits the univocity of being, however, we can say that God is included in the general notion of being; and to the extent that being motivates our intellect, God may be said to be an object naturally ordained to it. But in this case, being, rather than God, should be called the adequate object of the intellect.[56] Furthermore, Scotus argued, it is clear that God does not have a primacy of commonness in regard to all those objects that of themselves are intelligible to our intellect, since "God" cannot be predicated of everything we know. If he possessed any primacy of adequation in regard to our intellect, it would be one of virtuality, such as his divine nature has with respect to the divine intellect. But this is obviously false, for other things besides God are capable of moving our intellect in their own right. In no sense, then, can the divine essence be said to move us so that we can first know it and only then know all else besides God that can be known.[57]

Referring to the ten categories of Aristotle, Scotus pointed out that substance in general cannot be the primary object of our intellect, since accidents by virtue of their own nature motivate the mind. Substance does not primarily move the intellect to know it and through it to know all other things that are intelligible.[58]

What, then, is the adequate object of the intellect? What can be said to be commensurate to everything that is per se intelligible? Scotus admitted that there seems to be no single object that is virtually coextensive with what we can know. Neither is there any formal notion that can be predicated generally of all that we are able to know. By looking for something that combines a primacy of virtuality with that of common predication, however, it is possible to speak of some sort of adequate object in regard to our intellect.

The Twofold Primacy of Being

It is in being (ens) that we find just such an object. In being, Scotus pointed out, a twofold primacy concurs: a primacy of common predication and a primacy of virtuality. Neither taken singly is coextensive with all that can be known. Nevertheless, the combination of the two exhausts the realm of knowability. Since transcendental notions are all per se intelligible, an analysis of this twofold primacy of being will also throw light upon how the concept of being, as the subject of metaphysics, is related to the other transcendental notions.

Every genus, species, and individual and every essential part of a genus—and the uncreated being as well—include being quidditatively. Being, predicated *in quid* and as a noun, is regarded by the Scholastics as the first and fundamental concept in the essence of any real thing; it is the ultimate subject capable of existing outside the mind or imagination, the ultimate *quid*. It does not express the whole essence or entity of that of which it is predicated; rather, it only expresses the ultimate determinable and common element to be found in anything or any notion that is capable of being resolved into several simpler elements. Where concepts are concerned, it does not matter whether being is conceived distinctly, as in the composite concept "infinite being," or only indistinctly, as it is in simple but further resolvable concepts, such as substance or redness.

Scotus considered any concept to be simple that results from a simple act of apprehension, a simple grasp or understanding of the meaning of that concept. Not every simple concept is irreducibly simple, however. One element in every concept that is capable of further analysis will be common, the others will differentiate a given concept from others that share the common element. By continuing this process, we ultimately arrive at primary concepts incapable of further analysis—they cannot be broken down into two simpler concepts, one of which is determinable, the other qualifying. And it is such basic concepts that Scotus considered to be simple in an unqualified sense (*simpliciter simplex*). Aristotle and the Scholastics referred to concepts of this sort as "primarily diverse."[59]

Composite concepts result from a synthetic activity of the mind. Their reality is established either by finding some instance where both conceptual elements are realized, such as "living substance" or "kind person," or where these elements represent the subject and predicate of some valid rational inference. Examples of such would be the concepts "uncaused being" or "substantial being," where these are inferred conclusions of a demonstration that some being is uncaused and some being is substantial. The analysis of the intelligible concept of anything that one can call a real thing, and its resynthesis of these concepts in the form of a definition, will also yield a composite concept.

For a metaphysician, there is but one common and determinable element that is irreducibly simple, and that is the quidditative concept of being. In describing the primacy of common predication, however, Scotus was interested only in whether or not the concept in question is irreducibly simple. Being, he maintained, is contained *in quid* and univocally as part of the intelligible meaning of any concept that is not primary.

While "being" is the only irreducibly simple quidditative concept, there are as many differential concepts as there are ultimate differences, and they are all unique. What are these ultimate differences? Since Scotus gave the individual, the species, and the genus as examples of concepts that are not irreducibly simple, and since every such concept must contain an ultimate difference, we can distinguish several types of ultimate differences: an individuating difference, which Scotus refers to also as an individual's haecceity, or "thisness"; the ultimate specific difference[60] of anything; and the generic and transcendental differences that qualify "being" where it can be predicated univocally. Notions like infinite, finite, subsistent, accidental, material, or immaterial (in the sense of spiritual), would be examples of the third sort of difference.

The Primacy of Common Predication

The primacy of common predication does not extend to such ultimate differences, nor does it extend to notions that are predicated as proper attributes. Proper attributes, by reason of their grammatical or logical structure, are predicable *in quale*—or as modifications of a subject—rather than *in quid*—or as subsistent subjects. Hence Scotus says in his opening statement:

> I say ... since there can be nothing more common than being and that being cannot be predicated univocally *in quid* of all per se intelligibles, because it cannot be predicated of ultimate differences nor of its attributes, it follows that nothing is primary object of the intellect by reason of commonness *in quid* with respect to all per se intelligibles.

He goes on to argue, however, that since being, as well as substance and accident, can be predicated univocally of God and creatures—contrary to what Henry would admit—it follows that "every genus, species, and individual, and every essential part of a genus, and the uncreated being as well, include being quidditatively." He proves this "by the same two reasons used in the first question of this distinction to show that being is common to both created and uncreated being." Hence, "it is evident that being has a primacy of community to the first intelligibles, that is, to the quidditative concepts of genera, species, and individuals, and to all the essential parts of these—and to the concept of the uncreated being." The primary genus, however, according to

Aristotle, is the category of substance. Hence, Scotus devotes special attention in his second argument to show why being is univocal to substance and accidents. Only sense-perceptible accidents can be directly experienced, and hence if we cannot extract some common conception—such as the univocal concept of being—from such phenomena, we cannot infer the existence of some being that does not inhere in something more fundamental but rather subsists in itself. Such is the definition of a created substance as the underlying substratum of the material universe.

These arguments, however, "do not imply the univocation of being *in quid* with respect to the ultimate differences and attributes" which are grammatically and logically qualifying terms (*qualia*) rather than quiddities. Nevertheless, "it is not necessary that being be present to all of these concepts *in quid;* but it suffices if it is either so or is univocal to them as the determinable is to the determinant or what can be denominated to what denominates."

Though one cannot properly define primary qualifications, because of their simplicity, nevertheless one has to introduce the notion of their respective subject in some sense into a description of what they mean. And this creates the psychological impression that somehow, if they are not essentially a being, they are nothing. Aristotle, as Scotus points out, dealt with this logical conundrum in the *Posterior Analytics* and the *Metaphysics,* where he discussed the nature of ultimate differences and attributes that pertain to their respective subjects per se (*kath auto*).[61] "Number" does not enter into the definition of "odd" or "even" in the same way that "rational" and "animal" enter into the definition of a human being. "Rational" and "animal" are mutually exclusive terms and can be defined as such. But "odd" cannot be defined as excluding number, and yet "number" can be defined apart from "odd"; otherwise there could be no even numbers. And a similar case could be made for "even." The way the subject enters into the quasi-definition of what is fundamentally a primary qualification, Aristotle said, is "by addition" (*ek prostheseos,* which was translated as *sicut additum* in Latin). Since "being" as a *quid* and the ultimate differences or the proper attributes of being as basic *qualia* are all irreducibly simple terms, neither term is contained in the other as part of its essential meaning. Hence, if we need to explain that such *qualia* are qualifications of "being," we introduce "being" into such a description, says Scotus, only "as something added." Another primitive difference (such as "odd" with respect to number) that Aristotle gave would be "female" with respect to "animal." We are unable to give a strict definition of primitive notions such as "female" or "male" without introducing the notion of "animal," for "female" is "that quality by which an animal is female" and "male" is "that quality by which an animal is male." The peculiarity of such quasi-definitions, Aristotle said, is that they add something that lies outside their formal meaning. Only something that subsists as a subject in its own right is definable:

> If the other categories are also definable, it must be by addition of a determinant, e.g., the qualitative is defined thus, and so is the odd, for it cannot be defined apart from number; nor can female be defined apart from animal. (When I say "by addition" [*ek prostheseos*] I mean the expressions in which it turns out that we are saying the same thing twice, as in these instances.) And if this is true, coupled terms also, like "odd number," will not be definable (but this escapes our notice because our formulae are not accurate).[62]

In a similar way, Scotus argues that if "being" were predicable of ultimate differences and attributes essentially, or *in quid*, we would be asserting that they are not irreducibly simple terms. What is more, we would still have to introduce "being" *sicut additum—ek prostheseos*—into the definition of what is different; and if this means it is included essentially, this involves an endless repetition. "Consequently," Aristotle argued, "it is absurd that such things should have an essence; if they have, there will be an infinite regress."[63]

Nevertheless, they are qualifications of something that is a being and as such are not a "nothing." It is here that Scotus introduces the second primacy of being, that of virtuality.

The Primacy of Virtuality

The primacy of virtuality extends to all those intelligibles of which being is not predicable essentially, or *in quid*, but that are nevertheless characteristics of those objects of which being can be predicated *in quid*. Consequently, it is not the formal concept of being that contains the attributes or ultimate differences in the sense that these can be extracted or deduced from this notion, since it is irreducibly simple, according to Scotus. Rather, it is the concrete objects or physical entities—such as a man, God, or Paul— or the composite concepts that represent such objects—namely, the generic, specific, or individual concepts—which are not irreducibly simple, that can be said to contain virtually these secondary intelligibles. It is the concrete objects or physical entities to which our concepts refer that move or motivate the intellect, not only to form notions that can be said to contain being univocally but also to form concepts that express essential differences or attributes of quiddities. Because being can be given a univocal meaning, it can retain that univocal meaning when said to be that which these ultimate *qualia* qualify.[64] As Scotus puts it,

> every per se intelligible either includes the notion of being or is contained virtually or essentially in something that does include the notion of being essentially. For every genus, species, and individual, and every essential part of a genus, and the uncreated being as well, include being quidditatively; but all ultimate differences are included in these essentially, and all attributes of being are included in being and in its inferiors virtually. Therefore those of which being is not a univocal predicate *in quid* are included in those in which being is univocal in this way. And so it is evident that being has a primacy of community to the first intelligibles—that is, to the quidditative concepts of genera, species, and individuals, and to all the essential parts of these—and to the concept of the uncreated being; and it has a primacy of virtuality to all intelligibles included in the first intelligibles—that is, to those qualitative concepts of ultimate differences and proper attributes.

He concludes that since this double primacy concurs in whatever is itself a being or falls under the transcendental notion of being, this suffices to call being the primary object of the intellect, even though neither primacy alone extends to all per se intelligibles.

Practical Certitude and Refutation of Skepticism

Scotus, in his continuing critique of Henry's theory of knowledge, raised yet another question. He asked whether any certain and undiluted truth can be known naturally by the human intellect in the present life without some special influence on the part of God. In his *Lectura* Scotus explains more precisely what he means by "special influence" when he explains that "fire can burn the tarred hemp used for caulking with nothing more than God's general influence." As the creator of this dynamic cosmos, God concurs to some extent in its activity as well as in its continued existence. As a cognitive faculty, the intellect also has a certain natural activity that it can perform without any extra help on the part of God, Henry admitted. But he restricted this natural activity of the mind to simple apprehension, that is, to grasping the meaning of the words or terms we use in speaking. Aristotle spoke of this natural activity as the process whereby the intellect abstracts the general or common notions that we use to categorize or name things. Although this simple understanding of anything is actually knowledge of what is true, the human intellect does not recognize the truth value of this fact except by a further act of judgment.[65] And it is here, Henry insisted, that the mind needs some additional special influence on the part of God, a special illumination from what Augustine called the "Uncreated Light."[66] To know the truth itself, Henry argued, there are two exemplars, according to Plato in the *Timaeus:* one that is made or created and one that is not made. The created exemplar is the species of the universal caused by the thing. The uncreated exemplar is the idea in the divine mind that Augustine referred to. It is evident that if the human intellect is to have certain and infallible knowledge, it will not find this by looking at the created exemplar abstracted from the object through the senses.[67]

According to Henry, this is due to the thing from which the exemplar is abstracted, to the intellectual soul in which the created exemplar inheres, and to the created exemplar itself.[68] All of these are mutable, however, as Augustine explained:

> Everything which the bodily sense touches and which is called sensible is constantly changing. . . . But what does not remain stable cannot be perceived, for that is perceived which is grasped by knowledge, but that cannot be grasped which changes without ceasing. Therefore truth in any genuine sense is not something to be expected from the bodily senses.[69]

Furthermore, Henry argued, the soul itself is changeable and subject to error, and an exemplar that is even more changeable than the soul cannot correct this condition. Finally, the created exemplar itself can either represent itself as only a species and likeness of an object or present itself as an object, as it does in dreams. In the first case, there is truth; in the second, there is falsity. There is nothing about the species itself, however, that suffices to indicate which role this created exemplar may be playing. To distinguish truth from the appearance of truth, Henry concluded, one must look beyond this created exemplar to the uncreated exemplar itself.

In this life, however, we cannot gaze upon this exemplar directly, any more than our eye can look directly upon the burning face of the sun. Nevertheless, it is sunlight that directly or indirectly illuminates what we do see, and in a similar way this Uncreated Light indirectly illuminates our intellect. Scotus explains Henry's notion of its triple function more fully in his *Ordinatio* when he says:

> It is assumed, however, that the uncreated exemplar is related to the act of vision in three ways, namely, as a stimulating light, as a transforming species, and as a configuring character or exemplar. From this it is argued that a special influence is required. For just as we do not naturally see this [divine] essence in itself, neither do we see it naturally as the exemplar of any [created] essence. According to Augustine in *Seeing God*, it is in [God's] power to be seen: "If he wishes it, he is seen; if he does not wish it, he is not seen." Finally, it is added that perfect knowledge of the truth results when the two exemplar species concur in the mind: one inhering, namely, the created exemplar; the other flooding in, namely, the uncreated exemplar. And in this way we touch the word of truth perfectly.[70]

For this reason, Henry, following Augustine, argued that we need the help of the Uncreated Light from the exemplars in the divine mind:

> For unless our concepts are formed in us with the assistance of the eternal light, they remain without form, nor do they contain truth in an unqualified and undiluted fashion. Neither is the natural light of reason so potent that it suffices to enlighten one to conceive the truth unless it ascends to the eternal light itself.[71]

Scotus argues against Henry that if the object is mutable, then it does not help to know it as immutable, for there can be no certitude about knowing an object in some way other than as it truly is. Likewise, if the mutability of the exemplar in our intellect makes certitude impossible, it follows that nothing in the soul could prevent it from erring. If the understanding is even more mutable than the soul itself, then it will never be true or contain truth. Finally, if the species abstracted from the thing is a concurrent factor in all knowledge, and if we can never judge with certainty when we are awake, we shall never have any norm for distinguishing what is true from what appears to be true. In short, Henry's arguments only prove that nothing is certain, which is the opinion of the Academicians, whom, Augustine believed, he had refuted.

Scotus shows that Augustine was more consistent, since, unlike Henry, he did not try to combine the illumination theory with elements from Aristotle's theory of abstraction. Scotus quotes texts from Augustine to show that he admitted we can be certain of three types of knowledge. As to first principles, Augustine himself admitted: "Everyone concedes without hesitation that the proofs from the sciences are most true." Scotus then argues with Aristotle that first principles are known to all and that the laws of logic are evident, and hence one can use them to draw conclusions from first principles.[72] Furthermore, Augustine did not deny that we can obtain certitude from sense perception: "Far be it from us to doubt those things which we have learned are true through the senses of the body, for through them we have learned of the heavens, the earth, the sea and all that are in them."[73] Augustine insisted that we have certitude regarding our actions. In answer to the skeptic, who says: "Perhaps you are sleeping and you see in dreams," Augustine replies that one can still be certain that one lives and can always say: "'I know that I live'; whether he, therefore, sleeps, or whether he is awake, he lives. He cannot be deceived in his knowledge of this even by dreams, because to sleep and to see in dreams is characteristic of one who lives."[74] Scotus then goes on to show that there are three types of knowledge where we can have practical certitude. The first concerns those principles that we regard as self-evident and the logical conclusions we can draw from them. The second has to do with things known by experience, and the third is in regard to our actions.[75]

Certitude of First Principles

The first category consists of those fundamental truths about reality that we refer to as self-evident or as first principles. A principle, from the Latin *principium* (beginning), is the starting point for a rational deduction of whatever else we can know about a thing. Since the truth of such conclusions depends as much upon the truth of these initial propositions as upon the validity of our logical reasoning, Scotus sets as his first task to show why we can be certain of such analytical principles. "The terms of self-evident principles are so identical that it is evident that one necessarily includes the other."[76] In other words, if we understand the meaning of the subject and predicate terms of the proposition, we see that one meaning incorporates the other, so that if one is true, it follows that the other is true as well.

The most cogent argument that skeptics raise against intellectual knowledge is that it originates from sense perception, and therefore it is impossible to know anything with certitude. Scotus effectively shows that this in no way affects the certitude one has about the principle itself. The senses only provide the occasion for acquiring a concept; they are in no way the reason why we assent to the truth of the proposition. This is something that depends upon the meaning of the terms, and the intellect in understanding that meaning perceives the reason why the statement is true or not.

Since the laws of logic, like those of mathematics, do not depend upon empirical facts or judgments, the intellect can also judge whether conclusions deduced from principles that are evident from the analysis of the terms are true or false. The certitude of such propositions does not depend upon empirical data the way propositions such as "The earth is spherical" or "This flower is red" do.

Experiential Knowledge

The second type of knowledge concerns the things we need to know about the world in which we live. As a philosopher in the Aristotelian tradition, Scotus views all natural phenomena as governed by the law of cause and effect, something we discover experientially. As pattern perceivers, we have the natural ability to distinguish not only between fixed objects and static background but also between random behavior and dynamic regularities. And we regard these constant events as effects of natural causes. We begin with some awareness of the effect and then reason to the existence of its cause. Aristotle referred to this reasoning process as a demonstration (*apodeixis*), and to the conclusion as true or epistemic knowledge, quite different from mere opinion (*doxa*). Experiential knowledge becomes true and certain when we discover some principle from which it can be inferred as a conclusion. As Scotus reminds us, "one must realize that certain knowledge of the truth about both the conclusion and the principle is acquired through experience."

He is concerned to point out the reasoning process he believes we go through to arrive at a practical certitude regarding both conclusions and principles:

> About the conclusion, [certain knowledge] is acquired thus: One first has a knowledge of the simple fact that stems from perceiving that such an effect occurs frequently—for instance, when one sees the moon is eclipsed or that some herb frequently cures some infirmity. With this experience, however, the intellect has a self-evident proposition: "Whatever happens in most cases is a natural effect, and there is a natural cause that produces such an effect."

As we note in the next chapter, in his *Questions on the Metaphysics,* Scotus divides all efficient causes or active potencies into two metaphysical classes: nature and will. When he speaks here, then, of a "natural cause" and a "natural effect," he has in mind that the cause is not a free agent or a person who acts deliberately in a patterned way because it serves some rational end or purpose. In the *Ordinatio* he makes this idea explicit when he formulates this "self-evident" principle in the following way: "Whatever occurs in a great many instances by a cause that is not free is the natural effect of that cause." Since a natural cause is not free and yet for the most part acts regularly, and a natural effect is defined as "what happens in most cases" as the result of such a nonvoluntary cause, Scotus can speak of this proposition as analytical, or "self-evident." What he is saying is that we appeal to some general principle that can be said to be true simply by virtue of the meaning of its terms. He believes that this is how we either have, or can have, practical certitude about what we know from experience.

If we begin by noticing regularities in the behavior of things, which allows us to formulate statements that a philosopher of science might call a particular scientific fact or law, we tend to discover more general principles that would explain why these particular facts occur. We look for reasons or explanations why such regularities exist in nature. Such reasons or causes correspond to scientific theories and are related to the particular scientific law in the sense that the laws can be deduced from the theories. In contrast to this more familiar deductive approach, Scotus gives a different account, which we might call his theory of "scientific induction":

> What is more, the intellect that has such simple knowledge of this conclusion and knows that there is some natural cause of this then proceeds to inquire by way of division and, eliminating those things that are not causes nor could be causes, concludes that this particular one is the cause of it; and thus it has knowledge of the reason why the fact is so.

In Aristotelian terms, we move from a knowledge of a simple fact (*demonstratio quia*) to knowledge of the reasoned fact (*demonstratio propter quid*).[77] Scotus, following Aristotle, indicates the steps whereby one discovers the scientific cause of a solar eclipse, and suggests that by a similar procedure one learns other facts about the stars, measures the diameter or circumference of the earth geometrically, or discovers the medicinal properties of various herbs.

He also indicates that we can discover principles that govern sense perception, so that we can learn when our sense faculties are behaving normally and reliably. In this way he refutes the skeptical objection that the possibility of illusions proves that the senses can never give us practical certitude. He expands this explanation considerably in his *Ordinatio,* where he asks: "But how can one have certitude about those things that fall under the acts of the senses, for instance, that something outside is white, or hot, such as it appears to be?"[78] It is worth quoting his detailed reply at length, for it contains the basic principles whereby we become scientifically aware of the natural deficiencies of the senses and how we learn to judge when they cannot be trusted.

> I reply: either the same such object appears opposite to diverse senses or not, because all the senses that perceive it make the same judgment about it. If the second occurs, one has certainty about the truth of such through the testimony of the senses together with this proposition mentioned earlier: "What occurs in most cases by something, this is its natural cause, if it is not a free agent." Therefore, when from this, being present, such a change in the senses occurs for the most part, it follows that this change, or the image produced, is the natural effect of such a cause, and so such an external thing will be white or hot, or such as it is represented to us through the species produced by this [particular cause] for the most part.
>
> But if the judgments based on different senses diverge in regard to what they perceive outside—for example, if sight says the staff that is partly in water and partly in air is broken, or if sight says, as it always does, that the sun is smaller in size than it actually is, or each thing viewed from a distance is not as large as it really is, in such cases there is still certitude as to what is true and which sense is in error by virtue of a proposition residing in the soul that is more certain than the judgment of any sense, together with the concurrent testimony of more than one sense. Thus there is always some proposition setting the intellect aright regarding the acts of the senses, so it knows which is true and which is false. As regards this proposition, the intellect does not depend upon the sense as the cause [of its truth] but as an occasion [to recall or know it to be true]. For example, the intellect has this proposition residing in it: "Nothing harder is broken by the touch of something soft that gives way before it." This is so self-evident from the meaning of its terms that even if they were derived from erring senses, the intellect could not doubt this proposition. Indeed, its opposite includes a contradiction. But the fact that the staff is harder than water and that water recedes before it is something confirmed by both senses, that of sight and that of touch. It follows therefore that "the staff is not broken," as the sense [of sight] judges it to be. And so in regard to the broken staff, the intellect judges by something more certain than an act of sense perception. Likewise in the other case [of an apparent diminished size]: "a measure used to measure remains equal to itself"[79] is something known to the intellect, no matter how much the meaning of the terms may have been derived from erring senses;

but both the sense of sight and that of touch attest that the same measure could be applied to something seen, whether it be near or far. And therefore, vision declaring it to be less, errs.

This conclusion is inferred from principles that are self-evident together with what is known from perceptions of two senses that usually render such testimony for the most part. And so wherever reason judges that the sense errs, this judgment does not depend upon knowledge acquired from the senses precisely as its cause, but only because some knowledge from the sense occasioned [the judgment], in which the intellect would not be deceived, even if all the senses were deceived. And in addition there would be some other knowledge acquired from the usual behavior of one or several senses, which are known to be true [i.e., reliable] by reason of the [inductive] proposition so frequently mentioned, namely, "What occurs in most cases by something [that is not free is the natural cause]," etc.[80]

Knowledge of Our Own Actions

Finally Scotus turns to the third area where we require and can have certain knowledge. As he says at the outset, this concerns "our own actions and works, for if we did not need to know these, we would not be aware of what we are doing." Here he reminds us that "we need to consider how there can be certain knowledge about our acts, for example, how we know that we understand, feel sensations, or are asleep or awake, and so on."

Unlike necessary or analytic propositions, those asserting what we know of our own actions will have the logical form of a contingent proposition; and unlike necessary propositions, the evidence for their truth value does not stem from an analysis of the abstract meaning of the terms. Scotus recalls what he said in the prologue about the logical nature of contingent propositions.[81] They cannot be deduced from any set of necessary propositions. Consequently, either we have an infinite regress, or we admit that some contingent propositions are primitive. If we know them to be true, then we do so immediately on the basis of either personal experience or information we learn or have learned from what others have reported. The primitive contingent propositions that we can be most certain of, however, concern our own actions; and these, Scotus tells us, are or can be self-evident, and in the *Ordinatio*, he adds, "we are as certain of many of these as we are of the first and self-evident propositions, as is clear from [Aristotle]."[82]

In what sense are such propositions self-evident? They are evident because we are intuitively aware of the existential situation in which we are when we experience such actions in ourselves.

Scotus explains elsewhere that our intellect is not only the faculty whereby we abstract those characteristics that a sense-perceptible object has in common with other similar individuals; but in addition to this abstract knowledge, he insists, the intellect has a less well recognized type of knowledge that he refers to as intuitive cognition. "Intuition" is defined by Webster as the direct knowledge of something without the conscious use of reasoning; it is a form of immediate apprehension or understanding.[83] Etymologically, the word is derived from the Latin verb *intueri,* to look at or observe. As Scotus points out, it refers to viewing something that exists as present here and now. As the bodily eye sees what exists before it, so the intellect, as the eye of the mind, knows directly what exists and is immediately present to it. This includes the simple awareness of myself as an acting person. In a proposition asserting some such instance of self-awareness, the pronoun "I" is used as the subject of my statement. These actions of which I am aware can be either of an intellectual or a sense-perceptual nature, and they are expressed as verbs in the present tense. For example, I understand, I doubt, I choose, I regret, I am ashamed; or I hear, I feel, I smell. The basis for our certainty about such judgments does not stem from knowing the meaning of the terms but rather from some prior simple awareness of the situation expressed verbally in the form of a statement or proposition. What is immediately present to the intellect in this case is not the external object—such as the white plastic chair that I refer to when I point to it and assert, in answer to some question, perhaps: "I see something white." Rather, it is the fact that "I see"—my own activity, of which I am conscious. This is what is "present here and now" in its existential state to my intellect. And it is this activity that, Augustine insisted, is so immediate to us and so absolutely certain that in no way can we reasonably doubt it. As he expressed it in *The Trinity* 15.12, "I know that I live" because "to sleep or to see in dreams is characteristic of one who lives."

Even stronger than these statements in *The Trinity* is Augustine's refutation of the skeptics of the New Academy in his work *Against the Skeptics* (*Contra Academicos*): "I see no way that the academician can refute one who says: 'I know this looks white to me. I know I like what I hear and enjoy what I smell. I know this tastes sweet to me and that feels cold to me.'"[84] So long as one restricts such assertions to what one is intuitively aware of and does not assert that others experience this, or that all persons perceive these same things in the same way, we can be most certain of our own actions, Augustine maintained.

In the text we have cited here, Scotus wants to show that this same doctrine can be found in Aristotle. In book 4 of his *Metaphysics* (1011a3–9), Aristotle reminds us that the principles of demonstration are self-evident and hence cannot be made any clearer by trying to demonstrate them from other, equal or less evident propositions. Consequently, skeptics who challenge one to do so are foolishly "seeking a reason for things that have no reason." Those who try to formulate some a priori proof, for instance, based on what we can know from reflecting upon our actions make a bad job of it. Our certainty that we are awake and not dreaming is greater than any unquestionable knowledge that we can gain through introspective reflection. Hence, Scotus concludes that "we are not deceived about those acts that are in our power," though we may well be ignorant or unaware of many of the living processes that go on in our bodies.

Skeptics argue that we cannot trust what we see with our own eyes, because after staring long at some object and the eye is shut, we retain an afterimage of what we saw. Furthermore, if, in darkness, a person's closed eye is pressed or moved violently, a flash of fire is seen. Scotus points out that Aristotle discussed this optical phenomenon in some detail in his tract *De sensu et sensato* (437a23–26). There Aristotle points out that some Greek philosophers tried to explain the nature of the sense organs with what they knew of the physical elements:

> Not finding it easy to coordinate the five senses with the four elements [earth, water, air, fire],[85] they are at a loss respecting the fifth sense. But they hold the organ of sight to consist of fire, being prompted by a certain sensory affection of whose true cause they are ignorant. This is, when the eye is pressed, fire appears to flash from it.

Aristotle then proceeded to give his own scientific explanation of why this optical phenomenon occurs, and concludes that the eye sees a part of itself in this phenomenon. It sees itself as object, however, though it is just as unaware of itself as the subject as it is in ordinary vision.

The point that Scotus is making is that this phenomenon, as well as that of afterimages, is an unusual but true instance of "seeing" if we accept Aristotle's account of how the eye is structured. According to Augustine, even though we may see certain afterimages when the eyes are closed, vision is not deceived; but we do truly "see" because our visual power is not in the pupil as its organ but in the bunch of optic nerves, and therefore vision can still see the likeness that is still in the pupil. It is similar when one's eye is pressed, and one sees something like a flash of fire, as is clear from book 1 of *De sensu et sensato*.

Hence we can agree with Scotus's initial statement: "I say that . . . in the class of contingent propositions there are some that are immediate . . . and self-evident, and such are the propositions that refer to our actions, such as 'I sleep' and 'I am awake.'"

Conclusion

While Scotus in this section shows that an Aristotelian like himself can arrive at conclusions similar to those of Augustine without accepting his special theory of illumination, he also anticipates the refutation of skepticism by Descartes, who employed roughly this same epistemological ploy with his famous "Cogito, ergo sum." Though Scotus is primarily concerned with analyzing the nature of our knowledge of God in distinction 3 of his *Sentences*-commentaries, he uses it to present the main features of his theory of knowledge and to show how it differs from Henry's.

Two of the more original contributions he makes to this aspect of Scholastic philosophy are his theory of univocity and that of intuitive intellectual cognition. Univocity is required for two reasons, he pointed out: if our mind is initially a tabula rasa, then univocity is needed to have any knowledge of God, apart from a special illumination by the divine ideas; and if being qua being is to enjoy any primacy of common predication as the primary adequate object of the intellect, it must be predicable univocally of God and creatures, substance and accident. Since the Scholastics' notion of substance is what we might call today a theoretical entity, whereas accidents are those phenomena that a logical positivist would claim are all we really observe, Scotus's explanation of how we can rationally explain our knowledge of imperceptible things that we regard as real yet are not experienced directly through the senses has broader philosophical applications. It resembles in many respects the way a philosopher of science in the tradition of realism might explain a physicist's knowledge of theoretical entities.[86] His technique of showing why we cannot know God intuitively yet can have a proper concept of him constructed from common notions became known to subsequent Scholastics as the distinction between "cognitio propria ex propriis" (that is, proper knowledge "by acquaintance") and "cognitio propria ex communibus" (proper knowledge based on common notions). In the twentieth century, we find Georg Cantor using this Scholastic distinction to explain to a friend that the concepts that a mathematician has of irrational and transfinite numbers represent "proper knowledge" only in the second sense.[87] They are formed from concepts common (*ex communibus*) to other things.

Scotus shows that intuitive cognition is something our intellect possesses, not merely something characteristic of the external senses. For that reason Scotus insists that this notion, originally attributed to sense-perceptible knowledge, must be extended to the intellect as well. Scotus views intellectual intuitive cognition as accompanying, in a kind of peripheral way, every conscious act that we perform. The reason that philosophers stress abstract knowledge as characteristic of the intellect is that our knowledge begins with sense perception, and what we are intellectually aware of in external objects is what they have in common with one another. Such potentially universal intelligible characteristics are independent of what is present here and now or what needs to be ongoing or existing. That is why Scotus points out in his *Quodlibet* that it is

> helpful to distinguish two acts of the intellect at the level of simple apprehension or intellection of a simple object. One is indifferent as to whether the object is existing or not, and also whether it is present in reality or not. We often experience this act in ourselves, for universals and the essences of things we grasp equally well whether they exist extramentally in some subject or not, or whether we have an instance of them actually present or not. . . . But there is another act of understanding, though we do not experience it in ourselves with equal certitude, but it is possible. It is knowledge precisely of a present object as present and of an existing object as existing. . . . Now this sort of intellection can properly be called intuitive because it is an intuition of a thing as existing and present.[88]

It is clear from the cautious and tentative way that Scotus introduces the theory and continued to develop and clarify it over the course of his academic career that he considers himself to be a pioneer in this matter. The reaction of William of Ockham and Peter Auriol confirm this. Ockham cited Scotus to prove that his own theory of an intellectual intuition of both sensible and intelligible objects was not a personal innovation of his. Auriol questioned whether in the present life we have any truly intellectual intuition, as Scotus and Ockham maintained. From the time of Scotus onward, this subject continued to be treated by the late

Scholastics. We find it surfacing in various controversial contexts until it is given a new twist by Major, John Calvin's teacher, where it became a turning point in the history of theology.[89]

NOTES

1. See Robert Mulligan, "*Ratio Superior* and *Ratio Inferior:* The Historical Background"; Mulligan, "*Portio Superior* and *Portio Inferior* in the Writings of St. Bonaventure"; and John F. Quinn, *The Historical Constitution of St. Bonaventure's Philosophy,* esp. pt. 3, "Certitude and Illumination of Knowledge."

2. See "Agent Intellect" in Wippel and Wolter, *Medieval Philosophy,* 421–44. The Islamic philosophers, such as Avicenna and Averroes, identified it with one of the separate or bodiless substances (intelligences) associated (as final cause) with the movement of the celestial spheres. Among the Scholastics, Roger Bacon identified the agent intellect with God, but the later Scholastics, such as Bonaventure, Aquinas, Henry, and Scotus, regarded it as one of the natural powers possessed by the human soul. John Peckham, while admitting an active aspect to the human intellect, argued that "the agent intellect of which the Philosopher speaks is in no way part of the soul; rather as I believe, it is God who is the light of the Mind"; and again he says that Avicenna, who posited the agent intellect as a separated reality or Intelligence, did better than those who posit it as a part of the soul." See Etienne Gilson, *History of Christian Philosophy in the Middle Ages,* 360, 706.

3. The Arabian academy at Baghdad acquired from the Syrians, along with the genuine works of Aristotle, some pseudo-Aristotelian works, one of the most important of which was the Neoplatonic *Theology of Aristotle,* which is actually a series of excerpts from books 4–6 of the *Enneads* of Plotinus. See Ignatius Brady, *A History of Ancient Philosophy,* 194–95.

4. See note 9 below.

5. Gilson, *History of Christian Philosophy,* 408.

6. Since the condemnations of 1277 included a number of Aquinas's theses, many theologians, particularly in England—even Dominicans, such as Robert Kilwardby, but especially Franciscans, such as Roger Marston and John Peckham—reacted against Thomism as well as against the radical Aristotelianism of Siger and his followers. Henry was the leading representative of this reaction among the secular theologians at the University of Paris. Henry's conception of Aristotle was heavily influenced by Avicenna's earlier interpretation, which Neoaugustinians, such as Kilwardby and Peckham, could reconcile with the illumination theory of Augustine. Henry's highly personal synthesis has been described as a kind of Avicennian Augustinianism. See Wippel and Wolter, *Medieval Philosophy,* 376–77. For a treatment of Aquinas's role in the controversy, see Ralph McInerny's *Aquinas against the Averroists: On There Being Only One Intellect.*

7. Henry's advocates included the Franciscan Richard of Conington, who flourished around 1290–1310 and became a master at Oxford in 1305. He was a disciple of Henry and challenged Scotus's criticism of his master's theory of analogy. See Stephen F. Brown, "Richard of Conington and the Analogy of the Concept of Being."

8. This becomes clear in his treatment of truth and certitude: "Unde patet quod peccant qui ponunt quod prima principia et regulae speculabilium sunt impressiones quaedam a regulis veritatis aeternae et cum hoc non ponunt aliquam aliam impressionem fieri aut informationem in nostris conceptibus a luce aeterna quam illam solam qua sit a specie a re accepta adiutorio lucis naturalis ingenitae, nisi enim conceptus nostri a luce aeterna assistente nobis formarentur informes maneret nec veritatem vel simpliciter vel sinceram continerent, ut dictum est. Nec potens est lumen naturalis rationis ut ad ipsam concipiendam illuminare sufficiat nisi lumen aeternum ipsum accendat" (Henry of Ghent, *Summa quaestionum ordinariarum* art. 1, q. 3 [I, fol. 10G]).

9. Most of the Scholastics identified the agent intellect as a potency of the soul, whether they believed in some form of special illumination by divine ideas or not. Avicenna, however, believed that the agent intellect was a separate substance or intelligence that impressed transcendental notions in the possible intellect of the soul. See Avicenna, *Metaphysica* 1.6 in *Avicenna Latinus*, 1.5, pp. 31–32: "Dicemus igitur quod res et ens et necesse talia sunt quod statim imprimuntur in anima prima impressione, quae non acquiritur ex aliis notioribus se . . ." [We therefore say that "thing" and "being" and "necessary" are such that they are immediately impressed upon the soul by a first imposition that is not derived from anything better known than themselves]. Earlier Scholastics—such as Kilwardby and Roger Bacon—as believers in some form of divine illumination, considered God as the agent intellect and found it easier to identify with Avicenna's interpretation of Aristotle than with that of the radical Aristotelians, or of even Aquinas, who, like Scotus, believed that God gave human intellect all the illumination that was necessary to arrive at a rationally justified belief in God.

10. See Allan B. Wolter, "An Oxford Dialogue on Language and Metaphysics"; and Wolter, "A Scotistic Approach to the Ultimate Why-Question," esp. 113–16.

11. See Ignatius Brady, "St. Bonaventure's Doctrine of Illumination: Reactions Medieval and Modern."

12. Augustine, *The Trinity*, 8.3, pp. 247–48.

13. See Wolter, "Oxford Dialogue," 325–30; and Wolter, *The Philosophical Theology of John Duns Scotus*, 65–67.

14. Augustine, *The Trinity*, 9.6, p. 281. Just before, he pointed out: "Something similar takes place when I recall a beautifully and symmetrically intorted arch which I have seen, for example, in Carthage. In this case a certain reality, which was made known to my mind through the eyes and transferred to my memory, produces an imaginary view. But in my mind I behold something else, according to which that work pleases me; whence also, I should correct it if it displeased me. Therefore, we pass judgment upon these particular things according to that form of the eternal truth, and we perceive that form through the eye of the rational mind. But these particular things we touch, if present, with the bodily sense, or recall them, if absent, through the image fixed in our memory, or form images of things that are similar to them, such as we ourselves would also endeavor to construct, if we wished and were able. For we form images of bodies in our mind or see bodies through the body in one way, but we comprehend . . . etc." And in 7.12 (pp. 281–82), he continues: "With the eye of the mind, therefore, we perceive that eternal truth, from which all temporal things have been made, the form according to which we are, and by which we effect something either in ourselves or in bodies with a true and right reason. The true knowledge of things, thence conceived, we bear with us as a word, and beget by speaking from within; nor does it depart from us by being born. But in conversing with others we add the service of our voice or of some bodily sign to the word that remains within, in order to produce in the mind of the listener, by a kind of sensible remembrance, something similar to that which does not depart from the mind of the speaker."

15. Stephen Toulmin, *The Philosophy of Science*, 17–44; Norman R. Hanson, *Patterns of Discovery*, 4–30.

16. The Scholastics spoke of the goodness of creatures as "participated," since in creating them God communicated something of his own goodness to them. God's own goodness, by contrast, was said to be "unparticipated," since it was something that the divine nature possessed of itself and not from some extrinsic cause.

17. Avicenna, *Metaphysica* 1.6 (*Avicenna Latinus*, 31–32).

18. See Wippel and Wolter, *Medieval Philosophy*, 426, 430.

19. "[E]ven the godless think of eternity, and rightly condemn and rightly praise many things in the moral conduct of men. By what rules, pray, do they judge these things in which they see how each one ought to live, even though they themselves do not live in the same manner? Whence do they see them? For they do not see them in their own nature, since these things are doubtless in the mind, and their minds are admittedly changeable; . . . Where are these rules written in which even the unjust man recognizes what is just, and in which he perceives that he ought to have what he does not have? Where then, are they written except in the book of that light which is called Truth?" (Augustine, *The Trinity*, 14.15, pp. 440–41).

20. "Thus, when I call to mind the walls of Carthage which I have seen and form an image of those of Alexandria which I have not seen, and prefer some of these imaginary forms to others, I prefer them for a good reason; the judgment of the truth from above is strong and clear, and remains steadfast by the most incorruptible rules of its own right; and even if it is concealed by bodily images, as by a kind of cloud, still it is not hidden nor confused" (ibid., 9.6, p. 278).

21. It was not customary to mention the name of living or even recently deceased university masters whose views they were discussing, since the students he was addressing would be familiar with such.

22. "Ad hoc dicit quidam doctor sic: loquendo de cognitione alicuius, distingui potest, ex parte obiecti, quod potest cognosci per se vel per accidens, in particulari vel in universali. Realiter per accidens non cognoscitur Deus, quia quidquid de ipso cognoscitur, est ipse; tamen cognoscendo aliquod attributum eius, cognoscimus quasi per accidens quid est. Unde de attributis dicit Damascenus libro I cap. 4: 'Non naturam dicunt Dei sed quae circa naturam'" (*Ordinatio* I, d. 3, no. 20 ([Vat. 3:11]).

23. "In particulari non cognoscitur ex creaturis quia creatura est peregrina similitudo eius, sic quia tantum conformis ei quoad aliqua attributa, quae non sunt illa natura in particulari. Ergo cum nihil ducat in cognitionem alterius nisi sub ratione similis, sequitur etc." (ibid. [Vat. 3:20]).

24. "In universali etiam, puta in generali attributo, cognoscitur: non quidem in universali secundum predicationem quod dicatur de ipso—in quo nullum est universale, quia quiditas illa est de se singularis—sed in universali quod tantum analogice commune est sibi et creaturae; tamen quasi unum a nobis concipitur, propter proximitatem conceptuum, licet sint diversi conceptus" (ibid.).

25. "'Generalissime' tres habet gradus. Cognoscendo enim quodcumque ens ut hoc ens est, indistinctissime, concipitur ens quasi pars conceptus, et est primus gradus. Et amovendo 'hoc,' et concipiendo 'ens,' est secundus gradus; iam enim ut conceptum non ut pars, concipitur commune analogum Deo et creaturae" (*Ordinatio* I, d. 3, no. 21 [Vat. 3:12]).

26. "Quod si distinguatur conceptus entis qui Deo convenit, puta concipiendo ens indeterminatum negative, id est non determinabile a conceptu entis qui convenit analogice, quod est ens indeterminatum privative, iam est tertius gradus. Primo modo 'indeterminatum' abstrahitur ut forma ab omni materia, ut in se subsistens et participabilis; secundo modo 'indeterminatum' est universale abstractum a particularibus, quod est actu participatum in illis" (ibid. [Vat. 3:12–13]).

27. In *Ordinatio* IV, d. 8, q. 1, no. [2] (Vivès, 17.7) (Codex A, fol. 203rb), Scotus gives this descriptive definition: "ens, hoc est, cui non repugnat esse" [being, that is, that to which existence is not repugnant].

28. John Damascene likens God's perfections or attributes to drops of water that lose their separate identity when they are merged as a single sea of substance. In explaining the name God gave himself in Exodus 3:14, "Qui est" ("he who is"), he combines the idea of infinite or boundless perfection with the positive notion of its containing the whole of being, or *esse:* "Totum in seipso comprehendens habet esse, velut quoddam pelagus substantiae infinitum et indeterminatum" [He comprehends in himself the whole of being, as some kind of infinite and boundless sea of substance] (*De fide orthodoxa,* ed. E. M. Buytaert [St. Bonaventure, N.Y.: Franciscan Institute, 1955], chap. 9, 49).

29. Augustine, *The Trinity,* 9.12, [no. 18]. See, for example, Scotus *Lectura* I, d. 3, no. 26 (Vat. 16:234); *Ordinatio* I, d. 3, nos. 413, 550 (Vat. 3:250, 328); II, d. 3, no. 300 (Vat. 7:544).

30. Nec per speciem propriam cognoscitur, quia nihil est eo simplicius, sed ad modum aestimativae, per speciem aliquam alienam ex creaturis . . . (*Ordinatio* I, d. 3, no. 21 [Vat. 3:13]).

31. Scotus described Henry's unearthing process more fully in his earlier *Lectura* I, d. 3, no. 13 (Vat. 16:228); cf. Henry of Ghent, *Summa,* art. 1, q. 1 ad 7 (I, fol. 3K).

32. "Est ergo mens quaestionis ista, utrum aliquem conceptum simplicem possit intellectus viatoris naturaliter habere, in quo conceptu simplici concipiatur Deus" (*Ordinatio* I, d. 3, no. 19 [Vat. 3:11]).

33. Scotus uses *ens* (being) and *res* (thing) interchangeably. See his *Quodlibet,* q. 3, no. [2] (Vivès 25:13–14); and *God and Creatures* 3.8, p. 61.

34. In his *Quodlibet,* q. 3, no. 2 (*God and Creatures* 3.6–14, pp. 61–63), Scotus clarifies the various senses in which "being" or "thing" was used by philosophers in his day.

35. "Praeterea, omnes magistri et theologi videntur uti conceptu communi Deo et creaturae, licet contradicant verbo quando applicant, nam in hoc conveniunt omnes quod accipiunt conceptus metaphysicales

et removendo illud quod est imperfectionis in creaturis, attribuunt Deo quod est perfectionis, ut bonitatem, veritatem et sapientiam" (*Lectura* I, d. 3, no. 29 [Vat. 16:235]).

36. "Magistri etiam tractantes de Deo sive de his quae cognoscuntur de Deo et creaturis observant unitatem univocationis entis in doctrina seu in modo dicendi, sicut patet; licet in voce contradicunt" (*Reportatio* I A, d. 3; Merton College, Oxford, cod. 59, fol. 33v).

37. According to the anonymous Scotist of Vatican Latin MS 869, this argument was challenged by Richard of Conington, a Franciscan disciple of Henry's. This caused Scotus to add additional arguments in his revised *ordinatio*. In a marginal note recorded by the scribe of Codex A and two other manuscripts, he indicates that one could give as many as ten distinct arguments to prove univocation. See Vat. 3:29, line 3, which reads: "Nota, circa secundum sunt decem rationes: prima de conceptu certo et dubio" [Note: concerning the second point, there are ten arguments, the first of which (starts with the idea) of concepts that are certain and doubtful].

38. Pseudo-Dionysius was believed to have been the Athenian disciple whom the apostle Paul converted in his address to the Areopagus (Acts 17.34). Hence his writings were regarded with the highest respect.

39. *Quodlibet*, q. 14, no. 16. Cf. *God and Creatures*, 14.63, p. 332: "All such external motion consequently is contingent and hence has God's will itself as its immediate principle. No created intellect, consequently, is moved in a natural fashion by the essence as essence. All knowledge of this essence that is not caused by anything created is caused immediately by the divine will."

40. *Quodlibet*, q. 5. Cf. *God and Creatures*, 5.5, pp. 108–9.
41. Aristotle, *Physics* 3.4.203b 24–26.
42. Augustine, *The Trinity*, 9.6.
43. Scotus, *God and Creatures*, 5.6, pp. 109–10.
44. *God and Creatures*, 5.7, p. 109.
45. Aristotle, *Physics* 3.6.207a7–9.
46. *God and Creatures*, 5.8, p. 110.
47. *God and Creatures*, 5.9, p. 110.
48. *God and Creatures*, 5.9, pp. 110–11.
49. *God and Creatures*, 5.10, pp. 111–12.
50. *God and Creatures*, 5.11, p. 112.

51. "Dico quod conceptus conclusi per modum complexionis conveniunt Deo, nec conveniunt creaturae; huiusmodi sunt conceptus compositi, non autem simplices conceptus, cuiusmodi sunt conceptus entis, boni, etc., nam tales conceptus dicuntur univoce de Deo et creatura" [I say that concepts proper to God and not to creatures are concepts inferred by way of a proposition. Only complex concepts are of this sort—not simple ones, such as "being," "good," etc., for such simple concepts are said univocally of God and creatures] (*Collatio* 13, no. 4 [Vivès 5:202]).

52. *Ordinatio* I, d. 3, q. 3 (Vat. 3:68).
53. Scotus, *Ordinatio* I, d. 3, no. 117 (Vat. 3:72–73).
54. Augustine, *The Trinity*, 8.3, pp. 247–48.

55. "One always knows the essence that is in a creature by virtue of knowing that essence as it is in God. . . . For no one can know this [particular instance of] good or beauty, in its nature and essence—whether it is qualitative or quidditative being—except by knowing good and be-

ing absolutely. . . . This is the way participated good and being stand with respect to nonparticipated good and being" (Henry, *Summa,* art. 24, q. 8 [I, fol. 145P]).

56. Scotus, *Ordinatio* I, d. 3, no. 126 (Vat. 3:79).
57. Ibid., no. 127 (Vat. 3:79–80).
58. Ibid., no. 128 (Vat. 3:80).
59. According to Aristotle, things are said to be different (*diapheronta*) if they have something in common and to be other (*hetera*) if they have nothing in common. See *Metaphysics* 10.3.10054b 23–30. The *hetera* were what the Scholastics referred to as *primo diversa.*
60. Scotus distinguished ultimate specific differences from those that are not irreducibly simple. In a concept such as "living body," for example, he considered that what makes the body living is a soul, which is the form of the body and a distinct being, if predicated as a noun, of which being could be predicated *in quid.*
61. Aristotle, *Posterior Analytics* 1.4.73a 37–73b 5; *Metaphysics* 7.5.1031a 2–14.
62. Aristotle, *Metaphysics* 7.5.1031a 1–4.
63. Ibid., 1030b 34.
64. Since a subject is contained "as an addition" in the description of what these primitive differences or attributes mean, it can be said to be predicated of them "denominatively" or "derivatively." Scotus explains this in one of his Oxford *collationes,* for example, in answer to the objection that "if the common univocal concept is contracted, it is necessary that it be contracted by some addition. This addition is either a being or it is not a being. For it is necessary that whatever contracts another lies outside the notion of that which it contracts." (This is numbered as *collatio* 3 by C. R. S. Harris, *Duns Scotus,* 2:371–75, and as *collatio* 24 by C. Balić, "De Collationibus Ioannis Duns Scoti, Doctoris Subtilis ac Mariani," 215–16.) See Wolter, *Transcendentals,* 95–96.
65. For an exposition of Henry's doctrines on truth and illumination, see the studies of Jerome V. Brown: "Divine Illumination in Henry of Ghent," "Duns Scotus on the Possibility of Knowing Genuine Truth: The Reply to Henry of Ghent in the 'Lectura Prima' and in the 'Ordinatio,'" and "Sensation in Henry of Ghent: A Late Mediaeval Aristotelian-Augustinian Synthesis."
66. In order to bring out the engagement with the particulars of Henry's doctrine, Scotus worded this question somewhat differently when he revised his *lectura* as an *ordinatio.* In the final version of this work, the question reads: "Can the intellect of a pilgrim acquire some certain and unadulterated truth naturally without the special illumination of the uncreated light? [Utrum aliqua veritas certa et sincera possit naturaliter cognosci ab intellectu viatoris absque lucis increatae speciali illustratione]."
67. Henry, *Summa,* art 1., q. 2 (I, fol. 5F).
68. Ibid. (fol. 5E).
69. Augustine, *Eighty-three Different Questions,* q. 9, pp. 40–41.
70. Ponitur autem qualiter habeat triplicem rationem respectu actus videndi, scilicet: lucis acuentis, speciei immutantis et characteris sive exemplaris configurantis; et ex hoc concluditur ultra quod requiritur specialis influentia, quia sicut illa essentia non videtur naturaliter a nobis in se, ita, ut illa essentia est exemplar respectu alicuius creatu-

rae, naturaliter non videtur, secundum Augustinum *De videndo Deum*—in eius enim potestate est videri: 'si vult, videtur, si non vult non videtur.' Ultimo additur quod perfecta notitia veritatis est quando duae species exemplares concurrunt in mente: una inhaerens, scilicet creata, alia illapsa, scilicet non creata et sic contingimus verbum perfectae veritatis (Scotus, *Ordinatio* I, d. 3, nos. 216–17 [Vat. 3:131–32]).

71. Nisi enim conceptus nostri a luce aeterna assistente nobis formarentur, informes maneret nec veritatem vel simpliciter vel sinceram continerent, ut dictum est. Nec potens est lumen naturalis rationis ut ad ipsam concipiendam illuminare sufficiat nisi lumen aeternum ipsum accendat (Henry, *Summa,* art. 1, q. 3 [I, fol. 10G]).

72. *Lectura* I, d. 3, nos. 162–66 (Vat. 16:289–91); Augustine, *Soliloquia* 1.8.15; Aristotle, *Metaphysics* 1.1.993b4–5.

73. *Lectura* I, d. 3, no. 167 (Vat. 16:291); Augustine, *The Trinity,* 15.12.

74. Ibid., p. 481; Scotus cites this text in *Ordinatio* I, d. 3, no. 227 (Vat. 3:136).

75. We focus here on Scotus's Oxford *Lectura,* since it shows that he had already developed the rough outlines of his epistemology early in his academic career. Those interested can compare his account here with that in the *Ordinatio,* found in Allan B. Wolter, *John Duns Scotus: Philosophical Writings,* 106–15.

76. *Ordinatio* I, d. 3, no. 230 (Vat. 3:138–39).

77. On the difference between these two types of inferred knowledge, see Aristotle, *Posterior Analytics* 1.13.

78. Sed quomodo habetur certitudo eorum quae subsunt actibus sensus, puta quod aliquid extra est album vel calidum, quale apparet? (Scotus, *Ordinatio* I, d. 3, no. 240 [Vat. 3:146]).

79. Scotus seems to have in mind the case where the dimensions of a given object would seem to diminish if, when it is at a distance, it were held up to the same measuring staff used to measure it when it was close by.

80. Respondeo: Aut circa tale cognitum eadem opposita apparent diversis sensibus, aut non, sed omnes sensus cognoscentes illud, habent idem iudicium de eo. Si secundo modo, tunc certitudo habetur de veritate talis cogniti per sensus, et per istam propositionem praecedentem "quod evenit in pluribus ab aliquo, illud est causa naturalis eius, si non sit causa libera." Ergo cum ab isto, praesente, "ut in pluribus" evenit talis immutatio sensus, sequitur quod immutatio, vel species genita, sit effectus naturalis talis causae, et ita tale extra erit album vel calidum, vel tale aliquid quale natum est praesentari per speciem, genitam ab ipso "ut in pluribus."

Si autem diversi sensus habeant diversa iudicia, de aliquo viso extra—puta visus dicit baculum esse fractum, cuius pars est in aqua, et pars est in aere; visus semper dicit solem esse minoris quantitatis quam est, et omne visum a remotis esse minus quam sit—in talibus est certitudo, quid verum sit et quis sensus erret, per propositionem quiescentem in anima, certiorem omni iudicio sensus, et per actus plurium sensuum concurrentes, ita quod semper aliqua propositio rectificat intellectum de actibus sensus, quis sit verus et quis falsus, in qua propositione intellectus non dependet a sensu sicut a causa sed sicut ab occasione. Exemplum. Intellectus habet istam propositionem quiescentem: "nullum durius frangitur tactu alicuius mollis sibi cedentis." Haec est ita per se nota ex terminis quod, etiam si essent accepti a sensibus errantibus, non potest intellectus dubitare de illa, immo oppositum includit contradictionem. Sed quod baculus sit durior aqua et aqua sibi cedat, hoc dicit uterque sensus, tam visus quam tactus.

Sequitur ergo "baculus non est fractus," sicut sensus iudicat ipsum fractum, —et ita quis sensus erret et quis non, circa fractionem baculi, intellectus iudicat per certius omni actu sensus. Similiter, ex alia parte: quod "quantum applicatum quanto, omnino est aequale sibi," hoc est notum intellectui quantumcumque notitia terminorum accipiatur a sensu errante; sed quod idem "quantum" possit applicari viso propinquo et remoto, hoc dicit tam visus quam tactus; ergo "quantum," visum sive a prope sive a remotis, est aequale, —ergo visus dicens hoc esse minus, errat.

Haec conclusio concluditur ex principiis per se notis, et ex actibus duorum sensuum cognoscentium, "ut in pluribus" esse ita. Et ita ubicumque ratio iudicat sensum errare, hoc iudicat non per aliquam notitiam praecise acquisitam a sensibus ut causa, sed per aliquam notitiam occasionatam a sensu, in qua non fallitur etiam si omnes sensus fallantur, et per aliquam aliam notitiam, acquisitam a sensu vel a sensibus "ut in pluribus," quae sciuntur esse vera per propositionem saepe allegatam, scilicet "quod in pluribus evenit" etc. (Scotus, *Ordinatio* I, d. 3, nos. 240–45 [Vat. 3:146–48]).

81. Scotus, *Lectura*, prol., nos. 114–18 (Vat. 16:41–43).

82. Scotus, *Ordinatio* I, d. 3, no. 238 (Vat. 3:144): "Dico quod est certitudo de multis eorum sicut de primis et per se notis, —quod patet IV *Metaphysicae*."

83. Webster's *New World Dictionary of American English*, 3d College edition (New York: Simon and Schuster, 1988).

84. Augustine, *Contra Academicos* 3.11.26.

85. Aristotle's own view is that the eye is composed of water, the ear is composed of air, the organ of smell is composed of fire, the organ of touch is composed of earth, and taste is a form of touch (*De sensu et sensato* 438b 16–30).

86. See, for example, Mary Hesse, "Models and Analogies in Science."

87. Georg Cantor, *Gesammelte Abhandlungen*, 402–3; cf. Wolter, *Philosophical Theology*, 57–58.

88. Question 6, no. [7]; see *God and Creatures*, 6.17–18, pp. 135–37.

89. Wolter, *The Philosophical Theology of John Duns Scotus*, 98–122; Thomas F. Torrence, "Intuitive and Abstractive Knowledge from Duns Scotus to John Calvin."

CHAPTER FIVE | Two Metaphysical Questions

Text

1. Natura: Individualis, Universalis, et Indifferens

Sicut[1] dictum est in solutione primae quaestionis (de hac materia) quod natura prius est naturaliter quam haec natura, et unitas propria—consequens naturam ut natura—est prior naturaliter unitate eius ut haec natura; et sub ista ratione est consideratio metaphysica de natura, et assignatur definitio eius, et sunt propositiones per se primo modo. In eodem igitur quod est unum numero, est aliqua entitas, quam consequitur minor unitas quam sit unitas numeralis, et est realis; et illud cuius est talis unitas, formaliter est "de se unum" unitate numerali. Concedo igitur quod unitas realis non est alicuius exsistentis in duobus individuis, sed in uno. . . .

Ita[2] concedo quod quidquid est in hoc lapide, est unum numero,—vel primo, vel per se, vel denominative: "primo" forte, ut illud per quod unitas talis convenit huic composito; "per se" hic lapis, cuius illud quod est primo unum hac unitate, est per se pars; "denominative" tantum, illud potentiale quod perficitur isto actuali, quod quasi denominative respicit actualitatem eius. . . .

Et[3] si quaeras a me quae est ista "entitas individualis" a qua sumitur differentia individualis, estne materia vel forma vel compositum,—respondeo: Omnis entitas quiditativa—sive par-tialis sive totalis—alicuius generis, est de se indifferens "ut entitas quiditativa" ad hanc entitatem et illam, ita quod "ut entitas quiditativa" est naturaliter prior ista entitate ut haec est,—et ut prior est naturaliter, sicut non convenit sibi esse hanc, ita non repugnat sibi ex ratione sua suum oppositum; et

---

1. *Ordinatio* II, d. 3, no. 172 (Vat.7, 476).
2. *Ordinatio* II, d. 3, no. 175 (Vat. 7, 477–78).
3. *Ordinatio* II, d. 3, no. 187–88 (Vat. 7, 483–84).

Individuation, Universals, and Common Nature

As was stated in the solution to the first question on this matter [of individuation], nature is prior naturally to "this nature," and the unity proper—which follows on nature qua nature—is prior naturally to its unity qua this nature. And it is under this prior aspect that there is a metaphysical consideration of the nature, and its definition is assigned and propositions are true in the first mode of per se predication. And therefore in the same thing that is one in number, there is some entity to which is attributed a unity that is less than numerical, and that unity is real; and that to which such a unity pertains is made formally "one *de se*" by numerical unity. Therefore, I concede that this real unity is not something existing in two individuals but in one. . . .

And so I concede that whatever is in this stone is one numerically—either primarily or per se or derivatively. That [individuating difference or haecceity] through which such unity pertains to this composite would perhaps be such primarily; this stone would be such per se, [for] that which is primarily one by this unity [or individuating difference] is a per se part of the "this"; that potential [i.e., the stone-nature, in itself less than numerically one] which is perfected by this actual [individuating difference] is only derivatively one numerically with respect to its actuality. . . .

And if you ask me, What is this "individuating entity" from which the individual difference is taken? Is it matter or form or the composite? I give you this answer: Every quidditative entity—be it partial or total—of any sort is of itself indifferent as a quidditative entity to this entity and that, so that as a quidditative entity it is naturally prior to this entity as just *this*. Now just as, in this natural priority, it does not pertain to it to be this, neither is it repugnant to its essential nature to be other than

sicut compositum non includit suam entitatem (qua formaliter est "hoc") in quantum natura, ita nec materia "in quantum natura" includit suam entitatem (qua est "haec materia"), nec forma "in quantum natura" includit suam.

Non est igitur "ista entitas" materia vel forma vel compositum, in quantum quodlibet istorum est "natura,"—sed est ultima realitas entis quod est materia vel quod est forma vel quod est compositum; ita quod quodcumque commune, et tamen determinabile, adhuc potest distingui (quantumcumque sit una res) in plures realitates formaliter distinctas, quarum haec formaliter non est illa: et haec est formaliter entitas singularitatis, et illa est entitas naturae formaliter. Nec possunt istae duae realitates esse res et res, sicut possunt esse realitas unde accipitur genus et realitas unde accipitur differentia (ex quibus realitas specifica accipitur), —sed semper in eodem (sive in parte sive in toto) sunt realitates eiusdem rei, formaliter distinctae.

2. De Voluntate

"Palam[4] quia et potentiarum aliae erunt irrationabiles, aliae cum ratione, quapropter omnes artes et scientiae factivae potentiae sunt" [*Metaphysica* 9.2.1046b1–4].

Utrum differentia quam assignat Aristoteles inter potentias rationales et irrationales sit conveniens, scilicet quod istae sint oppositorum, hae unius oppositi. . . .

[V]idetur Aristoteles causam differentiae ponere talem, quia forma naturalis solummodo est principium assimilandi uni opposito similitudine naturali, sicut ipsa est ipsa et non opposita. Forma autem intellectus, puta scientia, est principium assimilandi oppositis similitudine intentionali, sicut et ipsa est virtualiter similitudo plurium oppositorum cognitorum, cum alterum contrariorum includat privationem alterius. Agens autem illius est activum, quod potest sibi assimilari secundum formam qua agit; ideo videtur Aristoteles ponere dictam differentiam. . . .

[S]ciendum est quod prima distinctio potentiae activae est secundum diversum modum eliciendi operationem. Quod enim circa hoc vel circa illud agat, etsi aliquo modo distinguat aut

---

4. *Quaestiones in Metaphysicam* IX, q. 15; text and English translation from *Duns Scotus on the Will and Morality*, 144–45, 148–49, 150–55, 168–69.

just *this*. And as the composite does not include qua nature its entity whereby it is this matter, nor does its form qua nature include its entity whereby it is this form.

This [individuating] entity, therefore, is not the matter or the form or the composite insofar as each of these is a "nature"; rather, it is the ultimate reality of the being that is the matter or that is the form or that is the composite; so that whatever is common and nevertheless determinable, no matter how much it is only one real thing, we can still distinguish further several formally distinct realities, of which this formally is not that; and this is formally the entity of singularity, and that is formally the entity of a nature. Nor can these two realities ever be two distinct real things, in the way that one reality might be that from which the genus is taken and another reality that from which the difference is taken (from which two realities the specific reality as a whole is taken); rather, in the same real thing there are always formally distinct realities (be they in the same real part or the same real whole).

I 2. On the Will

Text of Aristotle: "It is clear that some potencies will be nonrational, but others will be with reason. Hence, all the arts or productive sciences are potencies."

Is the difference that Aristotle assigns between the rational and irrational potencies appropriate, namely, that the former are capable of contrary effects but the latter produce but one effect? . . .

Aristotle seems to have understood the distinction to stem from the fact that a natural form is a principle for making only one pair of opposites, that which resembles itself naturally, just as this is this and not its opposite. But a form that is in the intellect, in the way that knowledge informs the mind, is a principle for representing opposites by an intentional likeness, just as knowledge is a virtual likeness of opposites [e.g., medical science is knowledge of both health and sickness], since one of the contraries includes the privation of the other. But the agent is active in regard to what can be modeled according to the form by which it acts. For this reason, then, Aristotle appears to have introduced the distinction. . . .

[K]eep in mind that the primary distinction of active potencies stems from the radically different way in which they elicit their respective operations [rather than from what they are concerned with]. For if we can somehow distinguish them because one acts in regard to this, another in regard to that, such a dis-

distinctionem ostendat, non tamen ita immediate. Non enim potentia ad obiectum circa quod operatur, comparatur nisi mediante operatione quam elicit, et hoc sic vel sic. Iste autem modus eliciendi operationem propriam non potest esse in genere nisi duplex: aut enim potentia ex se est determinata ad agendum, ita quod quantum est ex se, non potest non agere quando non impeditur ab extrinseco; aut non est ex se determinata, sed potest agere hunc actum vel oppositum actum, agere etiam vel non agere. Prima potentia communiter dicitur "natura," secunda dicitur "voluntas." Unde prima divisio principiorum activorum est in naturam et voluntatem. Iuxta quod Aristoteles in II *Physicorum* [cc. 4–6] duas ponit causas moventes per accidens: casum, iuxta naturam; et fortunam, iuxta propositum sive voluntatem.

Si ergo huius differentiae quaeritur causa (quare scilicet natura est unius tantum, hoc est, cuiuscumque vel quorumcumque sit, determinate ex se est illius vel illorum; voluntas autem est oppositorum, id est, ex se indeterminate huius actionis vel oppositae, seu actionis vel non actionis?), dici potest quod huius nulla est causa. Sicut enim effectus immediatus ad causam immediatam comparatur ex se et primo sine causa media, alioquin iretur in infinitum, ita causa activa ad suam actionem inquantum ipsam elicit videtur immediate se habere; nec est dare aliam causam quare sic elicit nisi quia est talis causa. Sed hoc est illud cuius causa quaerebatur. Sicut igitur calidum calefacit quia calidum, nec ista propositio "Calidum calefacit" est mediata, sed prima in quarto modo per se, ita et haec "Calidum ex se determinata calefacit." Similiter illa "Voluntas vult" et "Voluntas non vult determinate determinatione necessaria ex se."

[*Instantiae*] Contra ista obiicitur primo sic: ista propositio est contingens "Voluntas vult"; si voluntas non est ex se determinata ad volendum, quomodo illa propositio contingens est immediata?

tinction is not so immediate [i.e., radical or basic]. For a power or potency is related to the object in regard to which it acts only by means of some operation that it elicits in one way or another, and there is only a twofold generic way that an operation proper to a potency can be elicited. For either the potency of itself is determined to act, so that so far as it is concerned, it cannot fail to act when not impeded from without; or it is not of itself so determined but can perform either this act or its opposite or can either act or not act at all. A potency of the first sort is commonly called nature, whereas one of the second sort is called will. Hence, the primary division of active potencies is into nature and will—a distinction that Aristotle had in mind in book 2 of *Physics* when he assumed that there were two incidental, or *per accidens*, efficient causes: chance, which is reducible to nature; and fortune, which involves purpose or will.

Suppose someone seeks a further reason for this distinction. Just why does nature have to do with only one sort of action? That is, if it has to do with this or that, why is it determined of itself to cause just this effect or these effects, whatever they may be, whereas will, by contrast, has alternatives, that is, it is not intrinsically determined to this action or its opposite, or for that matter to acting or not acting at all? One could reply to such a question that there is no further reason for this. Just as any immediate effect is related to its immediate cause primarily and per se, without benefit of any mediating cause—otherwise one could go on ad infinitum looking for reasons—so an active cause [as opposed to a material or other cause] seems to be immediately related to the action that it elicits. One can give no other reason why it elicits its action in this way except that it is this sort of cause. Yet this is precisely what one is [foolishly] asking a reason for. "Heat heats" because it is heat, and the proposition "Heat heats" is not a mediate proposition [i.e., it is not a conclusion] but is rather a primary proposition in the fourth mode of per se predication, as is also the proposition "Heat is determined of itself to heat." "The will wills" and "The will does not will in a definite way by reason of some intrinsically necessary specification" would be similar sorts of statements.

[*Two objections*] Against this it is first objected that the proposition "The will wills" is contingent. If the will were not determined of itself to will, how would any contingent proposition be immediate?

Secundo sic, quare ponitur ista indeterminatio in voluntate, si non potest probari per naturam voluntatis?

[*Solutiones*] Ad primum responsio: ex necessariis non sequitur contingens. Patet: accipiatur aliqua contingens; si est immediata, habetur propositum; si non, detur medium; altera praemissa ad ipsam est contingens, alias ex necessariis inferetur contingens; illa praemissa contingens si est mediata, altera praemissa ad ipsam erit contingens, et sic in infinitum, nisi stetur in aliqua contingente immediata.

Confirmatur I *Posteriorum* ultimo [19.82a2–8]: vult Aristoteles quod contingit opinari "propter quid," scilicet per immediata, et "quia," per mediata; ita in propositio "Voluntas vult A." Si non est causa inter extrema, habetur propositum. Si est causa, puta "Voluntas vult B," ulterius procedetur. Stabitur alicubi! Ubi? Quare illud voluntas volet? Nulla est alia causa nisi quia est voluntas. Et tamen, si illa ultima propositio esse necessaria, non antecederet sola ad aliquam contingentem.

Ad secundum, a posteriori probatur. Experitur enim qui vult se posse non velle sive nolle, iuxta quod de libertate voluntatis alibi diffusius habetur.

[*Dubium*] Secundo, dubitatur circa praedicta: quomodo reducetur talis potentia ad actum, si indeterminata est ex se ad agendum et non agendum?

Responsio: est quaedam indeterminatio insufficientiae, sive ex potentialitate et defectu actualitatis, sicut materia non habens formam est indeterminata ad agendum actionem formae. Est alia superabundantis sufficientiae quae est ex illimitatione

Second, there is this objection. Why postulate this indeterminacy in the will if it cannot be proved to follow from the nature of the will? [In which case "The will wills" would be a conclusion and not a per se proposition of the fourth mode.]

[*Solutions*] The answer to the first is that the contingent does not follow from the necessary. This is clear if you consider some contingent proposition. If it is immediate, we have what we seek; if not, then there is some proposition that is intermediate; but this other premise from which it follows is also contingent; otherwise, a contingent proposition could be inferred from necessary premises [which is logically impossible]. But if this intermediate premise is contingent [according to the objector], there must be some further contingent proposition from which it follows; and so ad infinitum, unless one stops with some proposition that is admittedly immediate [or axiomatic].

What Aristotle says near the end of the *Posterior Analytics*, book 1, confirms this. There his meaning is that opining occurs both as a truth that is "propter quid" (that is, it is expressed in terms of a first principle or immediate proposition) and as a factual, or "quia," proposition that needs further proof. And so it is with the proposition under consideration, "The will wills A." If there is no further cause or mediate reason why this is the case, then our proposal is conceded [namely, that it is a first, or per se, proposition]. If there is some reason or cause, such as "Because the will wills B," then one inquires further. Somewhere, however, you must stop. Where? Why does the will will this last? There is no other cause to be found except that the will is will. And yet if this last proposition were necessary, it could not be the sole premise from which something contingent followed.

As for the second objection [i.e., that indeterminacy must be proved from the nature of the will and hence a priori], the proof here is a posteriori, for the person who wills [some object] experiences that he could have nilled or not willed what he did, according to what has been explained more at length elsewhere about the will's liberty.

[*A doubt*] A further doubt arises about the aforesaid. What reduces such a potency to act if it is of itself undetermined toward acting or not acting?

I reply: there is a certain indeterminacy of insufficiency, based on potentiality and a defect of actuality, in the way, for instance, that matter without a form is indeterminate as regards the actuation given by the form. There is another indeterminacy, however, that of a superabundant sufficiency, based on unlimited

actualitatis, vel simpliciter vel quodammodo. Primo modo indeterminatum non reducitur ad actum nisi prius determinetur ad formam ab alio. Secundo modo indeterminatum potest se determinare. Si enim posset hoc si haberet actum limitatum, quanto magis si illimitatum, cum nullo tunc careat quod fuit simpliciter principium agendi? Alioquin Deus, qui est summe indeterminatus ad quamcumque actionem indeterminatione illimitationis actualitatis, non posset aliquid ex se agere, quod est falsum. Exemplum huius: ignis est calefactivus, nec quaeritur extrinsecum a quo determinetur ad agendum; si tunc nulla diminutione facta in perfectione caloris daretur sibi perfectio frigoris, quare non ita ex se determinari posset ad calefaciendum, ut prius? . . . Indeterminatio autem quae ponitur in voluntate non est materialis, nec imperfectionis, inquantum ipsa est activa, sed est excellentis perfectionis et potestatis non alligatae ad determinatum actum. . . .

[*Ad Argumentum Principale*] [P]atet quod potentia rationalis, prout dicitur esse voluntas, est contrariorum non simul fiendorum, sed potest se determinare ad alterutrum; non sic intellectus. Cum arguitur contra, possum me non sedere nunc, supposito quod sedeam, dico quod in sensu compositionis propositio de possibili, componendo opposita, est falsa, quia notat potentiam ad opposita simul. In sensu divisionis autem dicerent aliqui quod quando est sessio, est necessario, iuxta illud I *Perihermenias*: "Omne quod est, quando est [necesse est esse]," et nihil pro tunc possibile, sed tantum pro instanti priori pro quo potuit non fore nunc. Et isti non videntur quod possint salvare voluntatem nunc esse potentiam ad oppositum eius quod inest. Huius positionis absurditas patet, quod scilicet necessitas et contingentia non sint proprie conditiones entium quando existunt, sed tunc necessitas et contingentia numquam, quia quando non est, nec est necessario nec contingenter. Quomodo etiam illa auctoritas I *Perihermenias* pro illis non facit propter fallaciam consequentis et figurae dictionis et propter secundum quid et simpliciter prolixum esset nunc explicare. Potest dici aliter quod voluntas quando est in aliqua volitione, tunc contingenter est in illa, et illa volitio tunc contingenter est ab ipsa;

actuality, either in an unqualified or in a qualified sense. The first sort of indeterminacy is not reduced to actuality unless it first is determined to some form by something else. Something indeterminate in the second sense, however, can determine itself. If this could occur where some limited actuality exists, how much more where the actuality is unlimited! For it would lack nothing required for an acting principle. Otherwise, God—who, in virtue of his indeterminacy of unlimited actuality, is supremely underdetermined in regard to any action whatsoever—would be unable to do anything of himself, which is false. Take this example: fire has the ability to heat, neither do we seek anything extrinsic to fire itself that determined it to burn. Suppose, without losing any of its perfection as heat, it were given the perfection of coldness, why should it not be able to determine itself to heat something, as before? . . . But the indetermination ascribed to the will is not like that of matter, nor, insofar as it is active, is it the indeterminacy of imperfection; rather it is the indeterminacy of surpassing perfection and power, not restricted to some specific act. . . .

[*Reply to an initial argument*] [I]t is clear that a rational potency, such as the will is said to be, does not have to perform opposites simultaneously but rather can determine itself to either alternative, which is something that the intellect cannot do. When it is objected that I am unable to be not seated, on the assumption I am sitting, my answer is this: A proposition about the possible would be false in the composite sense, because it would imply that I could do both at once. In the divided sense, however, some would say that when the sitting occurs, this is so necessarily, according to that principle in *De interpretatione,* "That which is must needs be when it is," and that nothing else is possible then but only at the moment before, when the present situation could have been otherwise. And these persons see no way of saving the claim that *now* the will has a potency for the opposite of the state it is actually in. This is absurd, however, for it would mean that necessity and contingency are not properly conditions of being at the time they exist. But if that were true, necessity and contingency would never exist, for when something is not existent, it is neither necessary nor contingent. It would take too long, however, to explain now why the *De interpretatione* principle does not support their claims, because their argument is invalid on three counts, being an instance of the fallacy of consequent, of figure of speech, and of the simple and qualified sense. To put the matter in another way, one could say that when the will is in a certain state of volition, it is in that state contingently, and that its present

nisi enim tunc, numquam, quia numquam alias est ab ipsa. Et sicut illa contingenter inest, ita voluntas tunc est potentia potens respectu oppositi, et pro tunc in sensu divisionis; non scilicet quod possit illud oppositum ponere simul cum isto, sed quod possit illud oppositum ponere in hoc intanti, non ponendo illud aliud in hoc instanti, quod tamen illud aliud divisim ponit in hoc instanti, et hoc non necessario sed contingenter.

volition stems from it contingently, for if it does not do so then, it will never do so, since at no other time does it proceed from the will. And just as this particular volition is contingently in the will, at that very moment the will is a potency with power over its opposite; and this holds for that moment in the divided sense—not that it could will the opposite at the same time as it wills this, but in the sense that it has the power to will the contrary at that very instant by not willing the other at that instant. For at this very instant it could, nevertheless, posit the other, in a divided sense, and do this not necessarily but contingently.

Commentary

Individuation, Universals, and Common Nature

Because Aristotle's theory of individuation by matter was regarded by many medieval theologians as unacceptable for several reasons, it became one of the more controversial issues in university circles, especially at Paris and Oxford in the latter portion of the thirteenth century. Scotus devoted a series of seven questions to a discussion of the various theories proposed by contemporaries in both his *Lectura* and *Ordinatio*. If we read any of his writings, however, it becomes clear that in raising these questions on individuation, he was less concerned with the problem of the metaphysical composition of matter than with a more fundamental epistemological and psychological question, namely, the objective nature of our intellectual knowledge.[1]

The problem arose because the human intellect, with its gift of generalization, invariably grasps some common or potentially universal characteristic of sense-perceptible objects and yet discovers no reason why this sortal aspect has to be associated with just *this* rather than *that* individual. If every descriptive word or phrase or every notion that the mind abstracts from an individual object or thing seems to be something that could be duplicated or multiplied indefinitely, then it cannot be what makes *this* uniquely individual. Rather, it represents some common property or feature that this individual shares with other individuals. Even if one grants that formal universality arises only when the concept in the intellect is perceived as common and predicable of many individuals, there still seems to be something in the nature of each thing that is isomorphic with the sort of thing we think it to be. This can best be expressed as an identity as to its form or intelligible nature. Scotus thinks that unless one admits the reality of the objective correlate prior to any actual intellection, the whole objectivity of our intellectual enterprise is threatened.

Scotus argues that the quiddity, in the sense of an individual's essential nature or definable characteristics, has its own integrity or unity as one *kind* of thing—for example, human nature—rather than one *instance* of this kind, such as Socrates or Plato. If each person's individuality or singularity is an instance of numerical unity, then this sortal unity, characteristic of their humanity or their "being human," is "less than numerical," where "less than" means less particularized and hence more general.

Though in Scotistic literature this quiddity or nature is often incorrectly referred to as "common nature" (*natura communis*), it has its "commonness"—at least potentially—only when conceived abstractly. As a "nature," however, it rather has the character of being "indifferent" either to being present in the individual or, when abstracted by the mind, to being "predicated of many." As Avicenna put it, "Equinity is just equinity—of itself it is neither one nor several, neither universal nor particular."[2] And in his comment on Avicenna's passage, Scotus says: "I understand: it is not of itself 'one' as not of itself 'numerically one,' nor 'several' as the opposite of this unity, nor universal as actual (in the manner, namely, by which something is universal as object of the intellect), nor is it particular of itself."[3] This view of Scotus is what Charles Sanders Peirce called "Scotistic realism," and he regarded it as a necessary foundation for scientific knowledge.

What individuates any specific nature in the concrete individual, Scotus claims, is some additional positive characteristic feature that he calls "its individuating difference." This principle has a twofold effect: it differentiates *this* individual from *that*—or any other—individual, and it is not a characteristic that can be duplicated in any way. On several occasions Scotus refers to this "entity" as an individual's "haecceity" (from the Latin word *haec,* "this"), which Scotus's followers popularized.

As our text indicates, in a given individual the quidditative entity and its haecceity are inseparable in reality and are only formally distinct. Formalities are objective aspects or characteristics of an extramental thing that can be conceived in principle, one without the other, but are inseparable in the individual thing where they occur. Though the formality that Scotus calls a thing's "haecceity" or "thisness" is intelligible to God and to an intellect that is not dependent upon sense perception, the human intellect is not able to grasp it as such. If it were, Scotus points out, then if one person were miraculously bilocated, we would not mistake this individual for a pair of identical twins. Conversely, if two identical objects were superimposed upon each other, we would still recognize the different haecceities of each and not mistake them for one and the same individual.[4]

On the Will

Commentators have long recognized the voluntarist strain in Scotistic thought, even though their interpretations of its significance have differed widely. In her Gifford lectures on the will,

Hannah Arendt featured Scotus as having one of the most rigorous doctrines of the will in the history of philosophy. His sustained, uncompromising account of contingency especially captured her attention.[5] The problem that the medievals faced with contingency was that it had to be rooted in a principle of indetermination that, perforce, cannot anchor the determinisms and universals of nature, which are required in classical accounts of scientific explanation. As a consequence, reason, which is attuned to such necessities, inevitably appears to conflict with faith, which tells the story of divine freedom. In appropriating Aristotelian and even Islamic Neoplatonic philosophies, the Christian theologians encountered a trenchant necessitarianism, which was inconsistent with revelation's account of creation. Many of Europe's best minds in the thirteenth century contributed to a protracted public debate on this conflict.[6] The dispute, somewhat resolved outside the halls of the universities by external authority in the famous condemnations of 1277, created one of the West's great intellectual watersheds. Though too young to be one of the participants, Scotus wrote in the shadows of the condemnations. His thought is best interpreted as an attempt to overcome the limitations of the pre-existing polarities of intellectualism and voluntarism, of Aristotelianism and Augustinianism. *On the Will* provides a case in point, for here Scotus carves out the basics of his metaphysics of the free will within the context of a sympathetic interpretation of Aristotle's *Metaphysics*. There is no question but that he amplifies Aristotle's doctrine, yet we have no reason to think he was insincere or manifestly wrong to see his work as a development of Aristotle's principles.

Our commentary begins with the problem of contingency. What we see here is the defense of a radical indeterminism in the nature of things, which Scotus traces to its source in the nature of the will as a distinctive species of active potency. Once the metaphysician's focus is directed to the free will as the responsible agent for the contingencies of the world, then the issue of freedom appears anew with a fresh set of concerns. One begins to wonder about the anthropological grounds and moral implications of free action. We shall briefly discuss these latter issues at the end of our commentary. Scotus himself specifically forged the connection of his metaphysical treatment of the will's freedom with its moral implications in question 18 of his *Quodlibet*. We do not find in his works, however, an integrated, philosophical ethics in any way comparable to his systematic consideration of metaphysical questions.

The Problem of Contingency

To say that an entity is contingent is to say of an actual being that at the instant it became, it could have been otherwise, or that although it now exists, its opposite is really possible. Contingency is thus a mode of actual being to be contrasted with necessity as its opposite. Taken as a disjunction, the pair contingent/necessary is a transcendental attribute of being. As modes of real existence, these attributes specify how existence belongs to the entity considered in its real possibility, in abstraction from actual existence.[7] If it is necessary, then there is no condition in which the entity did not exist: it is now, always was, and always will be. In chapter 3, we followed Scotus's argument that the real possibility of a first efficient cause entails its necessary existence. Most beings, however, exist contingently, and this signifies more than their temporality or mutability. Only someone excessively contentious would deny the fact that some being had come into existence after not being or that some already existent entity eventually will fall out of existence. When it comes to the further question whether the entity need have come to be when and as it did, the answer is not so unanimous. Might not all mutable things come and go with a metaphysical inevitability? Might it not be that all things that are, were, or will be exist of necessity, each in its own due time? If the universe is not deterministically fixed, what is the source of its indetermination? How do we explain that what is could have been otherwise?

Because determinism makes a strong claim on thoughtful minds, the first task is to show that something is contingent. One reason the dispute over freedom and determinism persists through the ages is because contingency cannot be proved in terms of something more evident to us than itself. It is a first principle, or a basic perception requisite to any further investigation.[8] Scotus puts the point forcefully:

> I do not see how it is possible to prove the contingency of things a priori. . . . The Philosopher also assumes that contingency exists in things; but he has not proved this a priori but a posteriori, because if contingency does not exist, there is no need to busy oneself or take counsel; that contingency does exist in things is known to everybody as much as, or more than, that a person must take pains and advice [about what may happen]. Therefore, it can be proved a posteriori, because otherwise neither virtues nor precepts nor admonitions nor rewards nor punishment nor honors would be necessary; and in short, all civility and human compassion would be destroyed. And against those who would deny this, one

should proceed with torments and with fire and such like, and they should be beaten until they confess that they are able not to be tormented, and thus admit they are tormented contingently and not necessarily, as Avicenna argues against those who deny a first principle [namely, noncontradiction]. For they, according to him, should be flogged until they recognize that it is not the same thing to be tortured as not to be tortured, burned as not to be burned.[9]

This is one case where the Subtle Doctor is not so subtle. For him the fact of contingency must be admitted as a basic and undeniable part of our experience in the realm of action, where virtue and vice, reward and punishment, advice and admonition, rule. Given that fact, the task is to provide an explanatory framework that makes the fact reasonable. This is the job of Scotus's doctrine of the will.[10]

Metaphysical Doctrine of the Will

On the Will, which is excerpted from the last of fifteen questions that Scotus raised with respect to book 9 of the *Metaphysics,* focuses on the basis of the distinction between the two fundamental kinds of agents, which Aristotle calls the rational and irrational and Scotus names wills and natures.[11] In the process of the argument, he defends the immediacy or irreducibility of contingent truths and locates the source of such realities in a very interesting kind of indetermination that is proper to wills. In effect, what Scotus achieves here is the opening up of conceptual space, which allows the philosopher and the theologian to proceed in discussions of freedom and contingency on firm metaphysical footing.

Consider the proposition "The will wills A," which Scotus uses as the paradigm of a contingent proposition. The subject (will) is a power that acts (wills) with respect to an object (A). As a power, the will had intrinsic to it at the time it willed A the capacity either to nill A or to will B or to not act at all. This means that the power is of itself undetermined with respect to its action; as Aristotle put it, it is open to contrary effects. In making the point, Scotus insists that the predicate inheres immediately in the subject,[12] that is, there is no cause or explanation outside of the power of the will itself that explains the option of willing over not willing, of willing over nilling, and of willing A over B. In other words, the will is the sufficient explanation of its effects. The problem, however, is that pointing to the will's power will not explain why the effect is *this* rather than *that.* Do we in fact, therefore, have an explanation of the effect? Does not an explanation identify the

determinate reason why something is *this* rather than *that*? So if
the will is intrinsically indeterminate regarding the alternatives
and there is no other decisive determining factor, how can that
which is indeterminate explain what is determinate?

The doubt expressed above calls into question the positive
reality of contingency. The very meaning of contingency is that
this actual entity has been chosen, and from an ontological point
of view, there is no reason for its existence other than that it was
willed at an instant when its opposite had the same real possibility. The will's action makes the difference. Moreover, the will's
decision is in no way predetermined. Scotus does not think he can
explain this in the sense of showing the will's operation to be the
result of some more basic factor. He does, however, think he can
clarify certain facts about the inner structure of the will. This
theoretical construct would allow us to understand the world as a
scene where freedom and the will have a place alongside necessity
and nature in the metaphysical account of things.

First of all, Scotus explains that in the most basic sense, contingency characterizes the modality by which the will elicits its
own acts. To understand what he is referring to, we need to review
briefly the basic lines of the action theory he employs. The main
idea is that an agent acts by extending or communicating its own
perfection in bringing about an effect. The action amounts to the
union of the power and its object. According to the theory of intentionality that informs Scotus's teaching, there is no volition except
that it be the love of some particular thing or person presented to
it as good. Although there are interesting questions to pursue in
sorting out the relationship between power and object,[13] Scotus
makes it clear that the interplay between the two is posterior to
the region where contingency is first found, in the internal workings of the power itself. Contingency characterizes what he calls
the will's immanent operation, by virtue of which it relates to its
object. In particular it specifies the manner in which the power
activates its own resources with respect to its object. Properly
speaking then, the noun "contingency" is an abstraction drawn
from a mode of action and would be best expressed as an adverb:
the will acts contingently. When the different elements are collected, we see the action that is the intentional union of the power
and its object; and with respect to the power there is its operation
and the modality with which it is elicited. Arriving at the mode of
operation, we come to a bedrock reality for which there is no accounting. Why does the will act this way? One can only answer,
"Because the will is a will."[14]

Many philosophers have had difficulty accepting the idea that a power could possess simultaneously the capacity for contrary effects. Their point is that by the law of noncontradiction, opposites cannot simultaneously exist in the same respect, and so it is absurd to impute to a power that which is impossible in actuality. To be sure, there would be no way to verify that the opposite of what was willed into existence was really possible. There are no retakes in history. In Scotus's response to such an objection, he first of all explains that the power for contrary effects is to be taken in the divided rather than the composed sense. In other words, he does not mean to say that the will could bring about the simultaneous existence of contrary effects—that, for example, I could both sit and stand in the same instant. He agrees that this is absurd. Rather, he means that when I am now sitting because I have so willed it, in that same "now" I have the possibility to be standing. From the objector's point of view, the clarification highlights the problem. How could a given moment of time, able to support only one actuality, be pregnant with the real possibility of its opposite? In reply Scotus gives two a posteriori arguments and then provides a supporting theoretical construct for what he thinks has to be the answer.

He argues first that if the objection is sustained, then contingency is not real; but contingency is required for the maintenance of civility and compassion in human affairs.[15] The argument for the minor premise was developed above in our treatment of the problem of contingency. The implication of the major premise seems true in that the objection does not try to provide an alternative account for contingency but rather to replace it with a deterministic explanation or to deny any modality to actual entities, be it contingency or necessity. Scotus's argument comes down to the claim that his volitional theory cannot be absurd if it is necessary to account for contingent existence. Scotus then points to the evidence of introspection. He says that in a volitional act—say, of willing A—we are aware that we could have nilled A or simply refrained from any act of will at all. Hence we have evidence from experience of a root indetermination from which our volitions proceed.[16]

In the final part of his reply, Scotus describes a principle of indetermination that would sustain the simultaneous possession of contrary effects in an active power. He says that one kind of indeterminacy is based on a defect of actuality. Matter, for instance, to the degree that it is devoid of form, is open to the reception of different and opposing forms. Its intrinsic insufficiency of actuality is overcome only by being determined by an extrinsic power. But there is a second kind of indeterminacy: "that of a superabundant sufficiency, based on unlimited actuality, either in an unqualified or in a qualified sense." The indeterminacy of the will is of this second sort. The idea is that whatever perfection is communicated by the will to its effect amounts to a delimitation of a preexisting actuality whose fullness can hardly be measured by its effect. The creative power of a poet illustrates the point: any individual poem derives from the actuality of the poet's art, but its actuality is relatively inexhaustible in comparison with any particular poem. Because this is so, any poem profiled in the mind's eye against the poet's fuller genius provides a particularly good example of something delimited, shaped, and formed out of superabundant resources. Although the typical volition may not have the splendor of a work of art, it proceeds from the same dynamic. Every volition is a delimitation of the will's own fuller reality. In such cases, although the agent is indeterminate with respect to its effects, it need not resort to any external cause because of a deficiency of actuality. Moreover, there would be no reason why such an agent could not determine itself to either of two contrary effects unless it were constituted, like a nature, to bring about only one sort of effect.[17]

Anthropological Doctrine of the Will

Up to this point, we have been considering the will as a potency. In this regard, Scotus has been intent on explaining how it is distinguished from a nature, the other species of active power, and how wills are the source of contingency in the world. Scotus's metaphysics of the will shows why a blanket determinism is wrong. It is evident from our text that Scotistic freedom, which describes the mode of the will's operation, has metaphysical implications. But it also has ethical consequences, since what eventuates from the free will could have been otherwise and becomes what it does because of our choice. Moreover, the origin of our moral responsibility lies in the will not simply because it has exercised its power to determine events one way rather than the other. What elevates this action to the moral realm is the fact that the will can operate with knowledge, but more especially because it is innately directed toward the upright or noble good. Within the context of moral discourse, "freedom" is the concrete ability of the will to deploy its distinctive metaphysical power on behalf of what is morally good. What is to be observed at this point is that the ground of this ability is an innate perfection of the will, which Scotus calls *affectio justitiae*.[18] Our brief synthesis will have the limited purpose of introducing the relevant anthropological or ethical dimensions of Scotistic voluntarism, of illuminating a second essential meaning of the term "free will." A fuller account of Scotus's doctrine of the will would need to integrate the anthropological and ethical with the metaphysical theories, for it becomes clear that one and the same subject, the free will, is the source of metaphysical contingency and moral responsibility.

Scotus himself seems to have drawn his basic ideas on this issue from Anselm of Canterbury, who had pointed out almost two hundred years earlier in his unfinished *De concordia* (3.11) the equivocal usages of the term "will." It can refer (1) to the "instrument" or power that acts, (2) to the affections or inclinations that direct it to one sort of object rather than another, and (3) to the actual uses or actions of the instrument acting on behalf of a desirable good. Anselm thought that human freedom, as an ethical category, depended upon the proper orientation or disposition of the instrument. With respect to the second meaning of "will," he identified two basic inclinations, which he called the *affectio ad volendum commoditatem* (the inclination to will what is beneficial) and the *affectio ad volendum rectitudinem* (the inclination to will what is right). His idea was that the objects of our volitions appear to us as desirable either because they satisfy some egoistic, self-perfecting desire or because we simply find the object of the action intrinsically worthy without regard to the advantage or disadvantage that it may bring to us. In addition, Anselm thought that human freedom precisely consisted in our capacity to opt for the just good even while being drawn toward the personally advantageous good. Scotus picks up on this distinction and uses it as a central anthropological principle in his ethical theory.

According to Scotus, when the will exercises its capacity for determining opposite possibilities, it is subject to two sorts of inclinations: *affectio commodi* (inclination for the advantageous good) and *affectio justitiae* (inclination for the just good). The first inclination judges the alternatives of action in terms of what personal advantage is to be gained in the transaction. Is my hunger satisfied? Will my reputation be tarnished? Will my pain be alleviated? In each case the measure of what is desirable or undesirable is keyed to the well-being of the acting self. By contrast, the other inclination directs the will to objects whose desirability consists simply in the fact that the action is intrinsically worthy. Scotus has in mind here the possibility of doing what is good or just, even when it is not of any personal benefit. Such action is therefore self-transcending. It becomes apparent that the basic dynamic of the moral life is a matter of exercising the will's power for action under the two drives. In this context, Scotus says that freedom consists in the ability of the acting persons to moderate their desire for the advantageous good. Indeed, it is the

> affection for justice that is the first check on the affection for the beneficial, inasmuch as we need not actually seek that toward which the latter affection inclines us, nor must we seek it above all else (namely, to the extent to which we are inclined by this affection for the advantageous)—this affection for what is just, I say, is the liberty innate to the will (*libertas innata voluntati*), since it represents the first check on this affection for the advantageous.[19]

Although Scotus insists that the inclination toward the just good is nobler than that toward the advantageous, he in no way denies the necessity and goodness of personally advantageous objects. In fact, he argues that there are circumstances when one in justice is required to act on behalf of those goods to which we are directed by our egoistic desires. The main point to the moral doctrine of freedom developed here, however, is that human action can transcend interests rooted in the deterministic side of our nature. The freedom from domination by our egoistic self liberates us on behalf of the good whose worth reposes in itself. In order to fill out an account of Scotus's moral theory, an ethics rooted in freedom, we would need to develop his doctrines of right reason and natural law. The first would explain the possibility of our rational access to moral truths,[20] and the second would establish the grounds for them.[21]

Even as Scotus introduces these features of his ethical theory to give form to the moral quality of our actions, he is careful to integrate them under his core insight into the radical indeterminism of the free will. We can imagine, for instance, an agent's will, fully cognizant of the moral law and aware through the dictate of right reason of its bearing on the particulars of a situation calling for action, standing with a metaphysical indifference before well-formed moral alternatives. This means that the splendor of a praiseworthy act and the ignobility of a blameworthy deed partially derive from the fact that they could have been otherwise. Human actions, precisely in their moral value, are the work of the free will—"free" because the will summons its own causal resources apart from any deterministic influences, but "free" also because it is open to the self-transcending claims of what is intrinsically good.

Moral goodness and moral evil, which Scotus understands as real qualities of the world, participate in the mystery of freedom and contingency,[22] which are essential principles of Scotistic metaphysics.

NOTES

1. For an understanding of the complex of issues in their historical development, see Jorge J. E. Gracia, *Introduction to the Problem of Individuation in the Early Middle Ages;* and *Individuation in Scholasticism: The Later Middle Ages and the Counter-Reformation, 1150–1650,* edited by Jorge J. E. Gracia.

2. Avicenna, *Metaphysica* 5.1 (*Avicenna Latinus,* 228).

3. *Ordinatio* II, d. 3, no. 31 (Vat. 7:403).

4. See also Allan B. Wolter, introduction to *Duns Scotus' Early Oxford Lecture on Individuation,* ix–xxvii; and Wolter, "Scotus' Individuation Theory."

5. Hannah Arendt, *The Life of the Mind,* vol. 2, *Willing,* 31, 120–42, 195.

6. For a discussion of the issue, see John F. Wippel, "The Condemnations of 1270 and 1277 at Paris." E. Fortin and P. O'Neill give a translation of the 1277 condemnations in *Medieval Political Philosophy: A Sourcebook,* ed. R. Lerner and M. Mahdi, 337–54. For the standard edition of the propositions, see H. Denifle and A. Chatelain, *Chartularium Universitatis Parisiensis,* 1:543–61. An English translation of the 1270 Parisian condemnations is in Wippel and Wolter, *Medieval Philosophy: From St. Augustine to Nicholas of Cusa,* 366; the original is in *Chartularium,* 1:486–87.

7. Wolter, *Transcendentals,* 150–52.

8. If the fact of contingency is a basic fact, then how could it be denied by serious thinkers throughout the ages? The question is an interesting one that leads to speculation on the limits of theoretical thought and its relation to one's form of life. Philosophers of science have shown convincingly how theory-laden our perceptions and basic insights are. With respect to the will, contingency, and freedom, Arendt has demonstrated how the philosophers' attachment to the categories of thought leads them to an almost inevitable denial of the categories of action (esp. *Willing,* 3–38). With regard to the general problem of the thinkers' theoretical bias or "overcommitment," which causes them to shortchange the intelligibility of personal aspects of reality typically celebrated in the arts and religion, see Stephen Toulmin, *The Return to Cosmology: Postmodern Science and the Theology of Nature.*

9. *Rep.* I A, d. 39–40 (Vienna, Österreichische Nationalbibliothek, cod. lat. 1453, fols. 115va–b).

10. See William A. Frank, "Duns Scotus' Concept of Willing Freely: What Divine Freedom beyond Choice Teaches Us"; and Allan B. Wolter, "Duns Scotus on the Will as Rational Potency," in *Philosophical Theology,* 163–80.

11. Scotus engages in some ingenious hermeneutics, showing that he and Aristotle were of one mind on this issue. Because some think that Aristotle had the intellect in mind as the primary rational power, Scotus took the opportunity to insist: "if 'rational' is understood to mean

'with reason,' then the will is properly rational, and it has to do with opposites, both as regards its own act and as regards the acts it controls. And it has to do with opposites not in the way that a nature, like the intellect, acts, which has no power to determine itself in any other way" (*Will and Morality,* 157).

12. In fact, he grants that a given contingent proposition may not be immediate. In such cases, however, the proposition is a conclusion that ultimately rests on basic premises, at least one of which is immediately contingent. The reasons are twofold: first, contingency is a positive perfection that requires some explanation for its existence; and second, one cannot infer a contingent proposition from a string of necessary premises.

13. Judgments concerning the role of the object in both volition and intellection were sharply debated among the Schoolmen. Scotus's own opinion seems to have been under development to the day he died. In general, however, he was anxious to preserve the active character of the power's causality, resisting every doctrine that would make the object the total efficient cause. His various treatments of *Sentences* II, d. 25 are the primary locus. See Bernardine M. Bonansea, "Duns Scotus' Voluntarism," and the *praefatio* to Scotus's *Lectura* II (Vat. 18:xi–xii).

14. See Scotus's treatment of the same matters in his *Quodlibet* q. 16; *God and Creatures,* 39–50.

15. Peter Strawson gives a contemporary version of this kind of argument in his influential essay "Freedom and Resentment."

16. Joseph M. Incandela, "Duns Scotus and the Experience of Human Freedom."

17. Our account of the will as the source of contingency is complemented by recent studies on related topics. One line of study develops Scotus's account of possibility. Ansgar Santogrossi ("Duns Scotus on Potency Opposed to Act in *Questions on the Metaphysics*") examines the ontological status of possibilities according to *Questions in Metaphysics.* The peculiar thing about potential beings is that they are nonexistent entities with objective reality. Santogrossi explains how these things—insofar as they both are and are not mind-dependent relations—find a place between pure nonbeing and full actuality. After the ontology of possibilities is established on philosophical grounds, there remains the task of explaining how they are reduced to the creative power of God. Allan Wolter explains how Scotus links the objective reality of possibilities to the creative power of God in "Scotus on the Divine Origin of Possibility."

18. On the perfection of the will, see especially John Boler, "The Moral Psychology of Duns Scotus: Some Preliminary Questions"; Boler, "Transcending the Natural: Duns Scotus on the Two Affections of the Will"; Mary Elizabeth Ingham, "Scotus and the Moral Order"; and Allan B. Wolter, "Native Freedom of the Will as a Key to the Ethics of Scotus" and "Duns Scotus on the Will and Morality."

19. *Ordinatio* II, d. 6, q. 2; *Duns Scotus on the Will and Morality,* 468–71.

20. *Quodlibet* 18 gives Scotus's most mature account of the source of moral goodness and the power of right reason to know it. Having described the moral goodness of an act as "consist[ing] in [the act] having all that the agent's right reason declares must pertain to the act or the

agent in acting," Scotus goes on to explain that a human agent is obligated to employ the ability that he or she possesses for judging the moral suitability of acts and to will in accordance with those judgments; indeed, one "must actually pass judgment upon the act and carry it out in accord with that judgment" (*God and Creatures,* 400, 402).

21. See Wolter's ample selection of Scotus's texts on natural law in *Duns Scotus on the Will and Morality,* esp. 263–318, 463–535.

22. In *Quodlibet* q.17 (*God and Creatures,* 388–98), Scotus develops the hierarchical constitution of actions. He explains how naturally good acts of the will are subsequently perfected as morally good, as naturally virtuous, and as supernaturally virtuous. All the later perfections of an act, however, are appropriated within the foundational contingency, which is the rudimentary perfection of any volition.

SELECT BIBLIOGRAPHY

Select Editions and Translations of Scotus

Joannis Duns Scoti, Doctor Subtilis, Ordinis Minorum, Opera omnia. 26 vols. Paris: apud Ludovicum Vivès, 1891–95. Reprint, Westmead, Farnborough, Hants.: Gregg International, 1969. [The Vivès edition is a republication of *R.P.F. Joannis Duns Scoti, Doctor Subtilis, Opera omnia,* 12 vols., edited by Luke Wadding (London: sumptibus Laurenti Durand, 1639).]

Doctoris Subtilis et Mariani Ioannis Duns Scoti, Ordinis Fratrum Minorum, Opera omnia. Vols. 1–8, 16–19. Vatican City: Typis Polyglottis Vaticanis, 1950– .

"Additiones magnae secundi libri: Dist. 25, q. 1." Edited by Charles Balić. Appendix 2 to Balić, *Les commentaires de Jean Duns Scot sur les quatre livres des Sentences,* 264–301. Louvain: Bureaux de la Revue, 1927.

Cuestiones Cuodlibetales. In *Obras del Doctor Sutil, Juan Duns Escoto.* Bilingual edition. Introduction, translation, and edition by Felix Alluntis. Madrid: Biblioteca de Autores Cristianos, 1963.

"Duns Scotus on the Necessity of Revealed Knowledge: Prologue to the *Ordinatio* of John Duns Scotus." Translated by Allan B. Wolter. *Franciscan Studies* 11 (1951): 231–72.

Duns Scotus on the Will and Morality. Selected and translated with an introduction by Allan B. Wolter. Washington, D.C.: The Catholic University of America Press, 1986.

Duns Scotus' Early Oxford Lecture on Individuation. Latin text and English translation by Allan B. Wolter. Santa Barbara, Calif.: Old Mission Santa Barbara, 1992.

"Duns Scotus' Parisian Proof for the Existence of God." Edition and translation by Allan B. Wolter and Marilyn McCord Adams. *Franciscan Studies* 42 (1982): 248–321.

Duns Scotus' Political and Economic Philosophy. Latin edition and English translation by Allan B. Wolter. Santa Barbara, Calif.: Old Mission Santa Barbara, 1989.

Joannis Duns Scoti Tractatus de Primo Principio. Edited by Marianus Mueller. Freiburg im Breisgau: Herder, 1941.

Johannes Duns Scotus, Abhandlung über das erste Prinzip. Translated with commentary by Wolfgang Kluxen. Darmstadt: Wissenschaftliche Buchgesellschaft, 1974.

John Duns Scotus, A Treatise on God as First Principle. Translated and edited with commentary by Allan B. Wolter. Chicago, Ill.: Franciscan Herald, 1984.

John Duns Scotus: Four Questions on Mary. Translation and introduction by Allan B. Wolter. Santa Barbara, Calif.: Old Mission Santa Barbara, 1988.

John Duns Scotus, God and Creatures: The Quodlibetal Questions. Translated with introduction, notes, and glossary by Felix Alluntis and Allan B. Wolter. Princeton, N.J.: Princeton University Press, 1975.

John Duns Scotus, Philosophical Writings: A Selection. Translated with introduction and notes by Allan Wolter. Foreword by Marilyn McCord Adams. Indianapolis, Ind.: Hackett, 1987.

Il Primo Principio degli esseri. Introduction, translation, and commentary by Pietro Scapin. Padua: Liviana Editrice, 1973.

"Une question inédite de J. Duns Scot sur la volonté." Edited by Charles Balić. Recherches de théologie ancienne et médiévale 3 (1931): 191–208.

Select Bibliographies

Cress, Donald A. "Toward a Bibliography on Duns Scotus on the Existence of God." Franciscan Studies 35 (1975): 45–65.

Gieben, Servus. "Bibliographia scotistica recentior (1953–1965)." Laurentianum 6 (1965): 492–522.

Schaefer, Odulfus. Bibliographia de Vita, Operibus et Doctrina Iohannis Duns Scoti, Doctoris Subtilis ac Mariani. Saec. XIX–XX. Rome: Orbis Catholicus-Herder, 1955.

———. "Resenha abreviada da bibliografia escotistica mais recente (1954–1966)." Revista portuguesa de filosofia 23 (1967): 338–63.

Recent Studies and Works Used

Acta Ordinis Minorum. Ad Claras Aquas, from before 1898; afterwards, Acta Ordinis Fratrum Minorum.

Adams, Marilyn McCord. "Duns Scotus on the Goodness of God." Faith and Philosophy 4 (1987): 486–507.

———. William Ockham. 2 vols. Notre Dame, Ind.: University of Notre Dame Press, 1987.

Anselm of Canterbury. De concordia praescientiae et praedestinationis et gratiae dei cum libero arbitrio. Vol. 2 of S. Anselmi Cantuariensis Archiepiscopi Opera omnia, edited by Franciscus Salesius Schmitt. 1940. Reprint, Stuttgart-Bad Cannstatt: Frommann, 1968.

———. Proslogion. Vol. 1 of S. Anselmi Cantuariensis Archiepiscopi Opera omnia, edited by Franciscus Salesius Schmitt. 1937. Reprint, Stuttgart-Bad Cannstatt: Frommann, 1968.

BIBLIOGRAPHY

Arendt, Hannah. *The Life of the Mind*. Vol. 2, *Willing*. New York and London: Harcourt, 1978.
Aristotle. *The Basic Works of Aristotle*. Edited by Richard McKeon. New York: Random, 1941.
Augustine. *Contra academicos*. Edited by Pius Knöll. Corpus Scriptorum Ecclesiaticorum Latinorum, vol. 67. Leipzig: Hölder-Pichler-Temsky, 1922.
―――. *De trinitate*. Edited by William John Mountain. Corpus Christianorum, Series Latina, vols. 50–50A. Turnholt: Brepols, 1968.
―――. *Eighty-three Different Questions*. Translated by David L. Mosher. Fathers of the Church, vol. 70. Washington, D.C.: The Catholic University of America Press, 1982.
―――. *Soliloquia*. In *Patrologiae cursus completus*, Series Latina, vol. 32, 869–904, edited by Jacques-Paul Migne. Paris, 1845.
―――. *The Trinity*. Translated by Stephen McKenna. Fathers of the Church, vol. 45. Washington, D.C.: The Catholic University of America Press, 1963.
Averroes. *Metaphysica*. Vol. 8 of *Aristotelis Opera cum Averrois Commentariis*. 1562–74. Reprint, Frankfurt am Main: Minerva, 1962.
―――. *Physica*. Vol. 4 of *Aristotelis Opera cum Averrois Commentariis*. 1562–74. Reprint, Frankfurt am Main: Minerva, 1962.
Avicenna. *Liber de Philosophia Prima sive Scientia Divina*. In *Avicenna Latinus*, edited by S. Van Riet. Louvain: Peeters; Leiden: Brill, 1977.
Balić, Charles. "De Collationibus Ioannis Duns Scoti, Doctor Subtilis ac Mariani." *Bogoslovni Vestnik* 9 (1929): 185–219.
―――. "The Life and Works of John Duns Scotus." In *John Duns Scotus, 1265–1965*, edited by John K. Ryan and Bernardine M. Bonansea, 1–27. Washington, D.C.: The Catholic University of America Press, 1965.
Balić, Charles, ed. *Ioannes Duns Scotus Doctor Immaculatae Conceptionis: Textus Auctores*. Rome: Academia Mariana Internationalis, 1954.
―――. *Iohannis de Polliaco et Iohannis de Neaopli, Quaestiones diputatae de immaculata conception Beatas Mariae Virginis*. Bibliotheca Mariana Medii Aevi. Sibenik: Ex typographia Kačić, 1931.
―――. *Ioannis Duns Scoti Doctoris mariani theologiae marianae elementa*. Bibliotheca Mariana Medii Aevi. Sibenik: Ex typographia Kačić, 1933.
Barth, Timotheus A. "Being, Univocity, and Analogy According to Duns Scotus." In *John Duns Scotus, 1265–1965*, edited by John K. Ryan and Bernardine M. Bonansea, 210–62. Washington, D.C.: The Catholic University of America Press, 1965.
Bettoni, Efrem. *Duns Scotus: The Basic Principles of His Philosophy*. Translated and edited by Bernardine Bonansea. Washington, D.C.: The Catholic University of America Press, 1961.
Boler, John. "The Moral Psychology of Duns Scotus: Some Preliminary Questions." *Franciscan Studies* 50 (1990): 31–56.
―――. "Transcending the Natural: Duns Scotus on the Two Affections of the Will." *American Catholic Philosophical Quarterly* 67 (1993): 109–26.

Bonansea, Bernardine M. "Duns Scotus' Voluntarism." In *John Duns Scotus, 1265–1965,* edited by John K. Ryan and Bernardine M. Bonansea, 83–121. Washington, D.C.: The Catholic University of America Press, 1965.

———. *Man and His Approach to God in John Duns Scotus.* Lanham, Md.: University Press of America, 1983.

Brady, Ignatius. "The Distinctions of Lombard's Book of Sentences and Alexander of Hales." *Franciscan Studies* 25 (1965): 90–116.

———. *A History of Ancient Philosophy.* Milwaukee, Wis: Bruce, 1959.

———. "St. Bonaventure's Doctrine of Illumination: Reactions Medieval and Modern." In *St. Bonaventure and Aquinas: Enduring Philosophers,* edited by Robert W. Shahan and Francis J. Kovach, 57–67. Norman: University of Oklahoma Press, 1976.

Brown, Jerome V. "Divine Illumination in Henry of Ghent." *Recherches de théologie ancienne et médiévale* 41 (1974): 177–99.

———. "Duns Scotus on the Possibility of Knowing Genuine Truth: The Reply to Henry of Ghent in the 'Lectura Prima' and in the 'Ordinatio.'" *Recherches de théologie ancienne et médiévale* 51 (1984): 136–82.

———. "John Duns Scotus on Henry of Ghent's Theory of Knowledge." *Modern Schoolman* 56 (1978): 1–29.

———. "Sensation in Henry of Ghent: A Late Mediaeval Aristotelian-Augustinian Synthesis." *Archiv für Geschichte der Philosophie* 53 (1971): 238–66.

Brown, Stephen F. "Avicenna and the Unity of the Concept of Being: The Interpretations of Henry of Ghent, Duns Scotus, Gerard of Bologna and Peter Aureoli." *Franciscan Studies* 25 (1965): 135–48.

———. "Richard of Conington and the Analogy of the Concept of Being." *Franziskanische Studien* 48 (1966): 297–307.

Brown, Stephen F., and Stephen D. Dumont. "The Univocity of the Concept of Being in the Fourteenth Century, III: An Early Scotist." *Mediaeval Studies* 51 (1989): 1–129.

Callebaut, André. "La maîtrise du bx. Jean Duns Scot en 1305: Son départ de Paris en 1307 durant la préparation du procès contre les Templiers." *Archivum Franciscanum Historicum* 21 (1928): 206–39.

———. "A propos du bx Jean Duns Scot de Litttledean: Notes et recherches historiques de 1265 à 1292." *Archivum Franciscanum Historicum* 24 (1931): 305–29.

Cantor, Georg. *Gesammelte Abhandlungen.* Edited by Ernst Zermelo. Berlin: Springer, 1932.

Catania, Francis J. "John Duns Scotus on *Ens Infinitum.*" *American Catholic Philosophical Quarterly* 63 (1993): 37–54.

Copleston, Frederick. *A History of Philosophy.* Vol. 2, *Mediaeval Philosophy,* part 2, "Albert the Great to Duns Scotus." Garden City, N.Y.: Image, 1962.

Courtenay, William J. "Scotus at Paris." In *Via Scoti: Methodologica ad Mentem Joannis Duns Scoti,* edited by Leonardo Sileo, 149–63. Rome: Antonianum, 1995.

Currey, Cecil B. *Reason and Revelation: John Duns Scotus on Natural Theology.* Synthesis Series. Chicago, Ill.: Franciscan Herald, 1977.

Daniels, Donald E. "Theology as a Science in Duns Scotus." In *Philosophy and Culture: Proceedings of the Seventeenth World Congress of Philosophy*, edited by Venant Cauchy, 837–40. Montreal: Montmorency, 1988.
Denifle, Henricus, and Aemilio Chatelain, eds. *Chartularium Universitatis Parisiensis*. 4 vols. Paris: Fratres Delalain, 1889–97.
De Saint-Maurice, Béraud. *John Duns Scotus: A Teacher for Our Times*. Translated by Columban Duffy. St. Bonaventure, N.Y.: Franciscan Institute, 1955.
Dixon, Richard Watson. *History of the Church of England from the Abolition of the Roman Jurisdiction*. 3d ed. 6 vols. Oxford: Oxford University Press, 1895–1903.
Dumont, Stephen. "The *Propositio Famosa Scoti:* Duns Scotus and Ockham on the Possibility of a Science of Theology." *Dialogue* 31 (1992): 415–29.
———. "Theology as a Science and Duns Scotus's Distinction between Intuitive and Abstractive Cognition." *Speculum* 64 (1989): 579–99.
———. "Transcendental Being: Scotus and Scotists." *Topoi* 11 (1992): 135–49.
———. "The Univocity of the Concept of Being in the Fourteenth Century: John Duns Scotus and William of Alnwick." *Mediaeval Studies* 49 (1987): 1–75.
Effler, Roy R. *John Duns Scotus and the Principle "Omne Quod Movetur Ab Alio Movetur."* St. Bonaventure, N.Y.: Franciscan Institute, 1962.
Falk, Arthur E. "The Forbearance of an Instantaneous Angel: Time, Possibility and Free Will." *Modern Schoolman* 61 (1984): 101–16.
Frank, William A. "Duns Scotus on Autonomous Freedom and Divine Co-Causality." *Medieval Philosophy and Theology* 2 (1992): 142–64.
———. "Duns Scotus' Concept of Willing Freely: What Divine Freedom beyond Choice Teaches Us." *Franciscan Studies* 42 (1982): 68–89.
Garver, Newton. "Subject and Predicate." In *The Encyclopedia of Philosophy*, 8:33–36. New York and London: Macmillan and Free Press, 1967.
Gilson, Etienne. *History of Christian Philosophy in the Middle Ages*. New York: Random, 1955.
———. *Jean Duns Scot: Introduction à ses positions fondamentales*. Paris: Vrin, 1952.
Glorieux, Palémon. *La littérature quodlibétique*. Bibliothèque thomiste, vol. 21. Paris: La Saulchoir, 1935.
Gracia, Jorge J. E. *Introduction to the Problem of Individuation in the Early Middle Ages*. 2d rev. ed. Munich: Philosophia Verlag, 1988.
Gracia, Jorge J. E., ed. *Individuation in Scholasticism: The Later Middle Ages and the Counter-Reformation, 1150–1650*. Albany: State University of New York Press, 1994.
Hamesse, Jacqueline, ed. *Les Auctoritates Aristotelis*. Louvain: Publications Universitaires; Paris: Béatrice-Nauwelaerts, 1974.

Hanson, Norman R. *Patterns of Discovery.* Cambridge: Cambridge University Press, 1958.
Harris, C. R. S. *Duns Scotus.* 2 vols. Oxford: Clarendon Press, 1927.
Heidegger, Martin. *An Introduction to Metaphysics.* Translated by Ralph Manheim. Garden City, N.Y.: Anchor, 1959.
Henry of Ghent. *Summa quaestionum ordinariarum.* 2 vols. 1520. Reprint, St. Bonaventure, N.Y.: Franciscan Institute, 1953.
Hesse, Mary. "Models and Analogies in Science." In *Encyclopedia of Philosophy,* 5:354–59. New York and London: Macmillan and Free Press, 1967.
Hobbes, Thomas. *Leviathan.* Edited by C. B. Macpherson. Harmondsworth: Penguin, 1968.
Incandela, Joseph M. "Duns Scotus and the Experience of Human Freedom." *Thomist* 56 (1992): 229–56.
Ingham, Mary Elizabeth. "*Ea Quae Sunt Ad Finem:* Reflections on Virtue as Means to Moral Excellence in Scotist Thought." *Franciscan Studies* 50 (1990): 177–96.
———. *Ethics and Freedom: An Historical-Critical Investigation of Scotist Ethical Thought.* Lanham, Md.: University Press of America, 1989.
———. "Scotus and the Moral Order." *American Catholic Philosophical Quarterly* 63 (1993): 127–50.
Kant, Immanuel. *Prolegomena to Any Future Metaphysics That Will Be Able to Come Forward as Science.* Translated by Paul Carus, rev. by James W. Ellington. Indianapolis, Ind.: Hackett, 1977.
Klibansky, Raymond. *Commentarium de Eckhardi Magisterio.* In *Magistri Eckardi Opera Latina.* Vol. 13. Leipzig: F. Meiner, 1944.
Lambert of Auxerre. *Logica (Summa Lamberti).* Edited by Franco Alessio. Florence: La Nuova Italia Editrice, 1971.
Lee, Patrick. "The Relation between Intellect and Will in Free Choice According to Aquinas and Scotus." *Thomist* 49 (1985): 321–42.
Lerner, Ralph, and Muhsin Mahdi, eds. *Medieval Political Philosophy: A Sourcebook.* Ithaca, N.Y.: Cornell University Press, 1963.
Little, Andrew G. *The Grey Friars in Oxford.* Oxford: Clarendon Press, 1892.
———. "Chronological Notes on the Life of Duns Scotus." *English Historical Review* 47 (1932): 568–82.
Little, Andrew G., and Franz Pelster, S.J. *Oxford Theology and Theologians circa A.D. 1282–1302.* Oxford: Clarendon Press, 1934.
Longpré, Efrem. "L'ordination sacerdotale du bx Jean Duns Scotus: Document du 17 mars 1291." *Archivum Franciscanum Historicum* 22 (1929): 54–62.
Loux, Michael J. "A Scotistic Argument for the Existence of a First Cause." *American Philosophical Quarterly* 21 (1984): 157–65.
Ludwig, Walter D. "Aristotle's Conception of the Science of Being." *New Scholasticism* 63 (1989): 379–404.
MacIntyre, Alasdair. *First Principles, Final Ends and Contemporary Philosophical Issues.* Aquinas Lecture, 1990. Milwaukee, Wis.: Marquette University Press, 1990.
———. *Three Rival Versions of Moral Enquiry, Encyclopaedia, Genealogy, Tradition, being Gifford Lectures delivered in the Univer-*

sity of Edinburgh in 1988. Notre Dame, Ind.: University of Notre Dame Press, 1990.

Mackey, Louis H. "Singular and Universal: A Franciscan Perspective." *Franciscan Studies* 39 (1979): 130–64.

Major, John. *A History of Greater Britain as Well England as Scotland Compiled from the Ancient Authorities by John Major, by Name Indeed a Scot, but by Profession a Theologian*. Translated by Archibald Constable. Edinburgh: Edinburgh University Press, 1892.

Malcolm, Norman. "Anselm's Ontological Arguments." *Philosophical Review* 69 (1960): 41–62. Reprinted in *The Ontological Argument: From St. Anselm to Contemporary Philosophers*, edited by Alvin Plantinga, 136–59. Garden City, N.Y.: Anchor, 1965.

Martinich, Alyosius P. "Scotus and Anselm on the Existence of God." *Franciscan Studies* 37 (1977): 139–52.

McInerny, Ralph. *Aquinas against the Averroists: On There Being Only One Intellect*. West Lafayette, Ind.: Purdue University Press, 1993.

Mulligan, Robert. "*Portio Superior* and *Portio Inferior* in the Writings of St. Bonaventure." *Franciscan Studies* 15 (1955): 332–49.

———. "*Ratio Superior* and *Ratio Inferior:* The Historical Background." *New Scholasticism* 29 (1955): 1–32.

Noone, Timothy B. "Scotus's Critique of the Thomistic Theory of Individuation and the Dating of the *Quaestiones in libros Metaphysicorum* VII, q. 13." In *Via Scoti: Methodologica ad Mentem Joannis Duns Scoti*, edited by Leonardo Sileo, 391–406. Rome: Antonianum, 1995.

Quine, Willard Van Orman. "Two Dogmas of Empiricism." In *From a Logical Point of View: Logico-Philosophical Essays*, 20–46. 2d, rev. ed. New York: Harper, 1961.

Quinn, John Francis. *The Historical Constitution of St. Bonaventure's Philosophy*. Toronto: Pontifical Institute of Mediaeval Studies, 1973.

Park, Woosuk. "Common Nature and Haecceitas." *Franziscanische Studien* 71 (1989): 188–92.

———. "The Problem of Individuation for Scotus: A Principle of Individuation or a Principle of Distinction." *Franciscan Studies* 48 (1988): 105–23.

Peirce, Charles Sanders. *Collected Papers of Charles Sanders Peirce*. Edited by Charles Hartshorne, Paul Weiss, and Arthur Burks. 8 vols. Cambridge, Mass.: Harvard University Press, 1931–35, 1958.

Pelster, Franz. "Handschriftliches zu Skotus mit neuen Angaben über sein Leben." *Franziskanische Studien* 10 (1923): 1–32.

Plantinga, Alvin. "Reason and Belief in God." In *Faith and Rationality: Reason and Belief in God*, edited by Alvin Plantinga and Nicholas Wolterstorff, 16–93. Notre Dame, Ind.: University of Notre Dame Press, 1983.

Peters, F. E. *Aristotle and the Arabs: The Aristotelian Tradition in Islam*. New York: New York University Press, 1968.

Prentice, Robert. *The Basic Quidditative Metaphysics of Duns Scotus as Seen in His "De Primo Principio."* Rome: Antonianum, 1970.
Richard St. Victor. *De trinitate: Texte critique avec introduction, notes et tables.* Edited by Jean Ribaillier. Paris: Vrin, 1958.
Roberts, Lawrence D. "Indeterminism in Duns Scotus' Doctrine of Human Freedom." *Modern Schoolman* 51 (1973): 1–16.
———. "John Duns Scotus and the Concept of Human Freedom." In *Deus et Homo ad Mentem,* edited by Camile Bérubé. Vol. 1, *Duns Scoti,* 317–25. Rome: Societas Internationalis Scotistica, 1972.
Ross, James. "Aquinas's Exemplarism: Aquinas's Voluntarism." *American Catholic Philosophical Quarterly* 64 (1990): 171–98.
Rudavsky, Tamar. "The Doctrine of Individuation in Duns Scotus." *Franziskanische Studien* 59 (1977): 320–77; 62 (1980): 62–83.
Ryan, John K., and Bernardine M. Bonansea, eds. *John Duns Scotus, 1265–1965.* Studies in the Philosophy and the History of Philosophy, vol. 3. Washington, D.C.: The Catholic University of America Press, 1965.
Sagüés-Azcona, Pius. "Apuntes para la historia del escotismo en España en el siglo XIV." In *De Doctrina Ioannis Duns Scoti,* edited by Camille Bérubé, 4:3–19. Rome: Societas Internationalis Scotistica, 1968.
Santogrossi, Ansgar. "Duns Scotus on Potency Opposed to Act in *Questions on the Metaphysics.*" *American Catholic Philosophical Quarterly* 67 (1993): 55–76.
Schufreider, Gregory. *Confessions of a Rational Mystic: Anselm's Early Writings.* West Lafayette, Ind. Purdue University Press, 1994.
Sellars, Wilfred. "Empiricism and the Philosophy of Mind." In Sellars, *Science, Perception, and Reality,* 127–93. London: Routledge and Kegan Paul, 1963.
Simon, Yves. *Definition of Moral Virtue.* Edited by Vukan Kuic. New York: Fordham University Press, 1986.
Strawson, Peter. "Freedom and Resentment." In *Freedom and Resentment and Other Essays,* 1–25. London: Methuen, 1974.
Stroick, Clemens. "Eine Pariser Disputation vom Jahre 1306: Die Verteidigung des thomistischen Individuationsprinzips gegen Johannes Duns Scotus durch Guillelmus Petri de Godino OP." In *Thomas von Aquino: Interpretation und Rezeption: Studien und Texte,* edited by Willehad Paul Eckert O.P, 559–608. Walberberger Studien, Philosophische Reihe, vol. 5. Mainz: Matthias-Grünewald-Verlag, 1974.
Tachau, Katherine H. *Vision and Certitude in the Age of Ockham: Optics, Epistemology and the Foundations of Semantics, 1250–1345.* Studien und Texte zur Geistesgeschichte des Mittelalters. Leiden: Brill, 1988.
Toulmin, Stephen. *The Philosophy of Science.* Hutchinson University Library. London: Hutchinson, 1953.
———. *The Return to Cosmology: Postmodern Science and the Theology of Nature.* Berkeley and Los Angeles: University of California Press, 1982.
Torrence, Thomas F. "Intuitive and Abstractive Knowledge from Duns Scotus to John Calvin." In *De doctrina Ioannis Duns Scoti,* ed-

ited by Camille Bérubé, 4:291–305. Rome: Societas Internationalis Scotistica, 1968.
Tweedale, Martin M. "Duns Scotus's Doctrine on Universals and the Aphrodisian Tradition." *American Catholic Philosophical Quarterly* 67 (1993): 77–94.
Van Steenberghen, Fernand. *Aristotle in the West: The Origins of Latin Aristotelianism*. Translated by Leonard Johnston. Louvain: Nauwelaerts, 1955.
Vorilong, William. *Opus super IV libros Sententiarum*. Venice, 1496.
Vos Jaczn, Anthonie, et al., eds. *Contingency and Freedom: John Duns Scotus, Lectural I 39*. Dordecht: Kluwer, 1994.
Wadding, Luke. *Annales Minorum seu trium Ordinum a S. Francisco institutuorum*. Vol. 6. Edited by Joseph Marie Fonseca ab Ebora. Ad Claras Aquas, 1931.
Wass, Meldon C. *The Infinite God and the "Summa Fratris Alexandri."* Chicago, Ill.: Franciscan Herald, 1964.
Weinberg, Julius R. *A Short History of Medieval Philosophy*. Princeton, N.J.: Princeton University Press, 1964.
Wippel, John F. "The Condemnations of 1270 and 1277 at Paris." *Journal of Medieval and Renaissance Studies* 7 (1977): 169–201.
———. *Metaphysical Themes in Thomas Aquinas*. Studies in Philosophy and the History of Philosophy, vol. 10. Washington, D.C.: The Catholic University of America Press, 1984.
———. "The Reality of Nonexisting Possibles According to Thomas Aquinas, Henry of Ghent, and Godfrey of Fontaines." *Review of Metaphysics* 34 (1981): 729–58. Reprinted as chap. 7 of his *Metaphysical Themes in Thomas Aquinas*. Washington, D.C.: The Catholic University of America Press, 1984.
Wippel, John F., and Allan B. Wolter, eds. *Medieval Philosophy: From St. Augustine to Nicholas of Cusa*. New York: Free Press, 1969.
Wittgenstein, Ludwig. *Tractatus Logico-Philosophicus*. Translated by D. F. Pears and B. F. McGuinness. London: Routlege and Kegan Paul, 1961.
Wolter, Allan B. "Duns Scotus at Oxford." In *Via Scoti: Methodologica ad Mentem Joannis Duns Scoti*, edited by Leonardo Sileo, 183–92. Rome: Antonianum, 1995.
———. "Duns Scotus on the Will and Morality." In *The Philosophical Theology of John Duns Scotus*, 181–208.
———. "Duns Scotus on the Will as Rational Potency." In *The Philosophical Theology of John Duns Scotus*, 163–80.
———. "God's Knowledge: A Study in Scotistic Methodology." In *Via Scoti: Methodologica ad Mentem Joannis Duns Scoti*, edited by Leonardo Sileo, 165–82. Rome: Antonianum, 1995.
———. "Native Freedom of the Will as a Key to the Ethics of Scotus." In *The Philosophical Theology of John Duns Scotus*, 148–62.
———. "An Oxford Dialogue on Language and Metaphysics." *Review of Metaphysics* 31 (1978): 615–48; 32 (1978): 323–48.
———. *The Philosophical Theology of John Duns Scotus*. Edited by Marilyn McCord Adams. Ithaca, N.Y.: Cornell University Press, 1990.
———. "Reflections on the Life and Works of Scotus." *American Catholic Philosophical Quarterly* 67 (1993): 1–36.

Wolter, Allan B. "A Scotistic Approach to the Ultimate Why-Question." In *Philosophies of Existence, Ancient and Medieval*, edited by Parviz Morewedge, 109–30. New York: Fordham University Press, 1982.

———. "Scotus' Individuation Theory." In *The Philosophical Theology of John Duns Scotus*, 68–97.

———. "Scotus on the Divine Origin of Possibility." *American Catholic Philosophical Quarterly* 67 (1993): 95–108.

———. *Transcendentals and Their Function in the Metaphysics of Duns Scotus*. St. Bonaventure, N.Y.: Franciscan Institute, 1946.

———. "The Unspeakable Philosophy of the Late Wittgenstein." *Proceedings of the American Catholic Philosophical Association* 34 (1960): 168–93.

Wolter, Allan B., and Blane O'Neill. *John Duns Scotus: Mary's Architect*. Quincy, Ill.: Franciscan Press, 1993.

Zimmermann, Albert. *Ontologie oder Metaphysik? Die Diskussion über den Gegenstand der Metaphysik im 13. und 14. Jahrhundert: Texte und Untersuchungen*. Leiden: Brill, 1965.

INDEX

Index of Names

Adam, 6, 7
Albert the Great, 8, 14
Albumazar, 3
Alexander of Aphrodisias, 135
Alexander of Hales, 76, 105
Alluntis, Felix, 9, 16, 106
Alnwick, William of, 10, 11, 15
Andreas, Antonius, 3, 15
Anselm of Canterbury, 64–65, 66–67, 97, 98–99, 100, 107, 206
Aquinas, Thomas, 8, 14, 76, 106, 137, 157, 176, 177
Arendt, Hannah, 198, 206
Aristotle, 3, 9, 10, 19, 27, 28, 29, 30, 32, 33, 37, 38, 39, 46–47, 56–57, 87, 89, 90, 92, 97, 101, 126–27, 130–31, 132, 134, 135, 136, 137, 138, 144, 145, 147, 151, 152, 155, 157, 158, 159, 160, 162, 163, 164, 166, 168, 169, 171, 173, 174, 176, 177, 180, 181, 182, 183, 186–87, 188–89, 190–91, 196, 198, 199, 200, 206
Augustine of Hippo, 43, 71, 97, 106, 132–33, 135, 136, 138, 139, 140, 142, 143, 145, 146, 152, 158, 165, 166, 167, 172, 173, 174, 176, 177, 178, 179, 180, 181, 182, 183
Auriol, Peter, 175
Averroes, 21, 23, 27, 32, 34, 36, 136, 176
Avicenna, 19, 21, 23, 27, 32, 34, 36, 44–45, 70–71, 102, 136, 137, 139, 140, 176, 177, 178, 197, 200, 206

Bacon, Roger, 176, 177
Balić, Charles, 11–12, 13, 16, 181
Benedict XI, pope, 5, 13
Boler, John, 207
Bonansea, Bernardine M., 207
Bonaventure, 2, 76, 135, 176, 177, 179
Boniface VIII, pope, 4, 5, 14
Brady, Ignatius, 105, 176, 177
Brockie, Marianus, 12
Brown, Jerome V., 181
Brown, Stephen F., 176

Callebaut, Andre, 12, 14
Calvin, John, 176, 183
Cantor, Georg, 175, 183
Chatelain, Aemilio. *See* Denifle, Henricus
Christ, 2, 6, 7
Conington, Richard of, 176, 180
Cromwell, Thomas, 11, 16

Dalderby, bishop, 4
Damascene, John, 141, 154–55, 178
Denifle, Henricus, 206
Descartes, 97, 137, 174
Dixon, R. W., 16
Dumont, Stephen, 105

Eckhart, Master, 4

Ferchius, Matthew (Ferkic), 14
Frank, William A., 206

Garver, Newton, 38
Gerard Calcariensis, 14
Gilles de Ligny, 5, 6, 13
Gilson, Etienne, 136, 176
Glorieux, P., 13
Godfrey of Fontaines, 13, 105, 106
Godin, William Peter, 6, 13
Gonsalvus of Spain, 4, 5, 8
Gracia, Jorge J. E., 206

Hanson, Norman R., 178
Harris, C. R. S., 16, 181
Henry of Ghent, 14, 79, 105, 106, 109, 115, 119, 135, 136, 137, 138, 139, 140, 141, 142, 143, 144, 145, 146, 149, 150, 155, 156, 157, 158, 159, 161, 164,

Henry of Ghent (*continued*)
    165, 166, 167, 174, 176, 177, 179, 180, 181, 182
Hesse, Mary, 183
Hobbes, Thomas, 91, 106
Hugh of Hertilpole, 4

Incandela, Joseph M., 207
Ingham, Mary Elizabeth, 207

John XXI, pope, 105
John the Baptist, 7
John Paul II, pope, 9
John Reynbold of Monte Ornato, 16

Kilwardby, Robert, 176, 177
Klibansky, Raymond, 13
Kluxen, Wolfgang, 16

Layton, Richard, 16
Little, Andrew, 8, 12, 13, 14
Longpré, Efrem, 12
Ludwig, Walter D., 37

MacIntyre, Alasdair, 38
Major, John, 2, 12, 176
Malcolm, Norman, 99, 106
Marston, Roger, 176
Mary, Mother of Christ, 6, 7, 8, 9, 13, 14
McInerny, Ralph, 176
Mueller, Max, 16
Mulligan, Robert, 176

Nédélec, Hervé de, 8
Nogaret, 4

Parmenides, 105
Paul, the apostle, 7, 9, 38, 139, 150, 164, 180
Peckham, John, 176
Peirce, Charles Sanders, 31, 38, 197
Pelster, Franz, 13
Peter Lombard, 3, 9, 31, 76, 134
Peters, F. E., 38
Philip IV, king (the Fair), 4, 5, 8, 14

Plantinga, Alvin, 38
Plato, 97, 110–11, 135, 137, 165, 196
Plotinus, 176
Pouilly, Jean de, 8, 13–14
Pseudo-Dionysius, 149, 180

Quine, Willard Van Orman, 38
Quinn, John F., 176

Richard St. Victor, 16, 39, 70–71, 102, 177
Roche, Evan, 16
Ross, James, 106
Russell, Bertrand, 141, 149

Sagüés-Azcona, Pius, 12
Santogrossi, Ansgar, 207
Scapin, Pietro, 16
Sellars, Wilfred, 37
Siger of Brabant, 136, 176
Simon, Yves, 37
Strawson, Peter, 207
Stroick, Clemens, 13
Sutton, bishop, 12

Tempier, Stephen, bishop, 105
Thomas of Erfurt, 15
Torrence, Thomas F., 183
Toulmin, Stephen, 178, 206

Urban VI, pope, 14

Van Steenberghen, Fernand, 38
Vital du Four, 15
Vorilong, William, 8, 14

Wadding, Luke, 8, 9, 10, 11, 12, 14, 15, 16
Wass, Meldon, C., 106
William of Ockham, 105, 175
Wippel, John F., 105, 106, 176, 178, 206
Wittgenstein, Ludwig, 97, 105–6
Wolter, Allan B., 13, 16, 38, 39, 105, 106, 176, 177, 178, 181, 182, 183, 206, 207, 208

Zimmermann, Albert, 37

Index of Subjects

Accidental order. *See* Essential order
Active intellect, 112–13, 135–36, 139, 144–45, 176, 177
Additiones magnae, 10–11, 15
Adequate object of the intellect. *See* Primary object of the intellect
Affectio commodi. *See* *Affectio justitiae*
Affectio justitiae, and freedom, 102–3, 204–5
Against the Skeptics (Contra Academicos) (of Augustine), 172, 183
Agent intellect. *See* Active intellect
Analogous concept, 108–15, 134, 137, 142–48, 158–59, 177, 179
Aristotelian abstraction, 97, 126–29, 135–38, 143–44, 167
Augustinian abstraction, 138–40, 143, 151–52, 158

Being (*ens*): fullness of, 79, 90, 92, 97, 104, 105, 143, 158; meaning of, 82, 143–44, 149; primacy by commonness and virtuality, 120–25, 159–64; quidditative concept of, 160–62, 164, 181; univocity of, 12, 28, 110–11, 120–25, 137, 147–48, 159, 161–62, 164

Cambridge, Scotus at, 4–5, 13
Categories, 30–31, 37–38, 56–57, 89–90, 159, 162–63
Categories (of Aristotle), 38
Causality: equivocal/univocal, 50–51, 60–61, 86; essential (*per se*)/accidental (*per accidens*), 44–47, 50–53, 82–83, 87, 94–95; natures/wills, 87, 168, 188–89, 198, 200, 203, 207
Certitude: Henry of Ghent's theory of, 164–66, 177, 182; and metaphysics, 18–19, 30, 36, 74; naturally acquired, 124–33, 134, 164–65, 167–74, 182–83; in proof of univocity, 108–11, 148–49, 180
Chimera, 66–67, 100

Collationes parisiensis et oxonienses, 11–12, 16, 106, 180, 181
Cologne, Scotus at, 1, 6, 8, 14, 15
Commentary on the *Sentences*: *lectura*, 3, 11, 75, 182; *ordinatio*, 3–4, 6, 10–11, 13, 15, 16, 75, 180, 182; *reportatio*, 3, 13, 75. *See also* *Sentences* of Peter Lombard
Common nature, 186–87, 197
Conceptual distinction, 155
Condemnations of 1277, 105, 136, 144, 176, 200, 208
Contingency: concept of, 201, 203; and demonstration, 44–45, 50–51, 80–82; expressed in an immediate proposition, 130–31, 171–72, 174, 188–91, 200, 207; irreducibility of, 199–200; reality of, 192–93, 199–202, 206; rooted in the will, 150, 180, 192–95, 198, 200–201, 203, 206, 207, 208; as a transcendental, 38, 192–93, 199

De interpretatione (of Aristotle), 192–93
Demonstration: as scientific knowledge, 32–35, 37, 39, 77, 80–81, 173; of the reasoned fact (*propter quid*), 38, 40–41, 77, 169; of the simple fact (*quia*), 33, 38, 40–41, 44–45, 50–51, 77, 81, 116–17, 169
De primo principio. *See* *Tractatus de primo principio*
De sensu et sensato (of Aristotle), 132–33, 173, 174, 183
De videndo Deum (Seeing God) (of Augustine), 166, 182
Divine ideas. *See* Exemplar, ideas
Divine Will. *See* Will, divine
Dunce, 31, 38

Eighty-three Different Questions (of Augustine), 165, 181
Eminence: order of, 37, 42–43, 78, 85, 88, 90, 92, 103–5, 154; way of, 144, 148–50. *See also* Preeminent Being

Ens infinitum. *See* Infinite Being
Essential order, 44–51, 54–57, 82–86, 88–89, 93, 105, 154
Estimative power, 118–21, 145–46, 179
Excellence. *See* Eminence
Exemplar: causality, 42–43, 52–53, 58–59, 79, 95; ideas, 62–63, 96–97, 106, 134–35, 137, 139, 151, 158, 165–66, 182. *See also* First Exemplar Cause

First Being (*Ens primum*), 24–25, 36, 40–41, 56–59, 66–67, 77, 88–90, 93, 95, 96, 104, 110–11
First Efficient Cause: infinity of, 58–63, 91–95; reality of, 40–67, 78–88, 106, 199
First Exemplar Cause: infinity of, 95–97; reality of, 52–55, 58–59, 62–63, 66–69, 78, 97, 106
First Final Cause: infinity of, 66–67; reality of, 52–59, 77–78, 87, 91, 106
First philosophy, 28, 36
Fly (*musca*), 50–51, 86
Formal distinction, 186–87
Foundational knowledge, 30, 37
Freedom. *See* Will

God: absolute properties of, 40–41, 77–78, 91; as end of metaphysics, 74, 104–5; quidditative knowledge of, 108–9, 146–47; relative properties of, 40–41, 77, 78, 91; self-sufficiency of, 97, 104, 105; and the subject of metaphysics, 20–28, 31–32, 35–36; unicity of, 56–57, 66–73, 77, 102–4; as voluntary object, 114–15, 150, 159. *See also* Knowledge of God
God and Creatures. See *Quodlibet*
Gold mountain, 66–67, 100, 118–19
Goodness, in the universe, 56–57, 89

Habitus, 22–23, 29, 31, 33, 34, 37, 74
Haecceity. *See* Individuation

Illumination, theory of, 97, 134–39, 145, 147, 151, 155–58, 165, 166, 174, 176, 177, 181–82
Immaculate conception, 6–9, 14
Indeterminacy of the will. *See* Will, indeterminacy of
Individuation, 6, 13, 106, 114–15, 161, 184–87, 196–97, 206
Infinite Being (*ens infinitum*), 37, 40–41, 58–67, 74, 77, 90–102, 143, 150–55
Infinite regress, 42–49, 56–57, 60–61, 80, 82, 163, 171, 188–91
Infinity: Aristotelian concept of, 151, 155; definition of, 92, 99, 154; as intrinsic mode of being, 116–19, 148–50, 155
Intellect, appeal to experience of, 97–100. *See also* Active intellect; Passive intellect
Intelligible species, 110–13, 118–19, 136, 144–46, 155–56
Intuitive cognition, 172–76

Knights Templar, 8, 14
Knowledge of God: Henry of Ghent's theory of, 140–44; Scotus's critique of Henry, 144–46; Scotus's theory of, 24–25, 40–41, 108–21, 146–56

Lectura, 13, 105, 124, 130, 164, 179, 180, 181, 182, 183, 196, 207. *See also* Commentary on the *Sentences*, *lectura*
Lectura cantabrigiensis, 13
Lectura completa, 15
Liber de Philosophia prima sive Scientia divina (of Avicenna), 18, 20
Liber Scoti, 11
Liberty. *See* Will

Metaphysica (of Averroes), 20
Metaphysica (of Avicenna), 20, 44–45, 70, 177
Metaphysics: good of, 74; science of, 18–21, 28–36, 74; subject of, 22–27, 31–36, 74, 140, 160; as a theologic, 74, 104–5. *See also* Transcendentals

INDEX

Metaphysics (of Aristotle), 18, 19, 20, 26, 27, 29, 32, 36, 37, 38, 46–47, 56–57, 62–63, 126–27, 130–31, 136, 162, 163, 173, 181, 182, 198, 207
Modal distinction, 155

Natural agent. *See* Causality, natures/wills
Neoplatonism, 83, 94, 135, 136, 137, 176, 198

Object, of scientific knowledge. *See* Scientific knowledge, subject of
On the Trinity (*De trinitate*) (of Augustine), 42–43, 138, 172, 177–82
On the Trinity (*De trinitate*) (of Richard St. Victor), 70–71
Ontological argument, 98–99. See also *Proslogion*
Opus oxoniense, 10, 15
Ordinary disputation, 6, 13
Ordinatio, 9–13, 75, 98, 101, 105–7, 108–25, 157, 165–66, 169, 170, 171, 178–83, 184, 196, 206, 207. *See also* Commentary on the *Sentences, ordinatio*
Original sin, 6, 7, 14
Oxford, Scotus at, 1, 3–6, 8, 10–11, 13–16, 75, 106, 198
Oxford Commentary. See *Opus oxoniense*
Oxford lectures, 3, 15, 75, 147–48, 151, 206

Paris, Scotus at, 1, 2, 3, 5
Paris Commentary. See *Reportata parisiensia*
Parsimony, principle of, 89, 104
Passive intellect, 113, 135–36, 144–45, 177
Perfection, fullness of. *See* Plenitude of perfection
Phantasm (sense image), 113, 127, 144–45
Physica (of Averroes), 22
Physics (of Aristotle), 22–25, 30, 34, 35, 36, 52–53, 58–59, 87, 92, 136, 153, 180, 188–89

Plenitude of perfection, 92, 94, 97, 104, 158, 205. *See also* Being, fullness of
Possibilities, necessity of, 48–51, 80–82, 99
Possible intellect. *See* Passive intellect
Posterior Analytics (of Aristotle), 22, 26–27, 32, 38, 39, 128–29, 162, 181, 182, 190–91
Preeminent Being: infinity of, 64–67, 92, 97–101, 154; reality of, 50–51, 56–57, 78, 85–87, 89–90
Primacy of Christ, 7
Primary object of the intellect, 120–25, 156–64
Prior Analytics (of Aristotle), 26–27
Priority and posteriority, concept of, 78
Proslogion (of Anselm), 64, 97, 98, 99
Pure perfections (*perfectio simpliciter*), 37, 38, 74, 92, 95, 116–17, 148–51, 152–56, 158

Quaestio (the genre), 12–13, 76, 79
Quaestiones super Metaphysicam Aristotelis. See *Questions on the Metaphysics*
Questions on the Metaphysics, 18, 28, 32, 39, 168, 186, 200, 207
Quidditative: concepts, 34, 100, 120–23, 146–47, 160–64; entity, 100, 184–87, 196–97
Quodlibet, 9–10, 15, 106, 107, 151, 155, 175, 179, 180, 183, 198, 207, 208
Quodlibetal disputation (*quodlibet*), 6

Radical Aristotelianism, 105, 136, 176
Real distinction, 155
Regent master, 2–6
Reportata parisiensia, 10, 13, 31, 147
Reportatio examinata, 10, 13
Reportatio I A, 10, 22–27, 25, 40–73, 75, 95, 98, 180, 206

Scientific knowledge (*scientia*): nature of, 22–23, 30, 33–34, 38–39, 77, 80, 128–29, 169, 197; subject (object) of, 20–21, 24–25, 32–35

Scotland, Scotus born in, 1–2

Self-evident proposition (*per se notum*), 35, 38, 40–41, 77, 128–31, 167, 169–74

Sense image. *See* Phantasm

Sensible species, 118–21, 126–27, 144–46

Sentences of Peter Lombard, 3, 4, 5, 9, 10, 11, 31, 76, 105, 134, 174, 207. *See also* Commentary on the *Sentences*

Sheep, in Henry of Ghent's illustration, 118–21, 145–46

Skepticism, 36, 38, 124–25, 134, 149, 164, 167–68, 169, 172–74

Soliloquia, 182

Stone, in Scotus's illustrations, 114–15, 184–85

Subject of science. *See* Scientific knowledge, subject of

Subtle Doctor, 1, 8, 14, 15, 31, 200

Summa quaestionum ordinariarum (of Henry of Ghent), 79, 177, 180, 181, 182

Summum cogitabile, 99–100

Theologism. *See* Metaphysics, as a theologic

Theology of Aristotle, 136

Theoremata, 15

Tractatus de primo principio (*Treatise on God as First Principle*), 11, 16, 75, 95, 98, 105

Transcendentals: being as, 31, 37, 38, 74, 90, 137, 160, 164; concept of, 30–31, 90; different kinds of, 37, 38, 161, 164, 199; in knowledge of God, 100, 118–19, 137, 156; as subject of metaphysics, 20–21, 28, 30–33, 37, 74–75, 160

Ultimate differences, 120–21, 124–25, 161, 162, 163, 164

Ultimate End. *See* First Final Cause

Univocal concept: definition of, 108–9, 149; in knowledge of God, 108–17, 134, 137, 142, 147–48, 156, 174, 180, 181. *See also* Being, univocity of

Will: an active power, 100, 101, 102, 186–89; divine, 68–71, 78, 95, 150, 180, 198; freedom of, 102, 190–91, 199, 201, 205; indeterminacy of, 143, 190–93, 202–3; potency for opposites, 192–95; a rational potency, 192–93; superabundant sufficiency of, 190–91, 203. *See also Affectio justitiae*

Wolf, in Henry of Ghent's illustration. *See* Sheep

www.ingramcontent.com/pod-product-compliance
Lightning Source LLC
Chambersburg PA
CBHW071712160426
43195CB00012B/1653